W9-ANR-572

An Introduction to
International Law

S14397
342
Kir

DISCARD

DISCARD
HIGH SCHOOL LIBRARY

An Introduction to

International

Law

Ronald B. Kirkemo

1975

LITTLEFIELD, ADAMS & CO.
Totowa, New Jersey

36660000006907

Published 1975 by

LITTLEFIELD, ADAMS & CO.

by arrangement with Nelson-Hall Company

Copyright © 1974 by Ronald B. Kirkemo

All rights reserved

Library of Congress Cataloging in Publication Data

Kirkemo, Ronald B.
  An Introduction to International Law

  (A Littlefield, Adams Quality Paperback No. 312)

  Reprint of the ed. published by Nelson-Hall, Chicago.

  Bibliography: p.

  1. International law.   I. Title.

JX3091.K55 1975   341   75–11636
ISBN 0–8226–0312–8

Printed in the United States of America

To my two mentors

William Y. Elliot &
Thomas F. Andrews

Maynard

$9.95 89/85

S 14397

Contents

Preface

International law is an important part of international politics but is misunderstood and disregarded by many in both academic and nonacademic communities. A typical attitude that international law is nebulous and pliable to the point of complete and total ineffectiveness is incorrect on the whole and, where the law is weak or uncertain, encourages governments and citizens to deemphasize concern with legal restraints.

Much creative thinking on the nature of international law and the means to strengthen its weaker portions has occurred in the last two decades, but methods for presenting to undergraduate students this new thinking and the general field of international law itself have been lacking. International law textbooks and casebooks are too long and expensive for use in world politics or foreign policy courses, and few undergraduates enroll in law courses. Collections of essays on international law are too theoretical and sophisticated for undergraduates and do not present in whole or in part the rules of the law. Textbooks on international politics normally devote one chapter to the topic of international law but overemphasize its political characteristics and do not present even a portion of the body of the law. In short, a gap exists in available material on international law for undergraduate courses in world politics—a gap that is itself detrimental to a realistic view of the law.

This book, although not a definitive work, is intended to fill that gap. Its purposes are to provide the student with an overall view of the corpus of the law, to give a feel of the law by using excerpts from cases and conventions, to provide some of the rationale for the law and specific rules, and to present some of the schools of thought on the nature and function of the law in the international system—all in the shortest length possible to make the book useful as supplemental text material.

This book makes no claims that international law can solve the problems of war, hatred, strife, oppression, and poverty in the world, but it does assume that law can and does provide effective regulations in some areas, and that it will become increasingly important as international affairs become increasingly interdependent and institutionalized. If this book can aid undergraduate students in gaining a realistic (neither overly optimistic *nor* overly pessimistic) perspective on the possible contributions of international law to solution of the world's problems, then it will be worthwhile.

I wish to thank Ms. Ruth Stone for her superb typing of the manuscript, Dr. William Roberts of the Catholic University of America who labored to educate me in the sociology of law, and Patti and Billy who spent a Christmas vacation and many subsequent nights alone while this manuscript was being created.

I
The Law
of
NATIONS

International law is a body of principles, rules, and judicial decisions applicable on the preponderant majority of its subjects—independent states and other subjects such as international organizations—or on those subjects involved in the specific activities that the law covers. It is developed by appropriate lawmakers through an appropriate lawmaking process. Although regional international law exists, this book will cover only worldwide or general international law.

THE SOURCES OF INTERNATIONAL LAW

The sources of international law are specified by the Statute of the International Court of Justice.

Article 38

1. The Court, whose function is to decide in accordance with international law such disputes as are submitted to it, shall apply:

a. international conventions, whether general or particular, establishing rules expressly recognized by the contesting states;

b. international custom, as evidence of a general practice accepted as law;

c. the general principles of law recognized by civilized nations;

d. subject to the provisions of Article 59, judicial decisions and the teachings of the most highly qualified publicists of the various nations, as subsidiary means for the determination of rules of law.

2. This provision shall not prejudice the power of the Court to decide a case *ex aequo et bono*, if the parties agree thereto.

Article 59

The decision of the Court has no binding force except between the parties and in respect of that particular case.

International conventions are treaties that may be bilateral between two nations or multilateral between three or more nations. Political leaders or their representatives negotiate and sign treaties, but the treaties do not come into effect as law until they have gained a certain number of ratifications from a certain majority of the nations by means of the appropriate constitutional process of each party. This process differentiates international law from resolutions and declarations of nations and the General Assembly of the United Nations.

International custom consists of rules that originate out of the common practices of nations and acquire an obligatory character. The use of custom is illustrated in the *Scotia* case, a dispute that arose when the American ship *Berkshire*, which did not display the colored lights that customary law of the sea requires, was struck by the British steamer *Scotia*, which did display the colored lights. Mr. Justice Strong delivered the opinion of the Supreme Court.

Undoubtedly, no single nation can change the law of the sea. That law is of universal obligation, and no statute of one or two nations can create obligations for the world. Like all the laws of nations, it rests upon the common consent of civilized communities. It is of force, not because it was prescribed by any superior power, but because it has been generally accepted as a rule of conduct. Whatever may have been its origin, whether in the usages of navigation or in the ordinances of maritime states, or in both, it has become the law of the sea only by the concurrent sanction of those nations who may be said to constitute the commercial world. . . .

When, therefore, we find such rules of navigation as are mentioned in the British orders in council of January 9th, 1863, and in our act of Congress of 1864, accepted as obligatory rules by more than thirty of the principal commercial states of the world, including almost all which have any shipping on the Atlantic Ocean, we are constrained to regard them as in part at least, and so far as relates to these vessels, the laws of the sea, and as having been the law at the time when the collision of which the libellants complain took place.

This is not giving to the statutes of any nation extra-territorial effect. It is not treating them as general maritime laws, but it is recognition of the historical fact that by common consent of mankind, these rules have been acquiesced in as of general obligation. Of that fact we think we may take judicial notice. Foreign municipal laws must indeed be proved as facts, but it is not so with the law of nations.

The consequences of this ruling are decisive of the case before us.

The substance of general principles of law that civilized nations recognize is disputed by the new nations, which reject the distinction between civilized and uncivilized and suspect any general principles advocated by nations that not long ago saw no injustice in colonialism. Though the provisions of the Statute seem to deemphasize the role of judicial decisions as precedents, such decisions are cited as precedents if they form a pattern and thus reflect a general principle or custom. Chief Justice Marshall, in the case of *Thirty Hogsheads of Sugar* v. *Boyle*, wrote:

The law of nations is the great source from which we derive those rules . . . which are recognized by all civilized and commercial states throughout Europe and America.

This law is in part unwritten, and in part conventional. To ascertain that which is unwritten, we resort to the great principles of reason and justice: but, as these principles will be differently understood by different nations under different circumstances, we consider them as being, in some degree, fixed and rendered stable by a series of judicial decisions. The decisions of the Courts of every country, so far as they are founded upon a law common to every country, will be received not as authority, but with respect. The decisions of the Courts of every country show how the law of nations, in the given case, is understood in that country, and will be considered in adopting the rule which is to prevail in this.

A case decided *ex aequo et bono* is decided on the principles of fairness and justice in the absence of any applicable rule of international law.

THE LEGAL NATURE OF INTERNATIONAL LAW

International law operates in an unconducive environment. The nations have a wide spectrum of motivations and policies, which prevents any consensus on legitimate ends and means of political power. The nations recognize no international legislature to make law for them. No international department of justice initiates legal action against a state involved in a violation of the law; no international juridical tribunal hears disputes between nations, nor are they compelled to submit to any. No international magistrate or police force provides protection and applies punishment or enforces a judicial ruling. Hence international law must be created by voluntary agreement among the nations and be enforced by their self-interest and their own efforts or not enforced at all.

If this international law cannot be swiftly and surely enforced, is it really law? Does the absence on the international level of such common national-level agencies as legislatures, police forces, and judicial systems negate the legal character of international law? The legality of international law has three alternative views. The *deniers* argue that international law is nothing more than international usages or quasi-authoritative communications, or that the test of a legal system is its ability to restrain the use of force, which international law obviously fails to do, or that the law, being so susceptible to nations' appropriation for their own policies and ends, is not autonomous enough to qualify as law. International law is not law because it is neither binding nor enforceable. The *restrainers* argue that international law is true law, binding and restraining on the nations. Adherents to this position postulate an international community that creates legal obligation, or an indestructible link between domestic and international law, or they emphasize the rhetoric of national spokesmen who profess adherence to international law. The *consenters* argue that international law really is law, but primitive law because the basis of obligation is mutual consent, and enforcement mechanisms are weak. The law is perceived as the result not of a world community but of state agreements to create legally binding regulations in those areas where their common interests are strong enough to support such formal means of regulation.

Before proceeding it is necessary to evaluate the case of the denier. The fundamental thrust of the deniers' attack is that the inability of international law to regulate the use of force and to impose sanctions for violations deprives the law of both authority and autonomy, thereby reducing it to impotence or a legal fiction that the states have created to justify rather than to regulate their policies. Those observations are not entirely false, but they do not destroy the legality of international law.

First, the restraint of force is not the only or even decisive criterion for ascertaining the existence of law. The use of force is only one aspect of social activity, and not the only aspect subject to legal regulation. In domestic societies the use of force between individuals is outlawed but not abolished. And the law performs functions other than just regulation: it allocates and defines responsibilities, obligations, and competencies for subjects; it establishes institutions and authorizes activities and programs; it is a tool of social engineering. In short, although law may become precarious to the point of temporary disappearance during times of acute social crisis and upheaval, order and stability are not the results of law alone, and the existence of law in other areas of social activity does not have to await the legal control of conflict.

Second, enforcement and punishment mecha-

nisms need not be inevitably and consistently operative for a legal system to exist. In domestic societies
many cases are settled out of court; pardons, suspended sentences, and reprieves are utilized to suspend punishment; and the application of enforcement and punishment can vary on the basis of the
defendant's race, status, wealth, or political allegiance. Additionally, sanctions can exist in the form
of loss of benefits through exclusion from mutual
efforts.

Third, judicial organs such as public prosecutors
and courts with exclusive jurisdiction to provide
inescapable indictments and binding legal pro-
nouncements and decisions are not necessary for a
legal system. In domestic societies, whether a prose-
cutor will or will not initiate judicial proceedings may
be based on political considerations. Additionally, he
has wide flexibility in specifying the charge to be
brought—for example, whether he will ask for a
first-degree or manslaughter charge against a defendant in a murder trial. Likewise, reconciliation
may be reached outside of court proceedings, and
political leaders may set aside court decisions. However, such judicial organs are not entirely lacking on
the international level; the United Nations has procedures for fulfilling these functions, but they, like
their domestic counterparts, may become dead-
locked, biased, or short-circuited.

In short, the legal nature of international law
can be denied if one sets up standards that are not
met in domestic systems, or emphasizes only certain

sections of the law, or mistakenly fails to separate the legal system from the judicial system. But if one assumes that law is a body of rules from various sources (custom, precedent, legislation), is consciously created by the appropriate legislator for the society (dictator, parliament, or the subjects themselves) for various purposes (regulating behavior, defining rights and duties, authorizing actions), and has widespread support and compliance, then international law really is law. It is more than international morality because it is more than just principles. It is more than political leaders' public relations rhetoric, for nations are held accountable for compliance and do voluntarily submit to international courts and arbiters and abide by the results. And it is more than utopian designs and abstract formulations over irrelevant topics, for it operates upon some of the most pressing problems of international relations.

THE STUDY OF INTERNATIONAL LAW

International law is the creation of independent nations that have constant and long-term interchange with one another. Its relatively recent development occurred after the breakup of the old Roman Empire, but in the process of development the nations and writers utilized various antecedents from the ancient and Roman worlds. Some of the earliest political communities in the Middle and Far East formalized their relationships through treaties. Roman authorities regulated the Empire, as distinct from Roman citizens alone, on the basis of a set of rules known as *jus gentium*, which came to be considered a kind of law of men or mankind. The Roman philosophers also developed the concept of law of nature or *jus naturale*, or law instituted by God to establish order and maintain harmony and justice in the world community of man. Legal scholars have developed various approaches to explain how and why this international law operates and is binding in the absence of a world government.

Natural Law Approach. The earliest writers on international law were theologians in Spain concerned with the legality and justness of Spain's wars in America. Such writers as Francisco de Vitoria (1480-1546) and Francisco Suarez (1548-1617), who represent the Spanish school, regarded transcendent natural law and the existence of an international community of states as the sources of international law and its binding nature. The law, derived from an idealized conception of international relations and discoverable through revelation and right reason, was binding because it was superior to the states and was normative because it conformed to the authors' *a priori* views of right international relationships. Samuel Pufendorf (1632-1694), a leader of the Naturalist school, argued that natural law was law derived in the Hobbesian prepolitical state of nature, a law that conformed not to an idealized standard of relations but to standards that were reasonable and good in society as it exists and operates.

Eclectic Approach. Later writers used treaties and custom as sources of international law, but did not deny the existence of natural law as a source. They combined the sources as complementary. Albert Gentilis (1552-1608) and Hugo Grotius (1583-1645) evolved this approach, recognizing that some international law existed which was binding law even though it did not derive from natural law.

Positivist Approach. A third approach completely rejected natural law as a source and recognized as international law only those laws voluntarily created by independent nations and expressed in treaties and custom. This approach increased precision of the law's substance but destroyed its inherently normative and obligatory characteristics in holding that the law consisted of only those rules the states consented to accept. Though positivism became the dominant approach down to the contemporary period, no satisfactory explanation of why states are bound to obey it has yet been developed. Early positivists such as Richard Zouche (1590-1660) and Cornelius von Bynkershoek (1673-1743) held the superficial view that states must obey the law because it was written and they had consented to it. Georg Jellinek, creator of the auto-limitation theory, argued that a government which creates binding domestic law can also voluntarily create binding and restrictive international law. Hans Kelson, desiring to develop a "pure theory of law," rejected all moral, historical and sociological factors to explain the law's binding character and developed the view that international and domestic law form a single system of law and rest on one common basis of obligation—the assertion that law ought to be obeyed. This basic norm is not a norm of positive law, however, but is an assertion, so the whole theory is founded upon a simple presupposition.

Sociological Approach. Some legal scholars reject the alternatives of naturalism and positivism and apply to international law the theories of Leon Duguit and Max Huber. Duguit believed that law is not an independent and autonomous phenomenon but a social artifact. Each society has its own inner order that reflects the social facts of that society—the power structure, behavior patterns and solidarity among the social groups. This inner order gives rise to norms of conduct called living law that maintain the inner order against disruption. Legal regulations are the juridical articulation of this living law and are binding because violational actions cause undesirable and costly social disturbances. Just as the substance of the law reflects the inner order of the society, so the effectiveness of the law reflects the degree of solidarity in the society.

Using this theory, Alejandro Alvarez of Argentina has postulated the existence of a specific American international law, and F.S.C. Northrop has advocated an international law built upon the common elements of the living law of different civilizations. In his classic *Theory and Reality in Public International Law*, Charles de Visscher argues that the conditions and needs of the present international society require an international law that will channel national power toward human ends rather than national ends. In the writings of these authors the crucial role of power relationships in society in determining the substance and fate of international law is correctly identified, but the writers incorrectly assume the existence of an international society and a spontaneously arising objective law, which in fact is not objective but implicitly embodies the values of the *status quo* or the author.

Current writers like Julius Stone and Stanley Hoffmann follow Max Huber in deemphasizing the living law of society and concentrate their study on the relationships between the political arrangements of the international order and the international law of that order. These writers concentrate not simply on the rules of the law but also on the degree to which specific rules are observed or violated, and then relate that study to the international hierarchy among the nations, the pattern of relations among the states, and the nature of transnational forces such as ideology and technology. Such a study can identify the gaps, evasions and ambiguities as well as the strengths and solidarity of the law, indicate the social factors producing that variation, and predict the areas in which law will grow or be subverted. Some writers in the sociological approach have adopted the concept of the international system as a framework for structuring data about the international social environment. Hoffmann employs that concept as do Morton Kaplan and Nicholas deB.

Katzenbach in *The Political Foundations of International Law.*

Policy Approach. Myres McDougal and his associates have developed a policy-oriented approach designed to analyze all the variables in the international and domestic environments that are relevant to the creation and maintenance of international law, and to identify those choices generated by the operation of those variables that policymakers can use to more completely achieve the democratic values and goals of American politics. The purpose of the policy-orientation is to make international law relevant rather than abstract, but the result implicitly incorporates the values and assumptions of social engineering and uses the law for the goals of a specific nation, thereby destroying the law's autonomy. Beyond their advice to the Prince, however, the authors have made a valuable contribution in rigorously specifying those factors and variables that affect the content and fate of the law. This expansion of the scope of inquiry has aided the incorporation of data from other fields and thereby further enriched the study of international law.

Richard Falk, a former student of McDougal, has adopted the policy-orientation of his mentor but diverted it away from the needs and goals of nations to the needs of the international system as a postulated autonomous global community. Falk and his associates are concerned to discover those choices and developments that could advance the prospects of peace, welfare, justice and dignity for the whole community and thereby serve national and international decision-makers who desire to engineer the international system to a more desirable state.

Where can one find current evidences and sources of international rules? Lengthy and detailed exposition of the law can be found in international law textbooks; a standard one is Charles Fenwick *International Law*, 5th edition (New York: Appleton-Century-Crofts, 1965). Fenwick has written one of the best organized and most comprehensive texts, has assumed the existence of an international society and the binding character of the law, but has not incorporated Soviet and non-Western perspectives.

In *Law Among Nations* (New York: Macmillan, 1965), Gerhard Von Glahn makes use of abstracts of important cases, thus allowing the reader to gain a concise understanding of the facts, issues, decisions, and reasoning of the more important cases in the law. Von Glahn gives a relatively long exposition of the law of war, unlike William Tung in *International Law in an Organizing World* (New York: Thomas Y. Crowell, 1968). The Tung book, clearly utilizing positivist theory, is extremely valuable in terms of its extensive footnotes and incorporation of non-Western and Communist perspectives on the law though he is sometimes quite terse in his exposition of the law itself. Hans Kelsen applies his "pure theory of law" to international law in *Principles of International Law*, 2nd edition, revised and edited by Robert W. Tucker (New York: Holt, Rinehart & Winston, 1966).

Two standard casebooks—collections of excerpts from such materials as speeches, treaties, judicial decisions, and textbooks—are Herbert Briggs *The Law of Nations: Cases, Documents, and Notes*, 2d edition, (New York: Appleton-Century-Crofts, 1952), and William Bishop *International Law: Cases and Materials*, 3d edition, (Boston: Little, Brown, 1971). The Briggs book incorporates more materials; Bishop includes extensive editorial notes and some materials from international organizations. A new casebook is Edward Collins, Jr., *International Law in a Changing World: Cases, Documents and Readings* (New York: Random House, 1970), which provides short commentaries at the beginning of each chapter and is half the size of the other two. Louis B. Sohn *Cases and Materials on United Nations Law* (Brooklyn, N.Y.: Foundation Press, 1956) provides ready reference to U.N. related law, and cases of the International Court of Justice are available in a 1952, 1958, and a three-volume 1966 compilation by Edvard Hambro, *The Case Law of the International Court* (Leyden: A. W. Sijthoff, 1966).

The latest digest of international law—a compilation of United States Executive Branch documents reflecting the positions of the U.S. on issues of international law—is Margret Whiteman *Digest of International Law*, published by the U.S. Government Printing Office. Fourteen volumes of the projected 16-volume set have already been published, and supersedes earlier sets by Wharton, Moore, and Hackworth. Cases from the American Supreme

Court, federal courts and state courts are compiled in a three-volume set by Francis Deak, *American International Law Cases, 1783-1968*, (Dobbs Ferry, N.Y.: Oceana, 1971 and 1972).

Among the numerous collections of treaties—which provide access to the texts of codified law—are the United Nations *Treaty Series* and the United States Department of State *Treaties and other International Agreements*. An annual index for the latter series is the State Department *Treaties in Force*. The International Court of Justice publishes an annual compilation *Reports of Judgments, Advisory Opinions and Orders*, and a short summary of its decisions in its annual *Yearbook*. Documents and scholarly articles on problems and issues of international law appear in such law journals as the *American Journal of International Law*, published by the American Society of International Law, and the quarterly journals of various law schools.

II
The Law
of
THE STATE

International law and its unique nature result from division of the world into independent states. States are the principal subjects of international law and recipients of its rights and protections; hence it is important for a political unit to gain the status of a state under international law. To do so a newly independent nation or a rebel group must have acquired four attributes: (1) a permanent population, (2) a defined territory, (3) sovereignty or effective rule within the territory, and (4) independence or the ability to carry on normal relations with other states.

These attributes differentiate a state from other political units, such as: The Vatican; vassal states, which have internal autonomy but do not control their foreign policy; domestic protectorates, as the Cherokee Nation in the United States, which is neither an independent state nor a state in the Union;

trust territories, former colonies of defeated World Wars I and II states, which other states now administered under the authority and direction of the United Nations; belligerent communities—rebel groups that have attained control over a portion of territory and can be accorded certain rights and duties under international law; and international organizations, some of which are regarded as juridic personalities. When a political group gains recognition as a state, it acquires certain rights, duties, and jurisdictional authorities.

RECOGNITION

Before formal relations can take place between states, each must recognize the other as a state. That recognition, once given, normally will remain despite changes in government, but any fundamental change in the government structure may require that other states recognize the new government before it is considered to be the representative of the state in foreign relations.

By the act of recognition a nation affirms that it will attribute certain rights and privileges to the state it is recognizing. It declares that it accepts the newly recognized state as possessing the four essential attributes of a state and that it will hold the recognized state responsible for abiding by international law, for adhering to previously signed treaties and other agreements, and for accepting responsibility for all acts of its officials that affect the interests of the recognizing state. In turn, the recognized state is accorded certain rights, among them the right to send ambassadors to other nations and international conferences, and to expect that those ambassadors will be extended courteous opportunities to represent the state and negotiate as equals on important matters of mutual concern. The recognized state receives the right to sue in the courts of the recognizing state for damages to its property or to nationals who reside in that state. It acquires title to the assets of its predecessor (if any) located in the territory of the recognizing state, including bank deposits, capital investments such as embassy buildings, the content of consular offices, and so on. It also succeeds as plaintiff in any legal claim of its predecessor government in the recognizing state.

Without recognition as a state, a political unit could legally be militarily violated or occupied and either absorbed or forced to accept certain agreements or conditions of servitude. Its properties at home, on the seas, or in another nation's territory could be seized and appropriated. Its people abroad would enjoy no legal protection from foreign governments. It could make no demand to be accepted as an equal in negotiations in any conferences on issues or actions that involved its vital interests. It would be without legal rights against any nonrecognizing state.

A new government that has come to power through such extraconstitutional means as a coup d'etat or revolution and intends to fundamentally change the policies of the preceding government must be recognized as a new government. The legal criteria for determining the appropriateness of recognition is the competency of the new government to represent the state in its foreign relations. Specifically, the criteria employed are:

1. Does the new government exercise de facto control over the administrative machinery of the nation?
2. Is the new government exercising its control without substantial internal opposition?
3. Does the new government appear to have the support of a substantial segment of public opinion in its country?

Differing policies and images lead some governments to use recognition for political purposes, resulting in two approaches for recognizing states and two approaches for recognizing governments. One approach to recognizing states holds that recognition is a constitutive act, that the state is created by other states' acts of recognition. The other approach, the declarative, holds that recognition is merely a public affirmation that the state exists and that its existence as a state is independent of any act of recognition by other states. One approach to recognizing governments is reflected in the Estrada Doctrine,[1] which holds that no considerations other than the three legal requirements should be involved in the determination to recognize a government. The other approach is reflected in the Tobar Doctrine,[2] which holds that such political factors as the means by which a government came into power or the foreign policies the new government intends to pursue should be considered in recognizing a new government. The following document is an example of this use of recognition for political purposes.

In the effort to block Peiping's attempts to extend Communist rule in Asia the withholding of diplomatic recognition is an important factor. The extension of diplomatic recognition by a great power normally carries with it not only increased access to international councils but enhanced international standing and prestige as well. Denial of recognition on the other hand is a positive handicap to the regime affected and one which makes it that much the more difficult for it to pursue its foreign policies with success . . . .

Those who advocate recognition of the Chinese Communists often assume that by the standards of international law applied to such cases the Peiping regime is "entitled" to diplomatic recognition. In the view of the United States diplomatic recognition is a privilege and not a right. Moreover, the United States considers that diplomatic recognition is an instrument of national policy which is both its right and its duty to use in the enlightened self-interest of the nation. However, there is reason to doubt that even by the tests often cited in international law the Chinese Communist regime qualifies for diplomatic recognition. It does not rule all China, and there is a substantial force in being which contests its claim to do so. The Chinese Communist Party, which holds mainland China in its grip, is a tiny minority comprising less than 2 percent of the Chinese people, and the regimentation, brutal repression, and forced sacrifices that have characterized its rule have resulted in extensive popular unrest. To paraphrase Thomas Jefferson's dictum, this regime certainly does not represent "the will of the populace, substantially declared." Finally, it has shown no intention to honor its international obligations. One of its first acts was to abrogate the treaties of the Republic of China, except those it chose to continue. On assuming power it carried out a virtual confiscation without compensation of the properties of foreign nationals, including immense British investments notwithstanding the United Kingdom's prompt recognition of it. It has failed to honor various commitments entered into since . . . .

Recognition may be *explicit*, when the recognizing state issues a formal statement, or may be *implicit*, when a state enters into a treaty with the new state or government, or receives its ambassador, or otherwise takes note of it. Recognition is normally *complete* but may also be *conditional*, as when the recognizing state explains in its statement of recognition that it expects certain types of actions or policies from the newly recognized state or government. It should be noted, however, that recognition may not be withdrawn if these expectations do not materialize. Recognition may be carried out *collectively*, as when the signatories to the Geneva Convention of 1954 extended collective recognition to the new states of Cambodia, Vietnam, and Laos. However, admission of a new state to the United Nations does not affect their recognition or nonrecognition by other member states of the UN. In summary, recognition is a political decision of the executive branch of government, a decision that carries certain legal consequences for the newly recognized state and is binding on the courts of the recognizing state.

RIGHTS AND DUTIES

International law is a tool to reinforce the states' own protection by bringing prediction into international relations through specific rules that authorize and prohibit certain actions. Besides specific rules of conduct, states have claimed that international law includes certain rights and duties. These rights and duties help to protect the states' essential attributes and solidify stability in world affairs.

The rights of states are those prerogatives of action and authority that a state may claim as natural, automatic, and inherent in its existence as a state. These rights grant the authority to take certain actions that the other nations will tolerate, if not approve, and for which the state cannot be held accountable. These actions and authorities are classified as rights in order to imply that they are natural and inherent to the state and to elevate them to a

EATON RAPIDS
HIGH SCHOOL LIBRARY

plane beyond the reach of policy whims of great powers or coalitions of powers; other nations recognize them in order to be attributed such rights themselves. The nations of the world assert and recognize four major rights.

1. Sovereignty—the concept that the state is its own master and may undertake acts and policies without the permission of any outside group. The very concept of sovereignty, however, is contrary to the existence of international law as well as to the conditions of economic and political interdependence in the modern world. Sovereignty remains a viable concept today and a right of international law when understood as the ability and authority of the state to have complete and exclusive rule over its citizens and territory without unrequested dictation and interference from other nations or organizations. As a reflection of the existence of sovereignty, the Act of State Doctrine holds that the courts of other states must accept as valid the acts of states in domestic affairs, even when those acts violate international law.

2. Independence—the authority of a state to pursue its own foreign policy without interference or dictation from another state. Within the limits of the U.N. Charter and international law states are free to pursue policies of their choice, associate with states of their choice, and change allies and policies when such change appears desirable.

3. Self-defense—a state's authority to take actions to protect itself from an imminent threat. Article 51 of the U.N. Charter specifies an inherent right of self-defense, and measures may be taken in exercise of that right.

4. Equality—a legal claim that economic, military, and political power do not confer special privileges in issues of international law. Equality is a claim made to counterbalance the reality of unequal power among nations and is the foundation for the demands of small states to be included in international deliberations, to share in the benefits that accrue from space and oceanic exploration, and to be accepted and respected as having inherent dignity, honor, and value.

The duties and obligations of states are specified in international law. This specification is important because, unlike national legal systems, no enforcement mechanism exists in the international legal order, no time lag for socialization between birth as a state and acceptance as a full equal with other states, and no international socialization agent. These duties, derived from custom, judicial precedent, and the U.N. Charter, may be classified into three categories.

1. Obligations that relate to the protection of the international legal order. A fundamental obligation is *pacta sunt servanda* (treaties must be observed), one of the oldest principles of international law.

That obligation to keep pacts agreed to is expanded by the obligation that stipulates that every state's conduct of relations with other nations must conform to international law. A third obligation in this category is to settle disputes by peaceful means.

2. Obligations that concern the protection of other states. Nonintervention in the internal affairs of other nations is an obligation designed to protect the sovereignty and independence of all nations, as is the similar obligation to refrain from military operations against another state except in self-defense or in accordance with the direction of the United Nations. In addition to its duty to refrain from direct activity against other nations, the state must also prevent within its territory the organization and functioning of any group that intends such direct intervention or operations. States are obligated to insure that activities within their territories do not pollute other nations' waters or air, and to prevent the counterfeiting of other nations' currencies, stamps, and securities within their own territories.

3. Obligations of the United Nations Charter. Those obligations are: (a) to refrain from giving assistance to any state against which the U.N. is taking enforcement action; (b) to make armed forces, facilities, and assistance available on call for Security Council use; (c) to hold immediately available national air force contingents for combined international enforcement action; and (d) to join in affording mutual assistance in carrying out measures decided on by the Security Council.

JURISDICTIONS

Persons

International law recognizes nationality as the tie that binds an individual in allegiance to a state. Domestic law defines citizenship as the tie between the individual and state. Nationality also binds the state to the protections and benefits that international law defines for the individual, though it allows the state to impose certain duties and limitations on the individual. Nationality is not automatically changed or lost when citizenship is changed or lost; so a person could be a national but not a citizen of a state.

States have the authority to determine who shall be its nationals, in what conditions nationality shall be conferred, who may be deprived of nationality, and in what conditions that nationality may be revoked. As nationals, individuals have the right to demand protection for themselves and their property against a foreign government's illegal acts.

Nationality may be acquired several ways. Some states follow the doctrine of the law of soil (*jus soli*), which holds that birth on the soil of a state automatically creates the bond of nationality of that state, irrespective of the parents' nationality. Other states follow the doctrine of the law of blood (*jus sanguinis*), which holds that the nationality of a child follows that of the parents, regardless of place of birth. With no universal adherence to one or the other doctrine a person could have two nationalities. The problems that such a lack of agreement creates can be seen in the plight of American nationals of Japanese descent who happened to be in Japan at the outbreak of war in 1941. They were nationals of the United States under *jus soli*, but under prevailing Japanese laws they were Japanese nationals under *jus sanguinis* and so were pressed into the Japanese armed services. Nationality also may be acquired voluntarily through the process of naturalization, or it may be lost through a denaturalization decree, or it may be changed by renunciation of nationality.

Corporations enjoy the status of juristic persons and so can be invested with nationality. The traditional criterion for determining the nationality of a corporation has been the place of domicile or residence of the state where incorporation took place, but events of the world wars led to a second criterion, the control test, which determined a corporation's nationality by place of residence of persons in control of the corporation.

A state's authority over nationals abroad includes the rights to punish for offenses committed abroad, tax for income earned abroad, summon home to assist in the prosecution of a crime, and prosecute for treasonable acts committed while abroad.

In regard to aliens residing within its territory a state may:

1. Exclude or admit aliens on the basis of any

criteria it deems appropriate in consequence of its sovereignty within its territory.

2. Tax and impose certain duties on alien individuals and corporations in return for enjoyed privileges and protections.
3. Try aliens for offenses committed on its territory.
4. Impose certain restrictions, such as purchase of land or admission to practice of certain professions.
5. Restrict certain political rights normally exercised by its own nationals.
6. Expropriate alien property if such property is to be used for public purposes and prompt compensation is provided.
7. Expect and demand from the alien temporary allegiance, which does not end if an enemy invades it. The alien may be tried for treason if he renders aid to the enemy.

In turn, the state must provide adequate means of redress to an alien who has been wronged and must observe due process when an alien has violated its laws. Failure to do so would constitute a denial of justice, which could occur if the state failed to punish an offending lower official, if due diligence was not taken in apprehending and prosecuting an offender, or if irregularities existed in court proceedings that resulted in a clearly unjust sentence.

A nation's jurisdiction over its nationals also includes the matters of asylum and extradition, which involve a national who has committed a civil or political crime in his home nation and has fled to another nation to escape the authority of his own. Asylum is the granting of shelter and protection to a political criminal or to a civil criminal in the absence of an extradition treaty. No general rule of international law governs extradition, in which the receiving nation apprehends and returns the fugitive to his home nation. A state may voluntarily surrender a fugitive but is under no legal obligation to do so unless it has signed an extradition treaty with the fugitive's home nation. Such treaties are quite common and share several common features.

1. Reciprocity and mutuality are the prime principles.
2. A fugitive surrendered cannot be tried for offenses not included in the extradition treaty or described in the extradition proceedings, or for a crime different from that stated at the time of extradition.
3. Extradition does not involve political criminals, and the receiving state determines whether or not the offense was politically motivated. Again, states will not be too free with this right because of the principle of reciprocity.

Territory

An essential attribute of a state is its possession and exclusive jurisdiction over a section of territory. That territory includes all land (including subterranean areas), waters (including rivers, lakes, and territorial sea), and airspace. Ships, aircraft, and embassy grounds abroad are not extensions of territory but extensions of a state's jurisdiction. Territory, besides being an integral part of the state's identity, is also a stake, a theater, and an environment;[3] so states have been concerned to specify rules governing acquisition of title, definition of boundaries, and degree of jurisdiction over their territory.

Five means exist for acquiring title to territory:

1. Occupation—the settlement of land not claimed by any other state.
2. Accretion—the gradual extension of territory through the geophysical process of soil deposits from a river or ocean that flows past a shore.
3. Prescription—continued occupation, over a long period of time and without protest by the original owner, of territory that belonged to another state.
4. Voluntary cession—formal transfer of title and sovereignty over a specific section of territory from one state to another.
5. Conquest and annexation—forceful occupation and absorption of another state's territory. The last mode, extensively used in the past, is generally considered to be illegal today. Those who claim its illegality point to such occurrences and conventions as the League of Nations' condemnation of Italy's

conquest of Ethiopia and application of sanctions, Article 10 of the Covenant of the League of Nations, the Kellogg-Briand Pact (see Chap.   ), and Articles 1 and 2 of the Charter of the United Nations. However, the Soviet Union's absorption of Lithuania, Latvia, and Estonia, India's of Goa, and China's of Tibet indicate that the law may have loopholes if absorption is accompanied by a plebiscite or claims of anticolonization.

Boundaries normally are determined through treaties, usually peace treaties such as Westphalia, Vienna, and Versailles. Bilateral treaties may be used to define a specific portion of a nation's boundaries, as between the United States and Mexico. If a river separates two nations the midchannel or thalweg becomes the boundary, which may change over time as erosion and accretion take place. If a mountain range separates two nations the watershed is the boundary. The seaward side of a coastal state is bounded by the edge of the territorial sea.

Jurisdiction over territory may be limited through a legal restriction called servitude; a binding obligation on the part of a given state to permit specified uses of all or parts of its territory by or in favor of another state or states. Servitudes can be positive, enabling a foreign state to exercise specific rights on the territory, or negative, in which the state that owns the territory refrains from certain specified actions on the territory. Examples of servitudes include: demilitarization of the Rhineland; prohibition of warships in the Black Sea; extraterritoriality, or the exempting of certain foreign nations from the jurisdiction of the state in whose territory they are located; leased territories, such as Guantanamo Bay in Cuba, in which administrative sovereignty is temporarily transferred from lessor to the lessee.

The Sea

A United Nations Conference on the Law of the Sea, held in Geneva in 1958, drafted and adopted four major conventions.

1. THE TERRITORIAL SEA AND THE CONTIGUOUS ZONE

The States Parties to this Convention
Have agreed as follows:

PART I

TERRITORIAL SEA

Section I. General

Article 1

1. The sovereignty of a State extends, beyond its land territory and its internal waters, to a belt of sea adjacent to its coast, described as the territorial sea.

2. This sovereignty is exercised subject to the provisions of these Articles and to other rules of international law.

Article 2

The sovereignty of a coastal State extends to the air space over the territorial sea as well as to its bed and subsoil.

Section II. Limits of the Territorial Sea

Article 3

Except where otherwise provided in these Articles, the normal baseline for measuring the breadth of the territorial sea is the low-water line along the coast as marked on large-scale charts officially recognized by the coastal State.

Article 4

1. In localities where the coastline is deeply indented and cut into, or if there is a fringe of islands along the coast in its immediate vicinity, the method of straight baselines joining appropriate points may be employed in drawing the baseline from which the breadth of the territorial sea is measured.
2. The drawing of such baselines must not depart to any appreciable extent from the general direction of the coast, and the sea areas lying within the lines must be sufficiently closely linked to the land domain to be subject to the régime of internal waters.

3. Baselines shall not be drawn to and from low-tide elevations, unless lighthouses or similar installations which are permanently above sea level have been built on them.

4. Where the method of straight baselines is applicable under the provisions of paragraph 1, account may be taken, in determining particular baselines, of economic interests peculiar to the region concerned, the reality and the importance of which are clearly evidenced by a long usage.

5. The system of straight baselines may not be applied by a State in such a manner as to cut off from the high seas the territorial sea of another State.

6. The coastal State must clearly indicate straight baselines on charts, to which due publicity must be given.

Article 5

1. Waters on the landward side of the baseline of the territorial sea form part of the internal waters of the State.

2. Where the establishment of a straight baseline in accordance with Article 4 has the effect of enclosing as internal waters areas which previously had been considered as part of the territorial sea or of the high seas, a right of innocent passage, as provided in Articles 14 to 23, shall exist in those waters.

Article 6

The outer limit of the territorial sea is the line every point of which is at a distance from the nearest point of the baseline equal to the breadth of the territorial sea.

Article 7

1. This Article relates only to bays the coasts of which belong to a single State.

2. For the purposes of these Articles, a bay is a well-marked indentation whose penetration is in such proportion to the width of its mouth as to contain landlocked waters and constitute more than a mere curvature of the coast. An indentation shall not, however, be regarded as a bay unless its area is as large as, or larger than, that of the semi-circle whose diameter is a line drawn across the mouth of that indentation.

3. For the purpose of measurement, the area of an indentation is that lying between the low-water mark around the shore of the indentation and a line joining the low-water mark of its natural entrance points. Where, because of the presence of islands, an indentation has more than one mouth, the semi-circle shall be drawn on a line as long as the sum total of the lengths of the lines across the different mouths. Islands within an indentation shall be included as if they were part of the water area of the indentation.

4. If the distance between the low-water marks of the natural entrance points of a bay does not exceed twenty-four miles, a closing line may be drawn between these two low-water marks, and the waters enclosed thereby shall be considered as internal waters.

5. Where the distance between the low-water marks of the natural entrance points of a bay exceeds twenty-four miles, a straight baseline of twenty-four miles shall be drawn within the bay in such a manner as to enclose the maximum area of water that is possible with a line of that length.

6. The foregoing provisions shall not apply to so-called 'historic' bays, or in any case where the straight baseline system provided for in Article 4 is applied.

Article 8

For the purpose of delimiting the territorial sea, the outermost permanent harbour works which form an integral part of the harbour system shall be regarded as forming part of the coast.

Article 9

Roadsteads which are normally used for the loading, unloading, and anchoring of ships, and which would otherwise be situated wholly or partly outside the outer limit of the territorial sea, are included in the territorial sea. The coastal State must clearly demarcate such roadsteads and indicate them on charts together with their boundaries to which due publicity must be given.

Article 10

1. An island is a naturally-formed area of land, surrounded by water, which is above water at high tide.
2. The territorial sea of an island is measured in accordance with the provisions of these Articles.

Article 11

1. A low-tide elevation is a naturally formed area of land which is surrounded by and above water at low-tide but submerged at high tide. Where a low-tide elevation is situ-

ated wholly or partly at a distance not exceeding the breadth of the territorial sea from the mainland or an island, the low-water line on that elevation may be used as the baseline for measuring the breadth of the territorial sea.

2. Where a low-tide elevation is wholly situated at a distance exceeding the breadth of the territorial sea from the mainland or an island, it has no territorial sea of its own.

Article 12

1. Where the coasts of two States are opposite or adjacent to each other, neither of the two States is entitled, failing agreement between them to the contrary, to extend its territorial sea beyond the median line every point of which is equidistant from the nearest points on the baselines from which the breadth of the territorial seas of each of the two States is measured. The provisions of this paragraph shall not apply, however, where it is necessary by reason of historic title or other special circumstances to delimit the territorial seas of the two States in a way which is at variance with this provision.

2. The line of delimitation between the territorial seas of two States lying opposite to each other or adjacent to each other shall be marked on large-scale charts officially recognized by the coastal States.

Article 13

If a river flows directly into the sea, the baseline shall be a straight line across the mouth of the river between points on the low-tide line of its banks.

Section III. Right of Innocent Passage

Sub-section A. Rules applicable to all ships

Article 14

1. Subject to the provisions of these Articles, ships of all States, whether coastal or not, shall enjoy the right of innocent passage through the territorial sea.
2. Passage means navigation through the territorial sea for the purpose either of traversing that sea without entering internal waters, or of proceeding to internal waters, or of making for the high seas from internal waters.
3. Passage includes stopping and anchoring, but only in so far as the same are incidental to ordinary navigation or are rendered necessary by *force majeure* or by distress.
4. Passage is innocent so long as it is not prejudicial to the peace, good order or security of the coastal State. Such passage shall take place in conformity with these Articles and with other rules of international law.
5. Passage of foreign fishing vessels shall not be considered innocent if they do not observe such laws and regulations as the coastal State may make and publish in order to prevent these vessels from fishing in the territorial sea.
6. Submarines are required to navigate on the surface and to show their flag.

Article 15

1. The coastal State must not hamper innocent passage through the territorial sea.

2. The coastal State is required to give appropriate publicity to any dangers to navigation, of which it has knowledge, within its territorial sea.

Article 16

1. The coastal State may take the necessary steps in its territorial sea to prevent passage which is not innocent.

2. In the case of ships proceeding to internal waters, the coastal State shall also have the right to take the necessary steps to prevent any breach of the conditions to which admission of those ships to those waters is subject.

3. Subject to the provisions of paragraph 4, the coastal State may, without discrimination amongst foreign ships, suspend temporarily in specified areas of its territorial sea the innocent passage of foreign ships if such suspension is essential for the protection of its security. Such suspension shall take effect only after having been duly published.

4. There shall be no suspension of the innocent passage of foreign ships through straits which are used for international navigation between one part of the high seas and another part of the high seas or the territorial sea of a foreign State.

Article 17

Foreign ships exercising the right of innocent passage shall comply with the laws and regulations enacted by the coastal State in conformity with these Articles and other rules of international law and, in particular, with such laws and regulations relating to transport and navigation.

Sub-section B. Rules applicable to merchant ships

Article 18

1. No charge may be levied upon foreign ships by reason only of their passage through the territorial sea.
2. Charges may be levied upon a foreign ship passing through the territorial sea as payment only for specific services rendered to the ship. These charges shall be levied without discrimination.

Article 19

1. The criminal jurisdiction of the coastal State should not be exercised on board a foreign ship passing through the territorial sea to arrest any person or to conduct any investigation in connexion with any crime committed on board the ship during its passage, save only in the following cases:

    (*a*) If the consequences of the crime extend to the coastal State; or

    (*b*) If the crime is of a kind to disturb the peace of the country or the good order of the territorial sea; or

    (*c*) If the assistance of the local authorities has been requested by the captain of the ship or by the consul of the country whose flag the ship flies; or

    (*d*) If it is necessary for the suppression of illicit traffic in narcotic drugs.

2. The above provisions do not affect the right of the coastal State to take any steps authorized by its laws for

the purpose of an arrest or investigation on board a foreign ship passing through the territorial sea after leaving internal waters.

3. In the cases provided for in paragraphs 1 and 2 of this Article, the coastal State shall, if the captain so requests, advise the consular authority of the flag State before taking any steps, and shall facilitate contact between such authority and the ship's crew. In cases of emergency this notification may be communicated while the measures are being taken.

4. In considering whether or how an arrest should be made, the local authorities shall pay due regard to the interests of navigation.

5. The coastal State may not take any steps on board a foreign ship passing through the territorial sea to arrest any person or to conduct any investigation in connexion with any crime committed before the ship entered the territorial sea, if the ship, proceeding from a foreign port, is only passing through the territorial sea without entering internal waters.

Article 20

1. The coastal State should not stop or divert a foreign ship passing through the territorial sea for the purpose of exercising civil jurisdiction in relation to a person on board the ship.

2. The coastal State may not levy execution against or arrest the ship for the purpose of any civil proceedings, save only in respect of obligations or liabilities assumed or incurred by the ship itself in the course or for the pur-

pose of its voyage through the waters of the coastal State.

3. The provisions of the previous paragraph are without prejudice to the right of the coastal State, in accordance with its laws, to levy execution against or to arrest, for the purpose of any civil proceedings, a foreign ship lying in the territorial sea, or passing through the territorial sea after leaving internal waters.

Sub-section C. Rules applicable to government ships other than warships

Article 21

The rules contained in sub-sections A and B shall also apply to government ships operated for commercial purposes.

Article 22

1. The rules contained in sub-section A and in Article 18 shall apply to government ships operated for non-commercial purposes.

2. With such exceptions as are contained in the provisions referred to in the preceding paragraph, nothing in these Articles affects the immunities which such ships enjoy under these Articles or other rules of international law.

Sub-section D. Rule applicable to warships

Article 23

If any warship does not comply with the regulations of the coastal State concerning passage through the territorial sea and disregards any request for compliance which is made to it, the coastal State may require the warship to leave the territorial sea.

PART II
CONTIGUOUS ZONE

Article 24

1. In a zone of the high seas contiguous to its territorial sea, the coastal State may exercise the control necessary to:

    (a) Prevent infringement of its customs, fiscal, immigration or sanitary regulations within its territory or territorial sea;

    (b) Punish infringement of the above regulations committed within its territory or territorial sea.

2. The contiguous zone may not extend beyond twelve miles from the baseline from which the breadth of the territorial sea is measured.

3. Where the coasts of two States are opposite or adjacent to each other, neither of the two States is entitled, failing agreement between them to the contrary, to extend its contiguous zone beyond the median line every point of which is equidistant from the nearest points on the baselines from which the breadth of the territorial seas of the two States is measured.

PART III
FINAL ARTICLES

Article 25

The provisions of this Convention shall not affect conventions or other international agreements already in force, as between States Parties to them.

Article 26

This Convention shall, until 31 October 1958, be open for signature by all States Members of the United Nations or of any of the specialized agencies, and by any other State invited by the General Assembly of the United Nations to become a party to the Convention.

Article 27

This Convention is subject to ratification. The instruments of ratification shall be deposited with the Secretary-General of the United Nations.

Article 28

This Convention shall be open for accession by any States belonging to any of the categories mentioned in Article 26. The instrument of accession shall be deposited with the Secretary-General of the United Nations.

Article 29

1. This Convention shall come into force on the thirtieth day following the date of deposit of the twenty-second instrument of ratification or accession with the Secretary-General of the United Nations.
2. For each State ratifying or acceding to the Convention after the deposit of the twenty-second instrument of ratification or accession, the Convention shall enter into force

on the thirtieth day after deposit by such State of its instrument of ratification or accession.

Article 30

1. After the expiration of a period of five years from the date on which this Convention shall enter into force, a request for the revision of this Convention may be made at any time by any Contracting Party by means of a notification in writing addressed to the Secretary-General of the United Nations.
2. The General Assembly of the United Nations shall decide upon the steps, if any, to be taken in respect of such request.

Article 31

The Secretary-General of the United Nations shall inform all States Members of the United Nations and the other States referred to in Article 26:

    (a) Of signatures to this Convention and of the deposit of instruments of ratification or accession, in accordance with Articles 26, 27, and 28;

    (b) Of the date on which this Convention will come into force, in accordance with Article 29;

    (c) Of requests for revision in accordance with Article 30.

Article 32

The original of this Convention, of which the Chinese, English, French, Russian, and Spanish texts are equally authentic, shall be deposited with the Secretary-General of the United Nations, who shall send certified copies thereof to all States referred to in Article 26.

In Witness Whereof the undersigned plenipotentiaries, being duly authorized thereto by their respective governments, have signed this Convention.

Done at Geneva, this twenty-ninth day of April one thousand nine hundred and fifty-eight.

2. THE HIGH SEAS

The States Parties to this Convention,

Desiring to codify the rules of international law relating to the high seas,

Recognizing that the United Nations Conference on the Law of the Sea, held at Geneva from 24 February to 27 April 1958, adopted the following provisions as generally declaratory of established principles of international law,

Have agreed as follows:

Article 1

The term 'high seas' means all parts of the sea that are not included in the territorial sea or in the internal waters of a State.

Article 2

The high seas being open to all nations, no State may validly purport to subject any part of them to its sovereignty. Freedom of the high seas is exercised under the conditions laid down by these articles and by the other rules of international law. It comprises, *inter alia*, both for coastal and non-coastal States:

(1) Freedom of navigation;
(2) Freedom of fishing;
(3) Freedom to lay submarine cables and pipelines;
(4) Freedom to fly over the high seas.

These freedoms, and others which are recognized by the general principles of international law, shall be exercised by all States with reasonable regard to the interests of other States in their exercise of the freedom of the high seas.

Article 3

1. In order to enjoy the freedom of the seas on equal terms with coastal States, States having no sea-coast should have free access to the sea. To this end States situated between the sea and a State having no sea-coast shall by common agreement with the latter and in conformity with existing international conventions accord:

(a) ‧ To the State having no sea-coast, on a basis of reciprocity, free transit through their territory; and

(b) To ships flying the flag of that State treatment equal to that accorded to their own ships, or to the ships of any other States, as regards access to seaports and the use of such ports.

2. States situated between the sea and a State having no sea-coast shall settle, by mutual agreement with the latter, and taking into account the rights of the coastal State or State of transit and the special conditions of the State having no sea-coast, all matters relating to freedom of

transit and equal treatment in ports, in case such States are not already parties to existing international conventions.

Article 4

Every State, whether coastal or not, has the right to sail ships under its flag on the high seas.

Article 5

1. Each State shall fix the conditions for the grant of its nationality to ships, for the registration of ships in its territory, and for the right to fly its flag. Ships have the nationality of the State whose flag they are entitled to fly. There must exist a genuine link between the State and the ship; in particular, the State must effectively exercise its jurisdiction and control in administrative, technical and social matters over ships flying its flag.
2. Each State shall issue to ships to which it has granted the right to fly its flag documents to that effect.

Article 6

1. Ships shall sail under the flag of one State only and, save in exceptional cases expressly provided for in international treaties or in these Articles, shall be subject to its exclusive jurisdiction on the high seas. A ship may not change its flag during a voyage or while in a port of call, save in the case of a real transfer of ownership or change of registry.
2. A ship which sails under the flags of two or more States, using them according to convenience, may not claim any of the nationalities in question with respect to

any other State, and may be assimilated to a ship without nationality.

Article 7

The provisions of the preceding Articles do not prejudice the question of ships employed on the official service of an intergovernmental organization flying the flag of the organization.

Article 8

1. Warships on the high seas have complete immunity from the jurisdiction of any State other than the flag State.
2. For the purposes of these Articles, the term 'warship' means a ship belonging to the naval forces of a State and bearing the external marks distinguishing warships of its nationality, under the command of an officer duly commissioned by the government and whose name appears in the Navy List, and manned by a crew who are under regular naval discipline.

Article 9

Ships owned or operated by a State and used only on government non-commercial service shall, on the high seas, have complete immunity from the jurisdiction of any State other than the flag State.

Article 10

1. Every State shall take such measures for ships under its flag as are necessary to ensure safety at sea with regard *inter alia* to:
   (a) The use of signals, the maintenance of communications and the prevention of collisions;

(b) The manning of ships and labour conditions for crews taking into account the applicable international labour instruments;

(c) The construction, equipment, and seaworthiness of ships.

2. In taking such measures each State is required to conform to generally accepted international standards and to take any steps which may be necessary to ensure their observance.

Article 11

1. In the event of a collision or of any other incident of navigation concerning a ship on the high seas, involving the penal or disciplinary responsibility of the master or of any other person in the service of the ship, no penal or disciplinary proceedings may be instituted against such persons except before the judicial or administrative authorities either of the flag State or of the State of which such person is a national.

2. In disciplinary matters, the State which has issued a master's certificate or a certificate of competence or licence shall alone be competent, after due legal process, to pronounce the withdrawal of such certificates, even if the holder is not a national of the State which issued them.

3. No arrest or detention of the ship, even as a measure of investigation, shall be ordered by any authorities other than those of the flag State.

Article 12

1. Every State shall require the master of a ship sailing

under its flag, in so far as he can do so without serious danger to the ship, the crew, or the passengers:

(a) To render assistance to any person found at sea in danger of being lost;

(b) To proceed with all possible speed to the rescue of persons in distress if informed of their need of assistance, in so far as such action may reasonably be expected of him;

(c) After a collision, to render assistance to the other ship, her crew and her passengers and, where possible, to inform the other ship of the name of his own ship, her port of registry and the nearest port at which she will call.

2. Every coastal State shall promote the establishment and maintenance of an adequate and effective search and rescue service regarding safety on and over the sea and—where circumstances so require—by way of mutual regional arrangements co-operate with neighbouring States for this purpose.

Article 13

Every State shall adopt effective measures to prevent and punish the transport of slaves in ships authorized to fly its flag, and to prevent the unlawful use of its flag for that purpose. Any slave taking refuge on board any ship, whatever its flag, shall, *ipso facto*, be free.

Article 14

All States shall co-operate to the fullest possible extent in the repression of piracy on the high seas or in any other place outside the jurisdiction of any State.

Article 15

Piracy consists of any of the following acts:

    (1) Any illegal acts of violence, detention or any act of depredation, committed for private ends by the crew or the passengers of a private ship or a private aircraft, and directed:

        (*a*) On the high seas, against another ship or aircraft, or against persons or property on board such ship or aircraft;

        (*b*) Against a ship, aircraft, persons, or property in a place outside the jurisdiction of any State;

    (2) Any act of voluntary participation in the operation of a ship or of an aircraft with knowledge of facts making it a pirate ship or aircraft;

    (3) Any act of inciting or of intentionally facilitating an act described in sub-paragraph 1 or sub-paragraph 2 of this article.

Article 16

The acts of piracy, as defined in Article 15, committed by a warship, government ship or government aircraft whose crew has mutinied and taken control of the ship or aircraft are assimilated to acts committed by a private ship.

Article 17

A ship or aircraft is considered a pirate ship or aircraft if it is intended by the persons in dominant control to be used for the purpose of committing one of the acts referred to in Article 15. The same applies if the ship or aircraft has been used to commit any such act, so long as it remains under the control of the persons guilty of that act.

Article 18

A ship or aircraft may retain its nationality although it has become a pirate ship or aircraft. The retention or loss of nationality is determined by the law of the State from which such nationality was derived.

Article 19

On the high seas, or in any other place outside the jurisdiction of any State, every State may seize a pirate ship or aircraft, or a ship taken by piracy and under the control of pirates, and arrest the persons and seize the property on board. The courts of the of the State which carried out the seizure may decide upon the penalties to be imposed, and may also determine the action to be taken with regard to the ships, aircraft or property, subject to the rights of third parties acting in good faith.

Article 20

Where the seizure of a ship or aircraft on suspicion of piracy has been effected without adequate grounds, the State making the seizure shall be liable to the State the nationality of which is possessed by the ship or aircraft, for any loss or damage caused by the seizure.

Article 21

A seizure on account of piracy may only be carried out by

warships or military aircraft, or other ships or aircraft on government service authorized to that effect.

Article 22

1. Except where acts of interference derive from powers conferred by treaty, a warship which encounters a foreign merchant ship on the high seas is not justified in boarding her unless there is reasonable ground for suspecting:

    (*a*) That the ship is engaged in piracy; or

    (*b*) That the ship is engaged in the slave trade; or

    (*c*) That, though flying a foreign flag or refusing to show its flag, the ship is, in reality, of the same nationality as the warship.

2. In the cases provided for in sub-paragraphs (*a*), (*b*) and (*c*) above, the warship may proceed to verify the ship's right to fly its flag. To this end, it may send a boat under the command of an officer to the suspected ship. If suspicion remains after the documents have been checked, it may proceed to a further examination on board the ship, which must be carried out with all possible consideration.

3. If the suspicions prove to be unfounded, and provided that the ship boarded has not committed any act justifying them, it shall be compensated for any loss or damage that may have been sustained.

Article 23

1. The hot pursuit of a foreign ship may be undertaken when the competent authorities of the coastal State

have good reason to believe that the ship has violated the laws and regulations of that State. Such pursuit must be commenced when the foreign ship or one of its boats is within the internal waters or the territorial sea or the contiguous zone of the pursuing State, and may only be continued outside the territorial sea or the contiguous zone if the pursuit has not been interrupted. It is not necessary that, at the time when the foreign ship within the territorial sea or the contiguous zone receives the order to stop, the ship giving the order should likewise be within the territorial sea or the contiguous zone. If the foreign ship is within a contiguous zone, as defined in Article 24 of the Convention on the Territorial Sea and the Contiguous Zone, the pursuit may only be undertaken if there has been a violation of the rights for the protection of which the zone was established.

2. The right of hot pursuit ceases as soon as the ship pursued enters the territorial sea of its own country or of a Third State.

3. Hot pursuit is not deemed to have begun unless the pursuing ship has satisfied itself by such practicable means as may be available that the ship pursued or one of its boats or other craft working as a team and using the ship pursued as a mother ship are within the limits of the territorial sea, or as the case may be within the contiguous zone. The pursuit may only be commenced after a visual or auditory signal to stop has been given at a distance which enables it to be seen or heard by the foreign ship.

4. The right of hot pursuit may be exercised only by warships or military aircraft, or other ships or aircraft on government service specially authorized to that effect.

5. Where hot pursuit is effected by an aircraft:
    (*a*) The provisions of paragraphs 1 to 3 of this article shall apply *mutatis mutandis*;
    (*b*) The aircraft giving the order to stop must itself actively pursue the ship until a ship or aircraft of the coastal State, summoned by the aircraft, arrives to take over the pursuit, unless the aircraft is itself able to arrest the ship. It does not suffice to justify an arrest on the high seas that the ship was merely sighted by the aircraft as an offender or suspected offender, if it was not both ordered to stop and pursued by the aircraft itself or other aircraft or ships which continue the pursuit without interruption.

6. The release of a ship arrested within the jurisdiction of a State and escorted to a port of that State for the purposes of an inquiry before the competent authorities may not be claimed solely on the ground that the ship, in the course of its voyage, was escorted across a portion of the high seas, if the circumstances rendered this necessary.

7. Where a ship has been stopped or arrested on the high seas in circumstances which do not justify the exercise of the rights of hot pursuit, it shall be compensated for any loss or damage that may have been thereby sustained.

Article 24

Every State shall draw up regulations to prevent pollution of the seas by the discharge of oil from ships or pipelines or resulting from the exploitation and exploration of the seabed and its subsoil, taking account of existing treaty provisions on the subject.

Article 25

1. Every State shall take measures to prevent pollution of the seas from the dumping of radioactive waste, taking into account any standards and regulations which may be formulated by the competent international organizations.
2. All States shall co-operate with the competent international organizations in taking measures for the prevention of pollution of the seas or air space above, resulting from any activities with radioactive materials or other harmful agents.

Article 26

1. All States shall be entitled to lay submarine cables and pipelines on the bed of the high seas.
2. Subject to its right to take reasonable measures for the exploration of the continental shelf and the exploitation of its natural resources, the coastal State may not impede the laying or maintenance of such cables or pipelines.
3. When laying such cables or pipelines the State in question shall pay due regard to cables or pipelines already in position on the sea-bed. In particular, possibilities of repairing existing cables or pipelines shall not be prejudiced.
Every State shall take the necessary legislative measures to provide that the breaking or injury by a ship flying its flag or by a person subject to its jurisdiction of a submarine cable beneath the high seas done wilfully or

through culpable negligence, in such a manner as to be liable to interrupt or obstruct telegraphic or telephonic communications, and similarly the breaking or injury of a submarine pipeline or high-voltage power cable shall be a punishable offence. This provision shall not apply to any break or injury caused by persons who acted merely with the legitimate object of saving their lives or their ships, after having taken all necessary precautions to avoid such break or injury.

Article 28

Every State shall take the necessary legislative measures to provide that, if persons subject to its jurisdiction who are the owners of a cable or pipeline beneath the high seas, in laying or repairing that cable or pipeline, cause a break in or injury to another cable or pipeline, they shall bear the cost of the repairs.

Article 29

Every State shall take the necessary legislative measures to ensure that the owners of ships who can prove that they have sacrificed an anchor, a net or any other fishing gear, in order to avoid injuring a submarine cable or pipeline, shall be indemnified by the owner of the cable or pipeline, provided that the owner of the ship has taken all reasonable precautionary measures beforehand.

Article 30

The provisions of this Convention shall not affect conventions or other international agreements already in force, as between States parties to them.

Article 31

This Convention shall, until 31 October 1958, be open for signature by all States Members of the United Nations or of any of the specialized agencies, and by any other State invited by the General Assembly of the United Nations to become a Party to the Convention.

Article 32

This Convention is subject to ratification. The instruments of ratification shall be deposited with the Secretary-General of the United Nations.

Article 33

This Convention shall be open for accession by any States belonging to any of the categories mentioned in Article 31. The instruments of accession shall be deposited with the Secretary-General of the United Nations.

Article 34

1. This Convention shall come into force on the thirtieth day following the date of deposit of the twenty-second instrument of ratification or accession with the Secretary-General of the United Nations.

2. For each ratifying or acceding to the Convention after the deposit of the twenty-second instrument of ratification or accession, the Convention shall enter into force on the

thirtieth day after deposit by such State of its instrument of ratification or accession.

Article 35

1. After the expiration of a period of five years from the date on which this Convention shall enter into force, a request for the revision of this Convention may be made at any time by any Contracting Party by means of a notification in writing addressed to the Secretary-General of the United Nations.

2. The General Assembly of the United Nations shall decide upon the steps, if any, to be taken in respect of such request.

Article 36

The Secretary-General of the United Nations shall inform all States Members of the United Nations and the other States referred to in Article 31:

(a) Of signatures to this Convention and of the deposit of instruments of ratification or accession, in accordance with Articles 31, 32, and 33;

(b) Of the date on which this Convention will come into force, in accordance with Article 34;

(c) Of requests for revision in accordance with Article 35.

Article 37

The original of this Convention, of which the Chinese, English, French, Russian, and Spanish texts are equally authentic, shall be deposited with the Secretary-General of the United Nations, who shall send certified copies thereof to all States referred to in Article 31.

In Witness Whereof the undersigned plenipotentiaries, being duly authorized thereto by their respective governments, have signed this Convention.

Done at Geneva, this twenty-ninth day of April one thousand nine hundred and fifty-eight.

4. THE CONTINENTAL SHELF

The States Parties to this Convention
Have agreed as follows:

Article 1

For the purpose of these Articles, the term 'continental shelf' is used as referring (*a*) to the seabed and subsoil of the submarine areas adjacent to the coast but outside the area of the territorial sea, to a depth of 200 metres or, beyond that limit, to where the depth of the superjacent waters admits of the exploitation of the natural resources of the said areas; (*b*) to the seabed and subsoil of similar submarine areas adjacent to the coasts of islands.

Article 2

1. The coastal State exercises over the continental shelf sovereign rights for the purpose of exploring it and exploiting its natural resources.

2. The rights referred to in paragraph 1 of this Article are exclusive in the sense that if the coastal State does not

explore the continental shelf or exploit its natural resources, no one may undertake these activities, or make a claim to the continental shelf, without the express consent of the coastal State.

3. The rights of the coastal State over the continental shelf do not depend on occupation, effective or notional, or on any express proclamation.

4. The natural resources referred to in these Articles consist of the mineral and other non-living resources of the seabed and subsoil together with living organisms belonging to sedentary species, that is to say, organisms which, at the harvestable stage, either are immobile on or under the seabed or are unable to move except in constant physical contact with the seabed or the subsoil.

Article 3

The rights of the coastal State over the continental shelf do not affect the legal status of the superjacent waters as high seas, or that of the air space above those waters.

Article 4

Subject to its right to take reasonable measures for the exploration of the continental shelf and the exploitation of its natural resources, the coastal State may not impede the laying or maintenance of submarine cables or pipelines on the continental shelf.

Article 5

1. The exploration of the continental shelf and the exploitation of its natural resources must not result in any unjus-

tifiable interference with navigation, fishing or the conservation of the living resources of the sea, nor result in any interference with fundamental oceanographic or other scientific research carried out with the intention of open publication.

2. Subject to the provisions of paragraphs 1 and 6 of this Article, the coastal State is entitled to construct and maintain or operate on the continental shelf installations and other devices necessary for its exploration and the exploitation of its natural resources, and to establish safety zones around such installations and devices and to take in those zones measures necessary for their protection.

3. The safety zones referred to in paragraph 2 of this Article may extend to a distance of 500 metres around the installations and other devices which have been erected, measured from each point of their outer edge. Ships of all nationalities must respect these safety zones.

4. Such installations and devices, though under the jurisdiction of the coastal State, do not possess the status of islands. They have no territorial sea of their own, and their presence does not affect the delimitation of the territorial sea of the coastal State.

5. Due notice must be given of the construction of any such installations, and permanent means for giving warning of their presence must be maintained. Any installations which are abandoned or disused must be entirely removed.

6. Neither the installations or devices, nor the safety zones around them, may be established where interference may be caused to the use of recognized sea lanes essential to international navigation.

7. The coastal State is obliged to undertake, in the safety zones, all appropriate measures for the protection of the living resources of the sea from harmful agents.

8. The consent of the coastal State shall be obtained in respect of any research concerning the continental shelf and undertaken there. Nevertheless, the coastal State shall not normally withhold its consent if the request is submitted by a qualified institution with a view to purely scientific research into the physical or biological characteristics of the continental shelf, subject to the proviso that the coastal State shall have the right, if it so desires, to participate or to be represented in the research, and that in any event the results shall be published.

Article 6

1. Where the same continental shelf is adjacent to the territories of two or more States whose coasts are opposite each other, the boundary of the continental shelf appertaining to such States shall be determined by agreement between them. In the absence of agreement, and unless another boundary line is justified by special circumstances, the boundary is the median line, every point of which is equidistant from the nearest points of the baselines from which the breadth of the territorial sea of each State is measured.

2. Where the same continental shelf is adjacent to the territories of two adjacent States, the boundary of the continental shelf shall be determined by agreement between them. In the absence of agreement, and unless another boundary line is justified by special circumstances, the

boundary shall be determined by application of the principle of equidistance from the nearest points of the baselines from which the breadth of the territorial sea of each State is measured.

3. In delimiting the boundaries of the continental shelf, any lines which are drawn in accordance with the principles set out in paragraphs 1 and 2 of this Article should be defined with reference to charts and geographical features as they exist at a particular date, and reference should be made to fixed permanent identifiable points on the land.

Article 7

The provisions of these Articles shall not prejudice the right of the coastal State to exploit the subsoil by means of tunnelling irrespective of the depth of water above the subsoil.

Article 8

This Convention shall, until 30 October 1958, be open for signature by all States Members of the United Nations or of any of the specialized agencies, and by any other State invited by the General Assembly of the United Nations to become a party to the Convention.

Article 9

This Convention is subject to ratification. The instruments of ratification shall be deposited with the Secretary-General of the United Nations.

Article 10

This Convention shall be open for accession by any States belonging to any of the categories mentioned in Article 8. The instruments of accession shall be deposited with the Secretary-General of the United Nations.

Article 11

1. This Convention shall come into force on the thirtieth day following the date of deposit of the twenty-second instrument of ratification or accession with the Secretary-General of the United Nations.
2. For each State ratifying or acceding to the Convention after the deposit of the twenty-second instrument of ratification or accession, the Convention shall enter into force on the thirtieth day after deposit by such State of its instrument of ratification or accession.

Article 12

1. At the time of signature, ratification or accession, any State may make reservations to Articles of the Convention other than to Articles 1 to 3 inclusive.
2. Any contracting State making a reservation in accordance with the preceding paragraph may at any time withdraw the reservation by a communication to that effect addressed to the Secretary-General of the United Nations.

Article 13

1. After the expiration of a period of five years from the date on which this Convention shall enter into force, a request for the revision of this Convention may be made at any time by any contracting party by means of a notification in writing addressed to the Secretary-General of the United Nations.

2. The General Assembly of the United Nations shall decide upon the steps, if any, to be taken in respect of such request.

Article 14

The Secretary-General of the United Nations shall inform all States Members of the United Nations and the other States referred to in Article 8:

(a) Of signatures to this Convention and of the deposit of instruments of ratification or accession, in accordance with Articles 8, 9 and 10;

(b) Of the date on which this Convention will come into force, in accordance with Article 11;

(c) Of requests for revision in accordance with Article 13;

(d) Of reservations to this Convention, in accordance with Article 12.

Article 15

The original of this Convention, of which the Chinese, English, French, Russian and Spanish texts are equally authentic, shall be deposited with the Secretary-General of the United Nations, who shall send certified copies thereof to all States referred to in Article 8.

In Witness Whereof the undersigned plenipotentiaries, being duly authorized thereto by their respective governments, have signed this Convention.

Done at Geneva, this twenty-ninth day of April one thousand nine hundred and fifty-eight.

Only the Convention on the High Seas is declaratory of general principles of international law, but the other sea conventions provide evidence of generally accepted rules. Despite this great amount of codification several problems remained.

1. No agreement was reached on the breadth of the territorial sea and coastal fishing jurisdiction.

2. No agreement was reached on the breadth of sovereign rights over the seabed resources of the Continental Shelf.

3. No appreciation of the dangers of pollution in the sea was expressed.

Another conference was held in 1960 to try to resolve these problems, but no agreements were reached. In the years since the 1958 and 1960 conferences supertankers have increased the danger of pollution from oilspills; methods of fishing have become more sophisticated, thereby increasing the danger of overfishing; technology for extracting the mineral resources of the Continental Shelf has increased; and states have enlarged their claims of jurisdiction over the seas, some claiming jurisdiction up to 200 miles from shore. In response to these developments another Law of the Sea Conference is scheduled for 1974.

Airspace and Outer Space

The airspace above a state has been considered an extension of the territory of that state and thus under its exclusive jurisdiction, for a state could be placed in mortal danger from the air. The boundary line between airspace and outer space is not commonly agreed on, but definite rules govern the use of both airspace and outer space. Following are the conventions and agreements that embody those rules.

ANNEX

RELEVANT ARTICLES OF THE CONVENTION ON INTERNATIONAL CIVIL AVIATION
(concluded at Chicago in 1944).

Preamble

Whereas the future development of international civil aviation can greatly help to create and preserve friendship and understanding among the nations and peoples of the world, yet its abuse can become a threat to the general security; and

Whereas it is desirable to avoid friction and to

promote that cooperation between nations and peoples upon which the peace of the world depends;

Therefore, the undersigned governments having agreed on certain principles and arrangements in order that international civil aviation may be developed in a safe and orderly manner and that international air transport services may be established on the basis of equality of opportunity and operated soundly and economically;

Have accordingly concluded this Convention to that end.

PART I—AIR NAVIGATION

Chapter I

GENERAL PRINCIPLES AND APPLICATION OF THE CONVENTION

Article 1

Sovereignty

The contracting States recognize that every State has complete and exclusive sovereignty over the air-space above its territory.

Article 2

Territory

For the purposes of this Convention the territory of a State shall be deemed to be the land areas and territorial waters adjacent thereto under the sovereignty, suzerainty, protection or mandate of such State.

Article 3

Civil and state aircraft

(*a*) This Convention shall be applicable only to civil aircraft and shall not be applicable to state aircraft.

(*b*) Aircraft used in military, customs and police services shall be deemed to be state aircraft.

(*c*) No state aircraft of a contracting State shall fly over the territory of another State or land thereon without authorization by special agreement or otherwise, and in accordance with the terms thereof.

(*d*) The contracting States undertake, when issuing regulations for their state aircraft, that they will have due regard for the safety of navigation of civil aircraft.

Article 4

Misuse of civil aviation

Each contracting State agrees not to use civil aviation for any purpose inconsistent with the aims of this Convention.

Chapter II

FLIGHT OVER TERRITORY OF CONTRACTING STATES

Article 5

Right of non-scheduled flight

Each contracting State agrees that all aircraft of the

other contracting States, being aircraft not engaged in scheduled international air services shall have the right, subject to the observance of the terms of this Convention, to make flights into or in transit non-stop across its territory and to make stops for non-traffic purposes without the necessity of obtaining prior permission, and subject to the right of the State flown over to require landing. Each contracting State nevertheless reserves the right, for reasons of safety of flight, to require aircraft desiring to proceed over regions which are inaccessible or without adequate air navigation facilities to follow prescribed routes, or to obtain special permission for such flights.

Such aircraft, if engaged in the carriage of passengers, cargo, or mail for remuneration or hire on other than scheduled international air services, shall also, subject to the provisions of Article 7, have the privilege of taking on or discharging passengers, cargo, or mail, subject to the right of any State where such embarkation or discharge takes place to impose such regulations, conditions or limitations as it may consider desirable.

Article 6

Scheduled air services

No scheduled international air service may be operated over or into the territory of a contracting State, except with the special permission or other authorization of that State, and in accordance with the terms of such permission or authorization.

Article 7

Cabotage

Each contracting State shall have the right to refuse permission to the aircraft of other contracting States to take on in its territory passengers, mail and cargo carried for remuneration or hire and destined for another point within its territory. Each contracting State undertakes not to enter into any arrangements which specifically grant any such privilege on an exclusive basis to any other State or an airline of any other State, and not to obtain any such exclusive privilege from any other State.

Article 8

Pilotless aircraft

No aircraft capable of being flown without a pilot shall be flown without a pilot over the territory of a contracting State without special authorization by that State and in accordance with the terms of such authorization. Each contracting State undertakes to insure that the flight of such aircraft without a pilot in regions open to civil aircraft shall be so controlled as to obviate danger to civil aircraft.

Article 9

Prohibited areas

(a) Each contracting State may, for reasons of military necessity or public safety, restrict or prohibit uniformly the aircraft of other States from flying over certain areas of its territory, provided that no distinction in this respect is made between the aircraft of the State whose territory is involved, engaged in international scheduled airline services, and the aircraft of the other contracting States likewise engaged. Such prohibited areas shall be of reasonable extent and location so as not to interfere unnecessarily with air navigation. Descriptions of such prohibited areas in the territory of a contracting State, as well as any subsequent alterations therein, shall be communicated as soon as possible to the other contracting States and to the International Civil Aviation Organization.

(*b*) Each contracting State reserves also the right, in exceptional circumstances or during a period of emergency, or in the interest of public safety, and with immediate effect, temporarily to restrict or prohibit flying over the whole or any part of its territory, on condition that such restriction or prohibition shall be applicable without distinction of nationality to aircraft of all other States.

(*c*) Each contracting State, under such regulations as it may prescribe, may require any aircraft entering the areas contemplated in subparagraphs (*a*) or (*b*) above to effect a landing as soon as practicable thereafter at some designated airport within its territory.

Article 10

Landing at customs airport

Except in a case where, under the terms of this Convention or a special authorization, aircraft are permitted to cross the territory of a contracting State without landing, every aircraft which enters the territory of a contracting State shall, if the regulations of that State so require, land at an airport designated by that State for the purpose of customs and other examination. On departure from the territory of a contracting State, such aircraft shall depart from a similarly designated customs airport. Particulars of all designated customs airports shall be published by the State and transmitted to the International Civil Aviation Organization established under Part II of this Convention for communication to all other contracting States.

Article 11
Applicability of air regulations

Subject to the provisions of this Convention, the laws and regulations of a contracting State relating to the admission to or departure from its territory of aircraft engaged in international air navigation, or to the operation and navigation of such aircraft while within its territory, shall be applied to the aircraft of all contracting States without distinction as to nationality, and shall be complied with by such aircraft upon entering or departing from or while within the territory of that State.

Article 12
Rules of the air

Each contracting State undertakes to adopt measures to insure that every aircraft flying over or maneuvering within its territory and that every aircraft carrying its nationality mark, wherever such aircraft may be, shall comply with the rules and regulations relating to the flight and maneuver of aircraft there in force. Each contracting

State undertakes to keep its own regulations in these respects uniform, to the greatest possible extent, with those established from time to time under this Convention. Over the high seas, the rules in force shall be those established under this Convention. Each contracting State undertakes to insure the prosecution of all persons violating the regulations applicable.

Article 13

Entry and clearance regulations

The laws and regulations of a contracting State as to the admission to or departure from its territory of passengers, crew or cargo of aircraft, such as regulations relating to entry, clearance, immigration, passports, customs, and quarantine shall be complied with by or on behalf of such passengers, crew or cargo upon entrance into or departure from, or while within the territory of that State.

Article 15

Airport and similar charges

Every airport in a contracting State which is open to public use by its national aircraft shall likewise, subject to the provisions of Article 68, be open under uniform conditions to the aircraft of all the other contracting States. The like uniform conditions shall apply to the use, by aircraft of every contracting State, of all air navigation facilities, including radio and meteorological services, which may be provided for public use for the safety and expedition of air navigation.

Any charges that may be imposed or permitted to be imposed by a contracting State for the use of such airports and air navigation facilities by the aircraft of any other contracting State shall not be higher,

(a) As to aircraft not engaged in scheduled international air services, than those that would be paid by its national aircraft of the same class engaged in similar operations, and

(b) As to aircraft engaged in scheduled international air services, than those that would be paid by its national aircraft engaged in similar international air services.

All such charges shall be published and communicated to the International Civil Aviation Organization: provided that, upon representation by an interested contracting State, the charges imposed for the use of airports and other facilities shall be subject to review by the Council, which shall report and make recommendations thereon for the consideration of the State or States concerned. No fees, dues or other charges shall be imposed by any contracting State in respect solely of the right of transit over or entry into or exit from its territory of any aircraft of a contracting State or persons or property thereon.

Chapter III

Nationality of Aircraft

Article 17

Nationality of aircraft

Aircraft have the nationality of the State in which they are registered.

Article 18

Dual registration

An aircraft cannot be validly registered in more than one State, but its registration may be changed from one State to another.

Article 19

National laws governing registration

The registration or transfer of registration of aircraft in any contracting State shall be made in accordance with its laws and regulations.

Article 20

Display of marks

Every aircraft engaged in international air navigation shall bear its appropriate nationality and registration marks.

Article 21

Report of registrations

Each contracting State undertakes to supply to any other contracting State or to the International Civil Aviation Organization, on demand, information concerning the registration and ownership of any particular aircraft registered in that State. In addition, each contracting State shall furnish reports to the International Civil Aviation Organization, under such regulations as the latter may prescribe, giving such pertinent data as can be made available concerning the ownership and control of aircraft registered in that State and habitually engaged in international air navigation. The data thus obtained by the International Civil Aviation Organization shall be made available by it on request to the other contracting States.

Treaty on Principles Governing the Activities of States in the Exploration and Use of Outer Space, Including the Moon and Other Celestial Bodies

The States Parties to this Treaty,

Inspired by the great prospects opening up before mankind as a result of man's entry into outer space,

Recognizing the common interest of all mankind in the progress of the exploration and use of outer space for peaceful purposes,

Believing that the exploration and use of outer space should be carried on for the benefit of all peoples irrespective of the degree of their economic or scientific development,

Desiring to contribute to broad international cooperation in the scientific as well as the legal aspects of the exploration and use of outer space for peaceful purposes,

Believing that such cooperation will contribute to the development of mutual understanding and to the strengthening of friendly relations between States and peoples,

Recalling resolution 1962 (XVIII), entitled 'Declaration of Legal Principles Governing the Activities of States in the Exploration and Use of Outer Space', which was adopted unanimously by the United Nations General Assembly on 13 December 1963,

Recalling resolution 1884 (XVIII), calling upon States to refrain from placing in orbit around the Earth any objects carrying nuclear weapons or any other kinds of weapons of mass destruction or from installing such weapons on celestial bodies, which was adopted unanimously by the United Nations General Assembly on 17 October 1963,

Taking account of United Nations General Assembly resolution 110 (II) of 3 November 1947, which condemned propaganda designed or likely to provoke or encourage any threat to the peace, breach of the peace or act of aggression, and considering that the aforementioned resolution is applicable to outer space,

Convinced that a Treaty on Principles Governing the Activities of States in the Exploration and Use of Outer Space, including the Moon and Other Celestial Bodies, will further the purposes and principles of the Charter of the United Nations,

Have agreed on the following:

Article 1

The exploration and use of outer space, including the Moon and other celestial bodies, shall be carried out for the benefit and in the interests of all countries, irrespective of their degree of economic or scientific development, and shall be the province of all mankind.

Outer space, including the Moon and other celestial bodies, shall be free for exploration and use by all States without discrimination of any kind, on a basis of equality and in accordance with international law, and there shall be free access to all areas of celestial bodies.

There shall be freedom of scientific investigation in outer space, including the Moon and other celestial bodies, and States shall facilitate and encourage international cooperation in such investigation.

Article 2

Outer space, including the Moon and other celestial bodies, is not subject to national appropriation by claim of sovereignty, by means of use or occupation, or by any other means.

Article 3

States Parties to the Treaty shall carry on activities in the exploration and use of outer space, including the Moon and other celestial bodies, in accordance with international law, including the Charter of the United Nations, in the interest of maintaining international peace and security and promoting international co-operation and understanding.

Article 4

States Parties to the Treaty undertake not to place in orbit around the Earth any objects carrying nuclear weapons or any other kinds of weapons of mass destruction, install such weapons on celestial bodies, or station such weapons in outer space in any other manner.

The Moon and other celestial bodies shall be used by all States Parties to the Treaty exclusively for peaceful purposes. The establishment of military bases, installations and fortifications, the testing of any type of weapons and the conduct of military manoeuvres on celestial bodies shall be forbidden. The use of military personnel for scientific research or for any other peaceful purposes shall not be prohibited. The use of any equipment or facility necessary for peaceful exploration of the Moon and other celestial bodies shall also not be prohibited.

Article 5

States Parties to the Treaty shall regard astronauts as envoys of mankind in outer space and shall render to them all possible assistance in the event of accident, distress, or emergency landing on the territory of another State Party or on the high seas. When astronauts make such a landing, they shall be safely and promptly returned to the State of registry of their space vehicle.

In carrying on activities in outer space and on celestial bodies, the astronauts of one State Party shall render all possible assistance to the astronauts of other States Parties.

States Parties to the Treaty shall immediately inform the other States Parties to the Treaty or the Secretary-General of the United Nations of any phenomena they discover in outer space, including the Moon and other celestial bodies, which could constitute a danger to the life or health of astronauts.

Article 6

States Parties to the Treaty shall bear international responsibility for national activities in outer space, including the Moon and other celestial bodies, whether such activities are carried on by governmental agencies or by non-governmental entities, and for assuring that national activities are carried out in conformity with the provisions set forth in the present Treaty. The activities of non-governmental entities in outer space, including the Moon and other celestial bodies, shall require authorization and continuing supervision by the appropriate State Party to the Treaty. When activities are carried on in outer space, including the Moon and other celestial bodies, by an international organization, responsibility for compliance with this Treaty shall be borne both by the international organization and by the States Parties to the Treaty participating in such organization.

Article 7

Each State Party to the Treaty that launches or procures the launching of an object into outer space, including the Moon and other celestial bodies, and each State Party from whose territory or facility an object is launched, is internationally liable for damage to another State Party to the Treaty or to its natural or juridical persons by such object or its component parts on the Earth, in air space or in outer space, including the Moon and other celestial bodies.

Article 8

A State Party to the Treaty on whose registry an object launched into outer space is carried shall retain jurisdiction and control over such object, and over any personnel thereof, while in outer space or on a celestial body. Ownership of objects launched into outer space, including objects landed or constructed on a celestial body, and of their component parts, is not affected by their presence in outer space or on a celestial body or by their return to the Earth. Such objects or component parts found beyond the limits of the State Party to the Treaty on whose registry they are carried shall be returned to that State Party, which shall, upon request, furnish identifying data prior to their return.

Article 9

In the exploration and use of outer space, including the Moon and other celestial bodies, States Parties to the Treaty shall be guided by the principle of co-operation and mutual assistance and shall conduct all their activities in outer space, including the Moon and other celestial bodies, with due regard to the corresponding interests of all other States Parties to the Treaty. States Parties to the Treaty shall pursue studies of outer space, including the Moon and other celestial bodies, and conduct exploration of them so as to avoid their harmful contamination and also adverse changes in the environment of the Earth resulting from the introduction of extraterrestrial matter and, where necessary, shall adopt appropriate measures for this purpose. If a State Party to the Treaty has reason to believe that an activity or experiment planned by it or its nationals in outer space, including the Moon and other celestial bodies, would cause potentially harmful interference with activities of other States Parties in the peaceful exploration and use of outer space, including the Moon and other celestial bodies, it shall undertake appropriate international consultations before proceeding with any such activity or experiment. A State Party to the Treaty which has reason to believe that an activity or experiment planned by another State Party in outer space, including the Moon and other celestial bodies, would cause potentially harmful interference with activities in the peaceful exploration and use of outer space, including the Moon and other celestial bodies, may request consultation concerning the activity or experiment.

Article 10

In order to promote international co-operation in the exploration and use of outer space, including the Moon and other celestial bodies, in conformity with the purposes of this Treaty, the States Parties to the Treaty shall consider on a basis of equality any requests by other States Parties to the Treaty to be afforded an opportunity to observe the flight of space objects launched by those States.
The nature of such an opportunity for observation and the conditions under which it could be afforded shall be determined by agreement between the States concerned.

Article 11

In order to promote international co-operation in the

peaceful exploration and use of outer space, States Parties to the Treaty conducting activities in outer space, including the Moon and other celestial bodies, agree to inform the Secretary-General of the United Nations as well as the public and the international scientific community, to the greatest extent feasible and practicable, of the nature, conduct, locations and results of such activities. On receiving the said information, the Secretary-General of the United Nations should be prepared to disseminate it immediately and effectively.

Article 12

All stations, installations, equipment and space vehicles on the Moon and other celestial bodies shall be open to representatives of other States Parties to the Treaty on a basis of reciprocity. Such representatives shall give reasonable advance notice of a projected visit, in order that appropriate consultations may be held and that maximum precautions may be taken to assure safety and to avoid interference with normal operations in the facility to be visited.

Article 13

The provisions of this Treaty shall apply to the activities of States Parties to the Treaty in the exploration and use of outer space, including the Moon and other celestial bodies, whether such activities are carried on by a single State Party to the Treaty or jointly with other States, including cases where they are carried on within the framework of international intergovernmental organizations.

Any practical questions arising in connexion with activities carried on by international intergovernmental organizations in the exploration and use of outer space, including the Moon and other celestial bodies, shall be resolved by the States Parties to the Treaty either with the appropriate international organization or with one or more States members of that international organization, which are Parties to this Treaty.

Article 14

1. This Treaty shall be open to all States for signature. Any State which does not sign this Treaty before its entry into force in accordance with paragraph 3 of this article may accede to it at any time.

2. This Treaty shall be subject to ratification by signatory States. Instruments of ratification and instruments of accession shall be deposited with the Governments of the Union of Soviet Socialist Republics, the United Kingdom of Great Britain and Northern Ireland and the United States of America, which are hereby designated the Depositary Governments.

3. This Treaty shall enter into force upon the deposit of instruments of ratification by five Governments including the Governments designated as Depositary Governments under this Treaty.

4. For States whose instruments of ratification or accession are deposited subsequent to the entry into force of this Treaty, it shall enter into force on the date of the deposit of their instruments of ratification or accession.

5. The Depositary Governments shall promptly inform all signatory and acceding States of the date of each signa-

ture, the date of deposit of each instrument of ratification of and accession to this Treaty, the date of its entry into force and other notices.

6. This Treaty shall be registered by the Depositary Governments pursuant to Article 102 of the Charter of the United Nations.

Article 15

Any State Party to the Treaty may propose amendments to this Treaty. Amendments shall enter into force for each State Party to the Treaty accepting the amendments upon their acceptance by a majority of the States Parties to the Treaty and thereafter for each remaining State Party to the Treaty on the date of acceptance by it.

Article 16

Any State Party to the Treaty may give notice of its withdrawal from the Treaty one year after its entry into force by written notification to the Depositary Governments. Such withdrawal shall take effect one year from the date of receipt of this notification.

Article 17

This Treaty, of which the Chinese, English, French, Russian and Spanish texts are equally authentic, shall be deposited in the archives of the Depositary Governments. Duly certified copies of this Treaty shall be transmitted by the Depositary Governments to the Governments of the signatory and acceding States.

In Witness Whereof the undersigned, duly authorized, have signed this Treaty.

Done in _____ , at the cities of London, Moscow and Washington, the _____ day of _____ one thousand nine hundred and _____ .

III

The Law
of
INTERNATIONAL
POLITICS

On the basis of general function, the law of international politics can be divided into four categories: procedure, suppression, regulation, and conflict resolution.

PROCEDURE

The law of procedure, which specifies the methods states use in communicating and cooperating with one another, is extensively codified and covers such subjects as diplomatic missions, treaties, and decision-making arrangements in international conferences and agencies. The agent of international transactions in peacetime, the diplomatic mission, is the subject of the 1961 Vienna Convention on Diplomatic Relations.

The States Parties to the present Convention,

Recalling that peoples of all nations from ancient times have recognized the status of diplomatic agents,

Having in mind the purposes and principles of the Charter of the United Nations concerning the sovereign equality of States, the maintenance of international peace and security, and the promotion of friendly relations among nations,

Believing that an international convention on diplomatic intercourse, privileges and immunities would contribute to the development of friendly relations among nations, irrespective of their differing constitutional and social systems,

Realizing that the purpose of such privileges and immunities is not to benefit individuals but to ensure the efficient performance of the functions of diplomatic missions as representing States,

Affirming that the rules of customary international law should continue to govern questions not expressly regulated by the provisions of the present Convention,

Have agreed as follows:

Article 1

For the purpose of the present Convention, the following expressions shall have the meanings hereunder assigned to them:

(a) the 'head of the mission' is the person charged by the sending State with the duty of acting in that capacity;

(b) the 'members of the mission' are the head of the mission and the members of the staff of the mission;

(c) the 'members of the staff of the mission' are the members of the diplomatic staff, of the administrative and technical staff and of the service staff of the mission;

(d) the 'members of the diplomatic staff' are the members of the staff of the mission having diplomatic rank;

(e) a 'diplomatic agent' is the head of the mission or a member of the diplomatic staff of the mission;

(f) the 'members of the administrative and technical staff' are the members of the staff of the mission employed in the administrative and technical service of the mission;

(g) the 'members of the service staff' are the members of the staff of the mission in the domestic service of the mission;

(h) a 'private servant' is a person who is in the domestic service of a member of the mission and who is not an employee of the sending State;

(i) the 'premises of the mission' are the buildings or parts of buildings and the land ancillary thereto, irrespective of ownership, used for the purposes of the mission including the residence of the head of the mission.

Article 2

The establishment of diplomatic relations between States, and of permanent diplomatic missions, takes place by mutual consent.

Article 3

1. The functions of a diplomatic mission consist *inter alia* in:

   (a) representing the sending State in the receiving State;
   (b) protecting in the receiving State the interests of the sending State and of its nationals, within the limits permitted by international law;
   (c) negotiating with the Government of the receiving State;
   (d) ascertaining by all lawful means conditions and developments in the receiving State, and reporting thereon to the Government of the sending State;
   (e) promoting friendly relations between the sending State and the receiving State, and developing their economic, cultural and scientific relations.

2. Nothing in the present Convention shall be construed as preventing the performance of consular functions by a diplomatic mission.

Article 4

1. The sending State must make certain that the

agre'ment of the receiving State has been given for the person it proposes to accredit as head of the mission to that State.

2. The receiving State is not obliged to give reasons to the sending State for a refusal of *agre'ment*.

Article 5

1. The sending State may, after it has given due notification to the receiving States concerned, accredit a head of mission or assign any member of the diplomatic staff, as the case may be, to more than one State, unless there is express objection by any of the receiving States.

2. If the sending State accredits a head of mission to one or more other States it may establish a diplomatic mission headed by a *charge' d'affaires ad interim* in each State where the head of mission has not his permanent seat.

3. A head of mission or any member of the diplomatic staff of the mission may act as representative of the sending State to any international organization.

Article 6

Two or more States may accredit the same person as head of mission to another State, unless objection is offered by the receiving State.

Article 7

Subject to the provisions of Articles 5, 8, 9 and 11, the sending State may freely appoint the members of the staff of the mission. In the case of military, naval or air attache's, the receiving State may require their names to be submitted beforehand, for its approval.

Article 8

1. Members of the diplomatic staff of the mission should in principle be of the nationality of the sending State.

2. Members of the diplomatic staff of the mission may not be appointed from among persons having the nationality of the receiving State, except with the consent of that State which may be withdrawn at any time.

3. The receiving State may reserve the same right with regard to nationals of a third State who are not also nationals of the sending State.

Article 9

1. The receiving State may at any time and without having to explain its decision, notify the sending State that the head of the mission or any member of the diplomatic staff of the mission is *persona non grata* or that any other member of the staff of the mission is not acceptable. In any such case, the sending State shall, as appropriate, either recall the person concerned or terminate his functions with the mission. A person may be declared *non grata* or not acceptable before arriving in the territory of the receiving State.

2. If the sending State refuses or fails within a reasonable period to carry out its obligations under paragraph 1 of this Article, the receiving State may refuse to recognize the person concerned as a member of the mission.

Article 10

1. The Ministry for Foreign Affairs of the receiving State, or such other ministry as may be agreed, shall be notified of:

- (a) the appointment of members of the mission, their arrival and their final departure or the termination of their functions with the mission;
- (b) the arrival and final departure of a person belonging to the family of a member of the mission and, where appropriate, the fact that a person becomes or ceases to be a member of the family of a member of the mission;
- (c) the arrival and final departure of private servants in the employ of persons referred to in sub-paragraph (a) of this paragraph and, where appropriate, the fact that they are leaving the employ of such persons;
- (d) the engagement and discharge of persons resident in the receiving State as members of the mission or private servants entitled to privileges and immunities.

2. Where possible, prior notification of arrival and final departure shall also be given.

Article 11

1. In the absence of specific agreement as to the size of the mission, the receiving State may require that the size of a mission be kept within limits considered by it to be reasonable and normal, having regard to circumstances

and conditions in the receiving State and to the needs of the particular mission.

2. The receiving State may equally, within similar bounds and on a nondiscriminatory basis, refuse to accept officials of a particular category.

Article 12

The sending State may not, without the prior express consent of the receiving State, establish offices forming part of the mission in localities other than those in which the mission itself is established.

Article 13

1. The head of the mission is considered as having taken up his functions in the receiving State either when he has presented his credentials or when he has notified his arrival and a true copy of his credentials has been presented to the Ministry for Foreign Affairs of the receiving State, or such other ministry as may be agreed, in accordance with the practice prevailing in the receiving State which shall be applied in a uniform manner.

2. The order of presentation of credentials or of a true copy thereof will be determined by the date and time of the arrival of the head of the mission.

Article 14

1. Heads of mission are divided into three classes, namely:

(a) that of ambassadors or nuncios accredited to Heads of State, and other heads of mission of equivalent rank;

(b) that of envoys, ministers and internuncios accredited to Heads of State;

(c) that of *charge' d'affaires* accredited to Ministers for Foreign Affairs.

2. Except as concerns precedence and etiquette, there shall be no differentiation between heads of mission by reason of their class.

Article 15

The class to which the heads of their missions are to be assigned shall be agreed between States.

Article 16

1. Heads of mission shall take precedence in their respective classes in the order of the date and time of taking up their functions in accordance with Article 13.

2. Alterations in the credentials of a head of mission not involving any change of class shall not affect his precedence.

3. This article is without prejudice to any practice accepted by the receiving State regarding the precedence of the representative of the Holy See.

Article 17

The precedence of the members of the diplomatic staff of the mission shall be notified by the head of the mission to the Ministry for Foreign Affairs or such other ministry as may be agreed.

Article 18

The procedure to be observed in each State for the reception of heads of mission shall be uniform in respect of each class.

Article 19

1. If the post of head of the mission is vacant, or if the head of the mission is unable to perform his functions, a *charge' d'affaires ad interim* shall act provisionally as head of the mission. The name of the *charge' d'affaires ad interim* shall be notified, either by the head of the mission or, in case he is unable to do so, by the Ministry for Foreign Affairs of the sending State to the Ministry for Foreign Affairs of the receiving State or such other ministry as may be agreed.
2. In cases where no member of the diplomatic staff of the mission is present in the receiving State, a member of the administrative and technical staff may, with the consent of the receiving State, be designated by the sending State to be in charge of the current administrative affairs of the mission.

Article 20

The mission and its head shall have the right to use the flag and emblem of the sending State on the premises of the mission, including the residence of the head of the mission, and on his means of transport.

Article 21

1. The receiving State shall either facilitate the acquisition on its territory, in accordance with its laws, by the sending State of premises necessary for its mission or assist the latter in obtaining accommodation in some other way.
2. It shall also, where necessary, assist missions in obtaining suitable accommodation for their members.

Article 22

1. The premises of the mission shall be inviolable. The agents of the receiving State may not enter them, except with the consent of the head of the mission.
2. The receiving State is under a special duty to take all appropriate steps to protect the premises of the mission against any intrusion or damage and to prevent any disturbance of the peace of the mission or impairment of its dignity.
3. The premises of the mission, their furnishings and other property thereon and the means of transport of the mission shall be immune from search, requisition, attachment or execution.

Article 23

1. The sending State and the head of the mission shall be exempt from all national, regional or municipal dues and

taxes in respect of the premises of the mission, whether owned or leased, other than such as represent payment for specific services rendered.

2. The exemption from taxation referred to in this Article shall not apply to such dues and taxes payable under the law of the receiving State by persons contracting with the sending State or the head of the mission.

Article 24

The archives and documents of the mission shall be inviolable at any time and wherever they may be.

Article 25

The receiving State shall accord full facilities for the performance of the functions of the mission.

Article 26

Subject to its laws and regulations concerning zones entry into which is prohibited or regulated for reasons of national security, the receiving State shall ensure to all members of the mission freedom of movement and travel in its territory.

Article 27

1. The receiving State shall permit and protect free communication on the part of the mission for all official purposes. In communicating with the Government and the other missions and consulates of the sending State, wherever situated, the mission may employ all appropriate

means, including diplomatic couriers and messages in code or cipher. However, the mission may install and use a wireless transmitter only with the consent of the receiving State.

2. The official correspondence of the mission shall be inviolable. Official correspondence means all correspondence relating to the mission and its functions.

3. The diplomatic bag shall not be opened or detained.

4. The packages constituting the diplomatic bag must bear visible external marks of their character and may contain only diplomatic documents or articles intended for official use.

5. The diplomatic courier, who shall be provided with an official document indicating his status and the number of packages constituting the diplomatic bag, shall be protected by the receiving State in the performance of his functions. He shall enjoy personal inviolability and shall not be liable to any form of arrest or detention.

6. The sending State or the mission may designate diplomatic couriers *ad hoc*. In such cases the provisions of paragraph 5 of this Article shall also apply, except that the immunities therein mentioned shall cease to apply when such a courier has delivered to the consignee the diplomatic bag in his charge.

7. A diplomatic bag may be entrusted to the captain of a commercial aircraft scheduled to land at an authorized port of entry. He shall be provided with an official document indicating the number of packages constituting the bag but he shall not be considered to be a diplomatic courier. The mission may send one of its members to take possession of the diplomatic bag directly and freely from the captain of the aircraft.

Article 28

The fees and charges levied by the mission in the course of its official duties shall be exempt from all dues and taxes.

Article 29

The person of a diplomatic agent shall be inviolable. He shall not be liable to any form of arrest or detention. The receiving State shall treat him with due respect and shall take all appropriate steps to prevent any attack on his person, freedom, or dignity.

Article 30

1. The private residence of a diplomatic agent shall enjoy the same inviolability and protection as the premises of the mission.
2. His papers, correspondence, and, except as provided in paragraph 3 of Article 31, his property, shall likewise enjoy inviolability.

Article 31

1. A diplomatic agent shall enjoy immunity from the criminal jurisdiction of the receiving State. He shall also enjoy immunity from its civil and administrative jurisdiction, except in the case of:
   (a) a real action relating to private immovable property situated in the territory of the receiving State, unless he holds it on behalf of the sending State for the purposes of the mission;

(b) an action relating to succession in which the diplomatic agent is involved as executor, administrator, heir or legatee as a private person and not on behalf of the sending State;

(c) an action relating to any professional or commercial activity exercised by the diplomatic agent in the receiving State outside his official functions.

2. A diplomatic agent is not obliged to give evidence as a witness.

3. No measures of execution may be taken in respect of a diplomatic agent except in the cases coming under subparagraphs (a), (b) and (c) of paragraph 1 of this Article, and provided that the measures concerned can be taken without infringing the inviolability of his person or of his residence.

4. The immunity of a diplomatic agent from the jurisdiction of the receiving State does not exempt him from the jurisdiction of the sending State.

Article 32

1. The immunity from jurisdiction of diplomatic agents and of persons enjoying immunity under Article 37 may be waived by the sending State.

2. Waiver must always be express.

3. The initiation of proceedings by a diplomatic agent or by a person enjoying immunity from jurisdiction under Article 37 shall preclude him from invoking immunity from jurisdication in respect of any counterclaim directly connected with the principal claim.

4. Waiver of immunity from jurisdiction in respect of civil

or administrative proceedings shall not be held to imply waiver of immunity in respect of the execution of the judgment, for which a separate waiver shall be necessary.

Article 33

1. Subject to the provisions of paragraph 3 of this Article, a diplomatic agent shall with respect to services rendered for the sending State be exempt from social security provisions which may be in force in the receiving State.

2. The exemption provided for in paragraph 1 of this Article shall also apply to private servants who are in the sole employ of a diplomatic agent, on conditions:

    (a) that they are not nationals of or permanently resident in the receiving State; and

    (b) that they are covered by the social security provisions which may be in force in the sending State or a third State.

3. A diplomatic agent who employs persons to whom the exemption provided for in paragraph 2 of this Article does not apply shall observe the obligations which the social security provisions of the receiving State impose upon employers.

4. The exemption provided for in paragraphs 1 and 2 of this Article shall not preclude voluntary participation in the social security system of the receiving State provided that such participation is permitted by that State.

5. The provisions of this Article shall not affect bilateral or multilateral agreements concerning social security concluded previously and shall not prevent the conclusion of such agreements in the future.

Article 34

A diplomatic agent shall be exempt from all dues and taxes, personal or real, national, regional or municipal, except:

(a) indirect taxes of a kind which are normally incorporated in the price of goods or services;

(b) dues and taxes on private immovable property situated in the territory of the receiving State, unless he holds it on behalf of the sending State for the purposes of the mission;

(c) estate, succession or inheritance duties levied by the receiving State, subject to the provisions of paragraph 4 of Article 39;

(d) dues and taxes on private income having its source in the receiving State and capital taxes on investments made in commercial undertakings in the receiving State;

(e) charges levied for specific services rendered;

(f) registration, court or record fees, mortgage dues and stamp duty, with respect to immovable property, subject to the provisions of Article 23.

Article 35

The receiving State shall exempt diplomatic agents from all personal services, from all public service of any kind whatsoever, and from military obligations such as those connected with requisitioning, military contributions and billeting.

Article 36

1. The receiving State shall, in accordance with such laws and regulations as it may adopt, permit entry of and grant exemption from all customs duties, taxes, and related charges other than charges for storage, cartage and similar services, on:

(*a*) articles for the official use of the mission;
(*b*) articles for the personal use of a diplomatic agent or members of his family forming part of his household, including articles intended for his establishment.

2. The personal baggage of a diplomatic agent shall be exempt from inspection, unless there are serious grounds for presuming that it contains articles not covered by the exemptions mentioned in paragraph 1 of this Article, or articles the import or export of which is prohibited by the law or controlled by the quarantine regulations of the receiving State. Such inspection shall be conducted only in the presence of the diplomatic agent or of his authorized representative.

Article 37

1. The members of the family of a diplomatic agent forming part of his household shall, if they are not nationals of the receiving State, enjoy the privileges and immunities specified in Articles 29 to 36.

2. Members of the administrative and technical staff of the mission, together with members of their families forming part of their respective households, shall, if they

are not nationals of or permanently resident in the receiving State, enjoy the privileges and immunities specified in Articles 29 to 35, except that the immunity from civil and administrative jurisdiction of the receiving State specified in paragraph 1 of Article 31 shall not extend to acts performed outside the course of their duties. They shall also enjoy the privileges specified in Article 36, paragraph 1, in respect of articles imported at the time of first installation.

3. Members of the service staff of the mission who are not nationals of or permanently resident in the receiving State shall enjoy immunity in respect of acts performed in the course of their duties, exemption from dues and taxes on the emoluments they receive by reason of their employment and the exemption contained in Article 33.

4. Private servants of members of the mission shall, if they are not nationals of or permanently resident in the receiving State, be exempt from dues and taxes on the emoluments they receive by reason of their employment. In other respects, they may enjoy privileges and immunities only to the extent admitted by the receiving State. However, the receiving State must exercise its jurisdiction over those persons in such a manner as not to interfere unduly with the performance of the functions of the mission.

Article 38

1. Except in so far as additional privileges and immunities may be granted by the receiving State, a diplomatic

agent who is a national of or permanently resident in that State shall enjoy only immunity from jurisdiction, and inviolability, in respect of official acts performed in the exercise of his functions.

2. Other members of the staff of the mission and private servants who are nationals of or permanently resident in the receiving State shall enjoy privileges and immunities only to the extent admitted by the receiving State. However, the receiving State must exercise its jurisdiction over those persons in such a manner as not to interfere unduly with the performance of the functions of the mission.

Article 39

1. Every person entitled to privileges and immunities shall enjoy them from the moment he enters the territory of the receiving State on proceeding to take up his post or, if already in its territory, from the moment when his appointment is notified to the Ministry for Foreign Affairs or such other ministry as may be agreed.

2. When the functions of a person enjoying privileges and immunities have come to an end, such privileges and immunities shall normally cease at the moment when he leaves the country, or on expiry of a reasonable period in which to do so, but shall subsist until that time, even in case of armed conflict. However, with respect to acts performed by such a person in the exercise of his functions as a member of the mission, immunity shall continue to subsist.

3. In case of the death of a member of the mission, the members of his family shall continue to enjoy the privileges and immunities to which they are entitled until the expiry of a reasonable period in which to leave the country.

4. In the event of the death of a member of the mission not a national of or permanently resident in the receiving State or a member of his family forming part of his household, the receiving State shall permit the withdrawal of the movable property of the deceased, with the exception of any property acquired in the country the export of which was prohibited at the time of his death. Estate, succession and inheritance duties shall not be levied on movable property the presence of which in the receiving State was due solely to the presence there of the deceased as a member of the mission or as a member of the family of a member of the mission.

Article 40

1. If a diplomatic agent passes through or is in the territory of a third State, which has granted him a passport visa if such visa was necessary, while proceeding to take up or to return to his post, or when returning to his own country, the third State shall accord him inviolability and such other immunities as may be required to ensure his transit or return. The same shall apply in the case of any members of his family enjoying privileges or immunities who are accompanying the diplomatic agent, or travelling separately to join him or to return to their country.

2. In circumstances similar to those specified in paragraph 1 of this Article, third States shall not hinder the passage of members of the administrative and technical or service staff of a mission, and of members of their families, through their territories.

3. Third States shall accord to official correspondence and other official communications in transit, including messages in code or cipher, the same freedom and protection as is accorded by the receiving State. They shall accord to diplomatic couriers, who have been granted a passport visa if such visa was necessary, and diplomatic bags in transit the same inviolability and protection as the receiving State is bound to accord.

4. The obligations of third States under paragraphs 1, 2 and 3 of this Article shall also apply to the persons mentioned respectively in those paragraphs, and to official communications and diplomatic bags, whose presence in the territory of the third State is due to *force majeure*.

Article 41

1. Without prejudice to their privileges and immunities, it is the duty of all persons enjoying such privileges and immunities to respect the laws and regulations of the receiving State. They also have a duty not to interfere in the internal affairs of that State.

2. All official business with the receiving State entrusted to the mission by the sending State shall be conducted with or through the Ministry for Foreign Affairs of the receiving State or such other ministry as may be agreed.

3. The premises of the mission must not be used in any manner incompatible with the functions of the mission as laid down in the present Convention or by other rules of general international law or by any special agreements in force between the sending and the receiving State.

Article 42

A diplomatic agent shall not in the receiving State practise for personal profit any professional or commercial activity.

Article 43

The function of a diplomatic agent comes to an end, *inter alia:*

(a)   on notification by the sending State to the receiving State that the function of the diplomatic agent has come to an end;

(b)   on notification by the receiving State to the sending State that, in accordance with paragraph 2 of Article 9, it refuses to recognize the diplomatic agent as a member of the mission.

Article 44

The receiving State must, even in case of armed conflict, grant facilities in order to enable persons enjoying privileges and immunities, other than nationals of the receiving State, and members of the families of such persons irrespective of their nationality, to leave at the earliest possible moment. It must, in particular, in case of need, place at their disposal the necessary means of transport for themselves and their property.

Article 45

If diplomatic relations are broken off between two States, or if a mission is permanently or temporarily recalled:

(a) the receiving State must, even in case of armed conflict, respect and protect the premises of the mission, together with its property and archives;

(b) the sending State may entrust the custody of the premises of the mission, together with its property and archives, to a third State acceptable to the receiving State;

(c) the sending State may entrust the protection of its interests and those of its nationals to a third State acceptable to the receiving State.

Article 46

A sending State may with the prior consent of a receiving State, and at the request of a third State not represented in the receiving State, undertake the temporary protection of the interests of the third State and of its nationals.

Article 47

1. In the application of the provisions of the present Convention, the receiving State shall not discriminate as between States.

2. However, discrimination shall not be regarded as taking place:

    (a) where the receiving State applies any of the provisions of the present Convention restrictively because of a restrictive application of that provision to its mission in the sending State;

    (b) where by custom or agreement States extend to each other more favourable treatment than is required by the provisions of the present Convention.

Article 48

The present Convention shall be open for signature by all States Members of the United Nations or of any of the specialized agencies or Parties to the Statute of the International Court of Justice, and by any other State invited by the General Assembly of the United Nations to become a Party to the Convention, as follows: until 31 October 1961 at the Federal Ministry for Foreign Affairs of Austria and subsequently, until 31 March 1962, at the United Nations Headquarters in New York.

Article 49

The present Convention is subject to ratification. The instruments of ratification shall be deposited with the Secretary-General of the United Nations.

Article 50

The present Convention shall remain open for accession

by any State belonging to any of the four categories mentioned in Article 48. The instruments of accession shall be deposited with the Secretary-General of the United Nations.

Article 51

1. The present Convention shall enter into force on· the thirtieth day following the date of deposit of the twenty-second instrument of ratification or accession with the Secretary-General of the United Nations.
2. For each State ratifying or acceding to the Convention after the deposit of the twenty-second instrument of ratification or accession, the Convention shall enter into force on the thirtieth day after deposit by such State of its instrument of ratification or accession.

Article 52

The Secretary-General of the United Nations shall inform all States belonging to any of the four categories mentioned in Article 48:

> (*a*) of signatures to the present Convention and of the deposit of instruments of ratification or accession, in accordance with Articles 48, 49 and 50;
> (*b*) of the date on which the present Convention will enter into force, in accordance with Article 51.

Article 53

The original of the present Convention, of which the

Chinese, English, French, Russian and Spanish texts are equally authentic, shall be deposited with the Secretary-General of the United Nations, who shall send certified copies thereof to all States belonging to any of the four categories mentioned in Article 48.

In Witness Whereof the undersigned Plenipotentiaries, being duly authorized thereto by their respective Governments, have signed the present Convention.

Done at Vienna, this eighteenth day of April one thousand nine hundred and sixty-one.

Decisions of international bodies can be significantly and decisively affected by such factors as who may deliberate, who may vote, how votes are weighted, and what type of vote is necessary for a decision. In special conferences the principle of equality of states usually results in each state's having one vote. Each individual conference, however, will decide its selection of chairman, rules of procedure, and whether a simple majority, absolute majority, or unanimity will be required for reaching a decision.

In the General Assembly of the United Nations all members are represented, each has one vote, and important questions are decided by a two-thirds vote and all other questions by a simple majority. The Security Council, which has primary responsibility for the maintenance of peace, has 5 permanent members and 10 nonpermanent members whom the General Assembly elects for 2-year terms. The Security Council presidency rotates among the members. Any one permanent member or any seven nonpermanent members may veto decisions on substantive questions, an arrangement intended to reflect the Great Powers' larger responsibility for the maintenance of peace and security.

SUPPRESSION

International law is used to suppress certain acts that endanger individuals and societies. While these acts may or may not be politically motivated, they are carried out by individuals without active governmental support or sanction and so are analogous to criminal acts in a community.

The 1929 Slavery Convention prohibits slavery and related arrangements—debt bondage, serfdom, child marriages. The treaty stipulates that all signatories are to adopt appropriate measures to prevent and suppress the slave trade, specify penalties for violations of those measures, and prevent forced labor arrangements from developing into conditions of slavery. The 1966 New York International Convention on the Elimination of all Forms of Racial Discrimination, designed to prevent racially-motivated violations of the inherent dignity and equality of all men, provides:

Part I

Article 2

1. States Parties condemn racial discrimination and un-

dertake to pursue by all appropriate means and without delay a policy of eliminating racial discrimination in all its forms and promoting understanding among all races, and, to this end:

(a) Each State Party undertakes to engage in no act or practice of racial discrimination against persons, groups of persons or institutions and to ensure that all public authorities and public institutions, national and local, shall act in conformity with this obligation;

(b) Each State Party undertakes not to sponsor, defend or support racial discrimination by any persons or organizations;

(c) Each State Party shall take effective measures to review governmental, national and local policies, and to amend, rescind or nullify any laws and regulations which have the effect of creating or perpetuating racial discrimination wherever it exists;

(d) Each State Party shall prohibit and bring to an end, by all appropriate means, including legislation as required by circumstances, racial discrimination by any persons, group or organization;

(e) Each State Party undertakes to encourage, where appropriate, integrationist multi-racial organizations and movements and other means of eliminating barriers between races, and to discourage anything which tends to strengthen racial division.

2. States Parties shall, when the circumstances so war-

rant, take, in the social, economic, cultural and other fields, special and concrete measures to ensure the adequate development and protection of certain racial groups or individuals belonging to them, for the purpose of guaranteeing them the full and equal enjoyment of human rights and fundamental freedoms. These measures shall in no case entail as a consequence the maintenance of unequal or separate rights for different racial groups after the objectives for which they were taken have been achieved.

Article 3

States Parties particularly condemn racial segregation and *apartheid* and undertake to prevent, prohibit and eradicate all practices of this nature in territories under their jurisdiction.

Article 4

States Parties condemn all propaganda and all organizations which are based on ideas or theories of superiority of one race or group of persons of one colour or ethnic origin, or which attempt to justify or promote racial hatred and discrimination in any form, and undertake to adopt immediate and positive measures designed to eradicate all incitement to, or acts of, such discrimination and, to this end, with due regard to the principles embodied in the Universal Declaration of Human Rights and the rights expressly set forth in Article 5 of this Convention, *inter alia:*

(a) Shall declare an offence punishable by law all dissemination of ideas based on racial superiority or hatred, incitement to racial discrimination, as well as all acts of violence or incitement to such acts against any race or group of persons of another colour or ethnic origin, and also the provision of any assistance to racist activities, including the financing thereof;

(b) Shall declare illegal and prohibit organizations, and also organized and all other propaganda activities, which promote and incite racial discrimination, and shall recognize participation in such organizations or activities as an offence punishable by law;

(c) Shall not permit public authorities or public institutions, national or local, to promote or incite racial discrimination.

Article 5

In compliance with the fundamental obligations laid down in Article 2 of this Convention, States Parties undertake to prohibit and to eliminate racial discrimination in all its forms and to guarantee the right of everyone, without distinction as to race, colour, or national or ethnic origin, to equality before the law, notably in the enjoyment of the following rights:

(a) The right to equal treatment before the tribunals and all other organs administering justice;

(b) The right to security of person and protection by the State against violence or bodily harm, whether inflicted by government officials or by any individual, group or institution;

(c) Political rights, in particular the rights to participate in elections—to vote and to stand for election—on the basis of universal and equal suffrage, to take part in the Government as well as in the conduct of public affairs at any level and to have equal access to public service;

(d) Other civil rights, in particular:

    (i) The right to freedom of movement and residence within the border of the State;

    (ii) The right to leave any country, including one's own, and to return to one's country;

    (iii) The right to nationality;

    (iv) The right to marriage and choice of spouse;

    (v) The right to own property alone as well as in association with others;

    (vi) The right to inherit;

    (vii) The right to freedom of thought, conscience and religion;

    (viii) The right to freedom of opinion and expression;

    (ix) The right to freedom of peaceful assembly and association;

(e) Economic, social and cultural rights, in particular:

    (i) The rights to work, to free choice of employment, to just and favourable conditions of work, to protection against unemployment, to equal pay for equal work, to just and favourable remuneration;

   (ii) The right to form and join trade unions;

   (iii) The right to housing;

   (iv) The right to public health, medical care, social security and social services;

   (v) The right to education and training;

   (vi) The right to equal participation in cultural activities;

 (f) The right of access to any place or service intended for use by the general public, such as transport, hotels, restaurants, cafés, theatres and parks.

Article 6

States Parties shall assure to everyone within their jurisdiction effective protection and remedies, through the competent national tribunals and other State institutions, against any acts of racial discrimination which violate his human rights and fundamental freedoms contrary to this Convention, as well as the right to seek from such tribunals just and adequate reparation or satisfaction for any damage suffered as a result of such discrimination.

Article 7

States Parties undertake to adopt immediate and effective measures, particularly in the fields of teaching, education, culture and information, with a view to combating prejudices which lead to racial discrimination and to promoting understanding, tolerance and friendship among nations and racial or ethnical groups, as well as to propagating the purposes and principles of the Charter of the United Nations, the Universal Declaration of Human Rights, the United Nations Declaration on the Elimination of All Forms of Racial Discrimination, and this Convention.

The 1961 Single Convention on Narcotic Drugs is designed to suppress non-medically related drug traffic. The signatories undertake to limit the production of opium, coca bush and cannabis to amounts consistent with national and international needs, to license and control all parties and enterprises engaged in the manufacture and the trade and distribution of drugs, and to take action against any illicit drug traffic.

The international concern to suppress airline hijacking by requiring penalties for hijacking and extradition or punishment for the hijacker is reflected in the following treaty.

Convention for the Suppression of Unlawful Seizure of Aircraft. Done at The Hague December 16, 1970

The States Parties to This Convention
Considering that unlawful acts of seizure or exercise of control of aircraft in flight jeopardize the safety of persons and property, seriously affect the operation of air services, and undermine the confidence of the peoples of the world in the safety of civil aviation;

Considering that the occurrence of such acts is a matter of grave concern;

Considering that, for the purpose of deterring such

acts, there is an urgent need to provide appropriate measures for punishment of offenders;

Have Agreed as follows:

Article 1

Any person who on board an aircraft in flight:
- (*a*) unlawfully, by force or threat thereof, or by any other form of intimidation, seizes, or exercises control of that aircraft, or attempts to perform any such act, or
- (*b*) is an accomplice of a person who performs or attempts to perform any such act, commits an offence (hereinafter referred to as "the offence").

Article 2

Each Contracting State undertakes to make the offence punishable by severe penalties.

Article 3

1. For the purpose of this Convention, an aircraft is considered to be in flight at any time from the moment when all its external doors are closed following embarkation until the moment when any such door is opened for disembarkation. In the case of a forced landing, the flight shall be deemed to continue until the competent authorities take over the responsibility for the aircraft and for persons and property on board.
2. This Convention shall not apply to aircraft used in military, customs or police services.

3. This Convention shall apply only if the place of take-off or the place of actual landing of the aircraft on board which the offence is committed is situated outside the territory of the State of registration of that aircraft; it shall be immaterial whether the aircraft is engaged in an international or domestic flight.

4. In the cases mentioned in Article 5, this Convention shall not apply if the place of take-off and the place of actual landing of the aircraft on board which the offence is committed are situated within the territory of the same State where that State is one of those referred to in that Article.

5. Notwithstanding paragraphs 3 and 4 of this Article, Articles 6, 7, 8 and 10 shall apply whatever the place of take-off or the place of actual landing of the aircraft, if the offender or the alleged offender is found in the territory of a State other than the State of registration of that aircraft.

Article 4

1. Each Contracting State shall take such measures as may be necessary to establish its jurisdiction over the offence and any other act of violence against passengers or crew committed by the alleged offender in connection with the offence, in the following cases:

    (a) when the offence is committed on board an aircraft registered in that State;

    (b) when the aircraft on board which the offence is committed lands in its territory with the alleged offender still on board;

    (c) when the offence is committed on board an aircraft leased without crew to a lessee who has his principal place of business or, if the lessee has no such place of business, his permanent residence, in that State.

2. Each Contracting State shall likewise take such measures as may be necessary to establish its jurisdiction over the offence in the case where the alleged offender is present in its territory and it does not extradite him pursuant to Article 8 to any of the States mentioned in paragraph 1 of this Article.

3. This Convention does not exclude any criminal jurisdiction exercised in accordance with national law.

Article 5

The Contracting States which establish joint air transport operating organizations or international operating agencies, which operate aircraft which are subject to joint or international registration shall, by appropriate means, designate for each aircraft the State among them which shall exercise the jurisdiction and have the attributes of the State of registration for the purpose of this Convention and shall give notice thereof to the International Civil Aviation Organization which shall communicate the notice to all States parties to this Convention.

Article 6

1. Upon being satisfied that the circumstances so warrant, any Contracting State in the territory of which the offender or the alleged offender is present, shall take him into custody or take other measures to ensure his pres-

ence. The custody and other measures shall be as provided in the law of that State but may only be continued for such time as is necessary to enable any criminal or extradition proceedings to be instituted.

2. Such State shall immediately make a preliminary enquiry into the facts.

3. Any person in custody pursuant to paragraph 1 of this Article shall be assisted in communicating immediately with the nearest appropriate representative of the State of which he is a national.

4. When a State, pursuant to this Article, has taken a person into custody, it shall immediately notify the State of registration of the aircraft, the State mentioned in Article 4, paragraph 1 (c), the State of nationality of the detained person and, if it considers it advisable, any other interested States of the fact that such person is in custody and of the circumstances which warrant his detention. The State which makes the preliminary enquiry contemplated in paragraph 2 of this Article shall promptly report its findings to the said States and shall indicate whether it intends to exercise jurisdiction.

Article 7

The Contracting State in the territory of which the alleged offender is found shall, if it does not extradite him, be obliged, without exception whatsoever, and whether or not the offence was committed in its territory, to submit the case to its competent authorities for the purpose of prosecution. Those authorities shall take their decision in the same manner as in the case of any ordinary offence of a serious nature under the law of that State.

Article 8

1. The offence shall be deemed to be included as an extraditable offence in any extradition treaty existing betwen Contracting States. Contracting States undertake to include the offence as an extraditable offence in every extradition treaty to be concluded betwen them.

2. If a Contracting State which makes extradition conditional on the existence of a treaty receives a request for extradition from another Contracting State with which it has no extradition treaty, it may at its option consider this Convention as the legal basis for extradition in respect of the offence. Extradition shall be subject to the other conditions provided by the law of the requested State.

3. Contracting States which do not make extradition conditional on the existence of a treaty shall recognize the offence as an extraditable offence between themselves subject to the conditions provided by the law of the requested State.

4. The offence shall be treated, for the purpose of extradition between Contracting States, as if it had been committed not only in the place in which it occurred but also in the territories of the States required to establish their jurisdiction in accordance with Article 4, paragraph 1.

Article 9

1. When any of the acts mentioned in Article 1 (a) has occurred or is about to occur. Contracting States shall take all appropriate measures to restore control of the aircraft to its lawful commander or to preserve his control of the aircraft.

2. In the cases contemplated by the preceding paragraph, any Contracting State in which the aircraft or its passengers or crew are present shall facilitate the continuation of the journey of the passengers and crew as soon as practicable, and shall without delay return the aircraft and its cargo to the persons lawfully entitled to possession.

Article 10

1. Contracting States shall afford one another the greatest measure of assistance in connection with criminal proceedings brought in respect of the offence and other acts mentioned in Article 4. The law of the State requested shall apply in all cases.
2. The provisions of paragraph 1 of this Article shall not affect obligations under any other treaty, bilateral or multilateral, which governs or will govern, in whole or in part, mutual assistance in criminal matters.

Article 11

Each Contracting State shall in accordance with its national law report to the Council of the International Civil Aviation Organization as promptly as possible any relevant information in its possession concerning:

(*a*) the circumstances of the offence;
(*b*) the action taken pursuant to Article 9;
(*c*) the measures taken in relation to the offender or the alleged offender, and, in particular, the results of any extradition proceedings or other legal proceedings.

Article 12

1. Any dispute between two or more Contracting States concerning the interpretation or application of this Convention which cannot be settled through negotiation, shall, at the request of one of them, be submitted to arbitration. If within six months from the date of the request for arbitration the Parties are unable to agree on the organization of the arbitration, any one of those Parties may refer the dispute to the International Court of Justice by request in conformity with the statute of that court.

2. Each State may at the time of signature or ratification of this Convention or accession thereto, declare that it does not consider itself bound by the preceding paragraph. The other Contracting States shall not be bound by the preceding paragraph with respect to any Contracting States having made such a reservation.

3. Any Contracting State having made a reservation in accordance with the preceding paragraph may at any time withdraw this reservation by notification to the Depositary Governments.

Article 13

1. This Convention shall be open for signature at The Hague on 16 December 1970, by States participating in the International Conference on Air Law held at The Hague from 1 to 16 December 1970 (hereinafter referred to as The Hague Conference). After 31 December 1970, the Convention shall be open to all States for signature in Moscow, London and Washington. Any State which does

not sign this Convention before its entry into force in accordance with paragraph 3 of this Article may accede to it at any time.

2. This Convention shall be subject to ratification by the signatory States. Instruments of ratification and instruments of accession shall be deposited with the Governments of the Union of Soviet Socialist Republics, the United Kingdom of Great Britain and Northern Ireland, and the United States of America, which are hereby designated the Depositary Governments.

3. This Convention shall enter into force thirty days following the date of the deposit of instruments of ratification by ten States signatory to this Convention which participated in The Hague Conference.

4. For other States, this Convention shall enter into force on the date of entry into force of this Convention in accordance with paragraph 3 of this Article, or thirty days following the date of deposit of their instruments of ratification or accession, whichever is later.

5. The Depositary Governments shall promptly inform all signatory and acceding States of the date of each signature, the date of deposit of each instrument of ratification or accession, the date of entry into force of this Convention and other notices.

6. As soon as this Convention comes into force, it shall be registered by the Depositary Governments pursuant to Article 102 of the Charter of the United Nations and pursuant to Article 83 of the Convention on International Civil Aviation (Chicago, 1944).

Article 14

1. Any Contracting State may denounce this Convention by written notification to the Depositary Governments.
2. Denunciation shall take effect six months following the date on which notification is received by the Depositary Governments.

In Witness Whereof the undersigned Plenipotentiaries, being duly authorized thereto by their Governments, have signed this Convention.

Done at The Hague, this sixteenth day of December, one thousand nine hundred and seventy, in three originals, each being drawn up in four authentic texts in the English, French, Russian and Spanish languages.

REGULATION

Weapon Regulation

As the international system has become more unified and warfare has become more destructive, the nations have found common cause to place some regulations on the production and deployment of weapons. These regulations reflect the attempt to make the system safer for smaller nations by preventing damage from occurring because of radioactive fallout, leakage of biological weapons, and other accidents. The regulations also reflect the attempt to make the system safer for large nations by restricting deployment in such areas as outer space and the seabed, which could pose significantly new dangers but, because an arms race inevitably would result there, could not significantly increase security.

No current regulations prohibit the production and stockpiling of specific weapons. An existing regulation prohibits certain testing of nuclear weapons.

Treaty Banning Nuclear Weapon Tests in the Atmosphere, in Outer Space, and Under Water, August 5, 1963

The Governments of the United States of America, the United Kingdom of Great Britain and Northern Ireland, and the Union of Soviet Socialist Republics, hereinafter referred to as the "original Parties",

Proclaiming as their principal aim the speediest possible achievement of an agreement on general and complete disarmament under strict international control in accordance with the objectives of the United Nations which would put an end to the armaments race and eliminate the incentive to the production and testing of all kinds of weapons, including nuclear weapons.

Seeking to achieve the discontinuance of all test explosions of nuclear weapons for all time, determined to continue negotiations to this end, and desiring to put an end to the contamination of man's environment by radioactive substances,

Have agreed as follows:

Article I

1. Each of the Parties to this Treaty undertakes to prohibit, to prevent, and not to carry out any nuclear weapon test explosion, or any other nuclear explosion, at any place under its jurisdiction or control:

(a) in the atmosphere; beyond its limits, including outer space; or underwater, including territorial waters or high seas; or

(b) in any other environment if such explosion causes radioactive debris to be present outside the territorial limits of the State under whose jurisdiction or control such explosion is conducted. It is understood in this connection that the provisions of this subparagraph are without prejudice to the conclusion of a treaty resulting in the permanent banning of all nuclear test explosions, including all such explosions underground, the conclusion of which, as the Parties have stated in the Preamble to this Treaty, they seek to achieve.

2. Each of the Parties to this Treaty undertakes furthermore to refrain from causing, encouraging, or in any way participating in, the carrying out of any nuclear weapon test explosion, or any other nuclear explosion, anywhere which would take place in any of the environments described, or have the effect referred to, in paragraph 1 of this Article.

Article II

1. Any Party may propose amendments to this Treaty. The text of any proposed amendment shall be

submitted to the Depositary Governments which shall circulate it to all Parties to this Treaty. Thereafter, if requested to do so by one-third or more of the Parties, the Depositary Governments shall convene a conference, to which they shall invite all the Parties, to consider such amendment.

2. Any amendment to this Treaty must be approved by a majority of the votes of all the Parties to this Treaty, including the votes of all of the Original Parties. The amendment shall enter into force for all Parties upon the deposit of instruments of ratification by a majority of all the Parties, including the instruments of ratification of all of the Original Parties.

Article III

1. This Treaty shall be open to all States for signature. Any State which does not sign this Treaty before its entry into force in accordance with paragraph 3 of this Article may accede to it at any time.

2. This Treaty shall be subject to ratification by signatory States. Instruments of ratification and instruments of accession shall be deposited with the Governments of the Original Parties—the United States of America, the United Kingdom of Great Britain and Northern Ireland, and the Union of Soviet Socialist Republics—which are hereby designated the Depositary Governments.

3. This Treaty shall enter into force after its ratification by all the Original Parties and the deposit of their instruments of ratification.

4. For States whose instruments of ratification or accession are deposited subsequent to the entry into

force of this Treaty, it shall enter into force on the date of the deposit of their instruments of ratification or accession.

5. The Depositary Governments shall promptly inform all signatory and acceding States of the date of each signature, the date of deposit of each instrument of ratification of and accession to this Treaty, the date of its entry into force, and the date of receipt of any requests for conferences or other notices.

6. This Treaty shall be registered by the Depositary Governments pursuant to Article 102 of the Charter of the United Nations.

Article IV

This Treaty shall be of unlimited duration.

Each Party shall in exercising its national sovereignty have the right to withdraw from the Treaty if it decides that extraordinary events, related to the subject matter of this Treaty, have jeopardized the supreme interests of its country. It shall give notice of such withdrawal to all other Parties to the Treaty three months in advance.

Article V

This Treaty, of which the English and Russian texts are equally authentic, shall be deposited in the archives of the Depositary Governments. Duly certified copies of this Treaty shall be transmitted by the Depositary Governments to the Governments of the signatory and acceding States.

In Witness Whereof the undersigned, duly authorized, have signed this Treaty.

Done in triplicate at the city of Moscow the fifth day of August, one thousand nine hundred and sixty-three.

For the Government of the United States of America	For the Government of the United Kingdom of Great Britain and Northern Ireland	For the Government of the Union of Soviet Socialist Republics
Dean Rusk	Home	A. Gromyko

The deployment of weapons is regulated in several ways.

Outer Space. The Outer Space Treaty of 1967 provides the following.

Article II

States Parties to the Treaty undertake not to place in orbit around the Earth any objects carrying nuclear weapons or other kinds of weapons of mass destruction, install such weapons on celestial bodies, or station such weapons in outer space in any manner.

The Moon and other celestial bodies shall be used by all States Parties to the Treaty exclusively for peaceful purposes. The establishment of military bases, installations and fortifications, the testing of any type of weapons and the conduct of military maneuvers on celestial bodies shall be forbidden. The use of military personnel for scientific research for any other peaceful purposes shall not be prohibited. The use of any equipment or facility necessary for peaceful exploration of the Moon and other celestial bodies shall also not be prohibited.

Antarctica. The Antarctic Treaty of 1959 provides the following.

Article I

1. Antarctica shall be used for peaceful purposes only. There shall be prohibited, *inter alia*, any measures of a military nature, such as the establishment of military bases and fortifications, the carrying out of military maneuvers, as well as the testing of any type of weapons.

2. The present Treaty shall not prevent the use of military personnel or equipment for scientific research or for any other peaceful purpose.

Article V

1. Any nuclear explosions in Antarctica and the disposal there of radioactive waste material shall be prohibited.

The Seabed. The Treaty on the Prohibition of the Emplacement of Nuclear Weapons and Other Weapons of Mass Destruction on the Seabed and the Ocean Floor, and in the Subsoil Thereof provides as follows.

The States Parties to this Treaty,

Recognizing the common interest of mankind in the progress of the exploration and use of the seabed and the ocean floor for peaceful purposes,

Considering that the prevention of a nuclear arms race on the seabed and the ocean floor serves the interests of maintaining world peace, reduces international tensions and strengthens friendly relations among States,

Convinced that this Treaty constitutes a step towards the exclusion of the seabed, the ocean floor and the subsoil thereof from the arms race,

Convinced that this Treaty constitutes a step towards a treaty on general and complete disarmament under strict and effective international control, and determined to continue negotiations to this end,

Convinced that this Treaty will further the purposes and principles of the Charter of the United Nations, in a manner consistent with the principles of international law and without infringing the freedoms of the high seas,

Have agreed as follows:

Article I

1. The States Parties to this Treaty undertake not to emplant or emplace on the seabed and the ocean floor and in the subsoil thereof beyond the outer limit of a seabed zone, as defined in article II, any nuclear weapons or any other types of weapons of mass destruction as well as structures, launching installations or any other facilities specifically designed for storing, testing or using such weapons.

2. The undertakings of paragraph 1 of this article shall also apply to the seabed zone referred to in the same paragraph, except that within such seabed zone, they shall not apply either to the coastal State or to the seabed beneath its territorial waters.

3. The States Parties to this Treaty undertake not to

assist, encourage or induce any State to carry out activities referred to in paragraph 1 of this article and not to participate in any other way in such actions.

Article II

For the purpose of this Treaty, the outer limit of the seabed zone referred to in article I shall be coterminous with the twelve-mile outer limit of the zone referred to in part II of the Convention on the Territorial Sea and the Contiguous Zone, signed at Geneva on April 29, 1958, and shall be measured in accordance with the provisions of part I, section II, of that Convention and in accordance with international law.

Article III

1. In order to promote the objectives of and insure compliance with the provisions of this Treaty, each State Party to the Treaty shall have the right to verify through observation the activities of other States Parties to the Treaty on the seabed and the ocean floor and in the subsoil thereof beyond the zone referred to in article I, provided that observation does not interfere with such activities.

2. If after such observation reasonable doubts remain concerning the fulfillment of the obligations assumed under the Treaty, the State Party having such doubts and the State Party that is responsible for the activities giving rise to the doubts shall consult with a view to removing the doubts. If the doubts persist, the State Party having such doubts shall notify the other States Parties, and the Parties concerned shall cooperate on such

further procedures for verification as may be agreed, including appropriate inspection of objects, structures, installations or other facilities that reasonably may be expected to be of a kind described in article I. The Parties in the region of the activities, including any coastal State, and any other Party so requesting, shall be entitled to participate in such consultation and cooperation. After completion of the further procedures for verification, an appropriate report shall be circulated to other Parties by the Party that initiated such procedures.

3. If the State responsible for the activities giving rise to the reasonable doubts is not identifiable by observation of the object, structure, installation or other facility, the State Party having such doubts shall notify and make appropriate inquiries of States Parties in the region of the activities and of any other State Party. If it is ascertained through these inquiries that a particular State Party is responsible for the activities, that State Party shall consult and cooperate with other Parties as provided in paragraph 2 of this article. If the identity of the State responsible for the activities cannot be ascertained through these inquiries, then further verification procedures, including inspection, may be undertaken by the inquiring State Party, which shall invite the participation of the Parties in the region of the activities, including any coastal State, and of any other Party desiring to cooperate.

4. If consultation and cooperation pursuant to paragraphs 2 and 3 of this article have not removed the doubts concerning the activities and there remains a serious question concerning fulfillment of the obligations assumed under this Treaty, a State Party may, in accordance with the provisions of the Charter of the United Na-

tions, refer the matter to the Security Council, which may take action in accordance with the Charter.

5. Verification pursuant to this article may be undertaken by any State Party using its own means, or with the full or partial assistance of any other State Party, or through appropriate international procedures within the framework of the United Nations and in accordance with its Charter.

6. Verification activities pursuant to this Treaty shall not interfere with activities of other States Parties and shall be conducted with due regard for rights recognized under international law, including the freedoms of the high seas and the rights of coastal States with respect to the exploration and exploitation of their continental shelves.

Article IV

Nothing in this Treaty shall be interpreted as supporting or prejudicing the position of any State Party with respect to existing international conventions, including the 1958 Convention on the Territorial Sea and the Contiguous Zone, or with respect to rights or claims which such State Party may assert, or with respect to recognition or nonrecognition of rights or claims asserted by any other State, related to waters off its coasts, including *inter alia*, territorial seas and contiguous zones, or to the seabed and the ocean floor, including continental shelves.

Article V

The Parties to this Treaty undertake to continue negotiations in good faith concerning further measures in the field of disarmament for the prevention of an arms race on the seabed, the ocean floor and the subsoil thereof.

Article VI

Any State Party may propose amendments to this Treaty. Amendments shall enter into force for each State Party accepting the amendments upon their acceptance by a majority of the States Parties to the Treaty and, thereafter, for each remaining State Party on the date of acceptance by it.

Article VII

Five years after the entry into force of this Treaty, a conference of Parties to the Treaty shall be held at Geneva, Switzerland, in order to review the operation of this Treaty with a view to assuring that the purposes of the preamble and the provisions of the Treaty are being realized. Such review shall take into account any relevant technological developments. The review conference shall determine, in accordance with the views of a majority of those Parties attending, whether and when an additional review conference shall be convened.

Article VIII

Each State Party to this Treaty shall in exercising its national sovereignty have the right to withdraw from this Treaty if it decides that extraordinary events related to the subject matter of this Treaty have jeopardized the supreme interests of its country. It shall give notice of such withdrawal to all other States Parties to the Treaty and to the United Nations Security Council three months in advance. Such notice shall include a statement of the extraordinary events it considers to have jeopardized its supreme interests.

Article IX

The provisions of this Treaty shall in no way affect the obligations assumed by States Parties to the Treaty under international instruments establishing zones free from nuclear weapons.

Article X

1. This Treaty shall be open for signature to all States. Any State which does not sign the Treaty before its entry into force in accordance with paragraph 3 of this article may accede to it at any time.

2. This Treaty shall be subject to ratification by signatory States. Instruments of ratification and of accession shall be deposited with the Governments of the United States of America, the United Kingdom of Great Britain and Northern Ireland, and the Union of Soviet Socialist Republics, which are hereby designated the Depositary Governments.

3. This Treaty shall enter into force after the deposit of instruments of ratification by twenty-two Governments, including the Governments designated as Depositary Governments of this Treaty.

4. For States whose instruments of ratification or accession are deposited after the entry into force of this

Treaty, it shall enter into force on the date of the deposit of their instruments of ratification or accession.

5. The Depositary Governments shall promptly inform the Governments of all signatory and acceding states of the date of each signature, of the date of deposit of each instrument of ratification or accession, of the date of the entry into force of this Treaty, and of the receipt of other notices.

6. This Treaty shall be registered by the Depositary Governments pursuant to Article 102 of the Charter of the United Nations.

Article XI

This Treaty, the English, Russian, French, Spanish and Chinese texts of which are equally authentic, shall be deposited in the archives of the Depositary Governments. Duly certified copies of this Treaty shall be transmitted by the Depositary Governments to the Governments of the States signatory and acceding thereto.

In Witness Whereof the undersigned, being duly authorized thereto, have signed this Treaty.

Done in triplicate, at the cities of Washington, London and Moscow, this eleventh day of February, one thousand nine hundred seventy-one.

Proliferation. The 1968 Nonproliferation Treaty undertakes to prevent the spread of nuclear weapons throughout the international system by prohibiting non-nuclear states from producing or acquiring them.

Treaty on the Nonproliferation of Nuclear Weapons, July 1, 1968

The States concluding this Treaty, hereinafter referred to as the "Parties to the Treaty,"

Considering the devastation that would be visited upon all mankind by a nuclear war and the consequent need to make every effort to avert the danger of such a war and to take measures to safeguard the security of peoples,

Believing that the proliferation of nuclear weapons would seriously enhance the danger of nuclear war,

In conformity with resolutions of the United Nations General Assembly calling for the conclusion of an agreement on the prevention of wider dissemination of nuclear weapons,

Undertaking to cooperate in facilitating the application of International Atomic Energy Agency safeguards on peaceful nuclear activities,

Expressing their support for research, development and other efforts to further the application, within the framework of the International Atomic Energy Agency safeguards system, of the principle of safeguarding effectively the flow of source and special fissionable materials by use of instruments and other techniques at certain strategic points,

Affirming the principle that the benefits of peaceful applications of nuclear technology, including any technological by-products which may be derived by nuclear-weapon States from the development of nuclear explosive devices, should be available for peaceful purposes to all Parties to the Treaty, whether nuclear-weapon or non-nuclear-weapon States,

Convinced that, in furtherance of this principle, all Parties to the Treaty are entitled to participate in the fullest possible exchange of scientific information for, and to contribute alone or in cooperation with other States to, the further development of the applications of atomic energy for peaceful purposes,

Declaring their intention to achieve at the earliest possible date the cessation of the nuclear arms race and to undertake effective measures in the direction of nuclear disarmament,

Urging the cooperation of all States in the attainment of this objective,

Recalling the determination expressed by the Parties to the 1963 Treaty banning nuclear weapon tests in the atmosphere in outer space and under water in its Preamble to seek to achieve the discontinuance of all test explosions of nuclear weapons for all time and to continue negotiations to this end,

Desiring to further the easing of international tension and the strengthening of trust between States in order to facilitate the cessation of the manufacture of nuclear weapons, the liquidation of all their existing stockpiles, and the elimination from national arsenals of nuclear weapons and the means of their delivery pursuant to a treaty on general and complete disarmament under strict and effective international control,

Recalling that, in accordance with the Charter of the United Nations, States must refrain in their international relations from the threat or use of force against the territorial integrity or political independence of any State, or in any other manner inconsistent with the Purposes of the United Nations, and that the establishment and mainte-nance of international peace and security are to be pro-moted with the least diversion for armaments of the world's human and economic resources,

Have agreed as follows:

Article I

Each nuclear-weapon State Party to the Treaty under-takes not to transfer to any recipient whatsoever nuclear weapons or other nuclear explosive devices, or control over such weapons or explosive devices directly, or indi-rectly; not to manufacture or otherwise acquire nuclear weapons or other nuclear explosive devices; and not to seek or receive any assistance in the manufacture of nu-clear weapons or other nuclear explosive devices.

Article II

Each non-nuclear-weapon State Party to the Treaty undertakes not to receive the transfer from any transferor whatsoever of nuclear weapons or other nuclear explo-sive devices or of control over such weapons or explosive devices directly, or indirectly; not to manufacture or other-wise acquire nuclear weapons or other nuclear explosive devices; and not to seek or receive any assistance in the manufacture of nuclear weapons or other nuclear explo-sive devices.

Article III

1. Each non-nuclear-weapon State Party to the

Treaty undertakes to accept safeguards, as set forth in an agreement to be negotiated and concluded with the International Atomic Energy Agency in accordance with the Statute of the International Atomic Energy Agency and the Agency's safeguards system, for the exclusive purpose of verification of the fulfillment of its obligations assumed under this Treaty with a view to preventing diversion of nuclear energy from peaceful uses to nuclear weapons or other nuclear explosive devices. Procedures for the safeguards required by this article shall be followed with respect to source or special fissionable material whether it is being produced, processed or used in any principal nuclear facility or is outside any such facility. The safeguards required by this article shall be applied on all source or special fissionable material in all peaceful nuclear activities within the territory of such State, under its jurisdiction, or carried out under its control anywhere.

2. Each State Party to the Treaty undertakes not to provide: (a) source or special fissionable material, or (b) equipment or material especially designed or prepared for the processing, use or production of special fissionable material, to any non-nuclear-weapon State for peaceful purposes, unless the source or special fissionable material shall be subject to the safeguards required by this article.

3. The safeguards required by this article shall be implemented in a manner designed to comply with article IV of this Treaty, and to avoid hampering the economic or technological development of the Parties or international cooperation in the field of peaceful nuclear activities, including the international exchange of nuclear material

and equipment for the processing, use or production of nuclear material for peaceful purposes in accordance with the provisions of this article and the principle of safeguarding set forth in the Preamble of the Treaty.

4. Non-nuclear-weapon States Party to the Treaty shall conclude agreements with the International Atomic Energy Agency to meet the requirements of this article either individually or together with other States in accordance with the Statute of the International Atomic Energy Agency. Negotiation of such agreements shall commence within 180 days from the original entry into force of this Treaty. For States depositing their instruments of ratification or accession after the 180-day period, negotiation of such agreements shall commence not later than the date of such deposit. Such agreements shall enter into force not later than eighteen months after the date of initiation of negotiations.

Article IV

1. Nothing in this Treaty shall be interpreted as affecting the inalienable right of all the Parties to the Treaty to develop research, production and use of nuclear energy for peaceful purposes without discrimination and in conformity with articles I and II of this Treaty.

2. All the Parties to the Treaty undertake to facilitate, and have the right to participate in, the fullest possible exchange of equipment, materials and scientific and technological information for the peaceful uses of nuclear energy. Parties to the Treaty in a position to do so shall also cooperate in contributing alone or together with other States or international organizations to the further devel-

opment of the applications of nuclear energy for peaceful purposes, especially in the territories of non-nuclear-weapon States Party to the Treaty, with due consideration for the needs of the developing areas of the world.

Article V

Each Party to the Treaty undertakes to take appropriate measures to ensure that, in accordance with this Treaty, under appropriate international observation and through appropriate international procedures, potential benefits from any peaceful applications of nuclear explosions will be made available to non-nuclear-weapon States Party to the Treaty on a nondiscriminatory basis and that the charge to such Parties for the explosive devices used will be as low as possible and exclude any charge for research and development, non-nuclear-weapon States Party to the Treaty shall be able to obtain such benefits, pursuant to a special international agreement or agreements, through an appropriate international body with adequate representation of non-nuclear-weapon States. Negotiations on this subject shall commence as soon as possible after the Treaty enters into force. Non-nuclear-weapon States Party to the Treaty so desiring may also obtain such benefits pursuant to bilateral agreements.

Article VI

Each of the Parties to the Treaty undertakes to pursue negotiations in good faith on effective measures relating to cessation of the nuclear arms race at an early date and to nuclear disarmament, and on a treaty on general and complete disarmament under strict and effective international control.

Article VII

Nothing in this Treaty affects the right of any group of States to conclude regional treaties in order to assure the total absence of nuclear weapons in their respective territories.

Article VIII

1. Any Party to the Treaty may propose amendments to this Treaty. The text of any proposed amendment shall be submitted to the Depositary Governments which shall circulate it to all Parties to the Treaty. Thereupon, if requested to do so by one-third or more of the Parties to the Treaty, the Depositary Governments shall convene a conference, to which they shall invite all the Parties to the Treaty, to consider such an amendment.

2. Any amendment to this Treaty must be approved by a majority of the votes of all the Parties to the Treaty, including the votes of all nuclear-weapon States Party to the Treaty and all other Parties which, on the date the amendment is circulated, are members of the Board of Governors of the International Atomic Energy Agency. The amendment shall enter into force for each Party that deposits its instrument of ratification of the amendment upon the deposit of such instruments of ratification by a majority of all the Parties, including the instruments of ratification of all nuclear-weapon States Party to the Treaty

and all other Parties which, on the date the amendment is circulated, are members of the Board of Governors of the International Atomic Energy Agency. Thereafter, it shall enter into force for any other Party upon the deposit of its instrument of ratification of the amendment.

3. Five years after the entry into force of this Treaty, a conference of Parties to the Treaty shall be held in Geneva, Switzerland, in order to review the operation of this Treaty with a view to assuring that the purposes of the Preamble and the provisions of the Treaty are being realized. At intervals of five years thereafter, a majority of the Parties to the Treaty may obtain, by submitting a proposal to this effect to the Depositary Governments, the convening of further conferences with the same objective of reviewing the operation of the Treaty.

Article IX

1. This Treaty shall be open to all States for signature. Any State which does not sign the Treaty before its entry into force in accordance with paragraph 3 of this article may accede to it at any time.

2. This Treaty shall be subject to ratification by signatory States. Instruments of ratification and instruments of accession shall be deposited with the Governments of the United States of America, the United Kingdom of Great Britain and Northern Ireland and the Union of Soviet Socialist Republics, which are hereby designated the Depositary Governments.

3. This Treaty shall enter into force after its ratification by the States, the Governments of which are desig-

nated Depositaries of the Treaty, and forty other States signatory to this Treaty and the deposit of their instruments of ratification. For the purposes of this Treaty, a nuclear-weapon State is one which has manufactured and exploded a nuclear weapon or other nuclear explosive device prior to January 1, 1967.

4. For States whose instruments of ratification or accession are deposited subsequent to the entry into force of this Treaty, it shall enter into force on the date of the deposit of their instruments of ratification or accession.

5. The Depository Governments shall promptly inform all signatory and acceding States of the date of each signature, the date of deposit of each instrument of ratification or of accession, the date of the entry into force of this Treaty, and the date of receipt of any requests for convening a conference or other notices.

6. This Treaty shall be registered by the Depositary Governments pursuant to article 102 of the Charter of the United Nations.

Article X

1. Each Party shall in exercising its national sovereignty have the right to withdraw from the Treaty if it decides that extraordinary events, related to the subject matter of this Treaty, have jeopardized the supreme interests of its country. It shall give notice of such withdrawal to all other Parties to the Treaty and to the United Nations Security Council three months in advance. Such notice shall include a statement of the extraordinary events it regards as having jeopardized its supreme interests.

2. Twenty-five years after the entry into force of the Treaty, a conference shall be convened to decide whether the Treaty shall continue in force indefinitely, or shall be extended for an additional fixed period or periods. This decision shall be taken by a majority of the Parties to the Treaty.

Article XI

This Treaty, the English, Russian, French, Spanish and Chinese texts of which are equally authentic, shall be deposited in the archives of the Depositary Governments. Duly certified copies of this Treaty shall be transmitted by the Depositary Governments to the Governments of the signatory and acceding States.

In Witness Whereof the undersigned, duly authorized have signed this Treaty.

Done in triplicate, at the cities of Washington, London and Moscow, this first day of July one thousand nine hundred sixty-eight.

Communication Regulation

The international exchange of publications is subjected to regulations in the 1955 Universal Copyright Convention designed to protect the rights of authors. The 1947 Paris Universal Postal Convention establishes the right of free transit for postal materials and regulates service charges and what types of material may be prohibited, such as obscenity. The 1958 Paris Convention Concerning the International

Exchange of Publications binds signatory states to encourage and facilitate the exchange between nations of educational, scientific, technical and cultural publications from governmental and non-governmental institutions. It also regulates customs arrangements, service charge rates, and conditions of transport.

The 1965 Montreux International Telecommunication Convention recognizes the right of the public to correspond by means of the international services of public correspondence, and requires that signatories establish and protect channels and installations of communication, prevent deceptive or false distress and identificiation calls, and give priority to any communication concerning safety at sea, on land, and in the air or outer space.

Environment and Resource Regulation

Protection of the environment and resources outside the territories of individual states is of increasing importance and growing concern among the nations. In attempting to prevent wasteful and destructive pollution of the environment and the unilateral exploitation of nonnational resources, the nations have formulated regulations to define their responsibilities.

A corpus of law provides regulations to prevent pollution of the sea by oil. The basic legislation is the International Convention for the Prevention of Pollution of the Sea by Oil, 1954, as amended.

Article II

(1) The present Convention shall apply to ships registered in any of the territories of a Contracting Government and to unregistered ships having the nationality of a Contracting Party, except:

(a) tankers of under 150 tons gross tonnage and other ships of under 500 tons gross tonnage, provided that each Contracting Government will take the necessary steps, so far as is reasonable and practicable, to apply the requirements of the Convention to such ships also, having regard to their size, service and the type of fuel used for their propulsion;

(b) ships for the time being engaged in the whaling industry when actually employed on whaling operations;

(c) ships for the time being navigating the Great Lakes of North America and their connecting and tributary waters as far east as the lower exit of St. Lambert Lock at Montreal in the Province of Quebec, Canada;

(d) naval ships and ships for the time being used as naval auxiliaries.

(2) Each Contracting Government undertakes to adopt appropriate measures ensuring that requirements equivalent to those of the present Convention are, so far as is reasonable and practicable, applied to the ships referred to in subparagraph (d) of paragraph (1) of this Article.

Article III

Subject to the provisions of Articles IV and V:

(*a*) the discharge from a ship to which the present Convention applies, other than a tanker, of oil or oily mixture shall be prohibited except when the following conditions are all satisfied:
  (i) the ship is proceeding en route;
  (ii) the instantaneous rate of discharge of oil content does not exceed 60 litres per mile;
  (iii) the oil content of the discharge is less than 100 parts per 1,000,000 parts of the mixture;
  (iv) the discharge is made as far as practicable from land;

(*b*) the discharge from a tanker to which the present Convention applies of oil or oily mixture shall be prohibited except when the following conditions are all satisifed:
  (i) the tanker is proceeding en route;
  (ii) the instantaneous rate of discharge of oil content does not exceed 60 litres per mile;
  (iii) the total quantity of oil discharged on a ballast voyage does not exceed 1/15,000 of the total cargo-carrying capacity;
  (iv) the tanker is more than 50 miles from the nearest land;

(*c*) the provisions of sub-paragraph (b) of this Article shall not apply to:
  (i) the discharge of ballast from a cargo tank which, since the cargo was last carried

therein, has been so cleaned that any effluent therefrom, if it were discharged from a stationary tanker into clean calm water on a clear day, would produce no visible traces of oil on the surface of the water; or

(ii) the discharge of oil or oily mixture from machinery space bilges, which shall be governed by the provisions of sub-paragraph (a) of this Article.

Article IV

Article III shall not apply to:

(a) the discharge of oil or of oily mixture from a ship for the purpose of securing the safety of a ship, preventing damage to a ship or cargo, or saving life at sea;

(b) the escape of oil or of oily mixture resulting from damage to a ship or unavoidable leakage, if all reasonable precautions have been taken after the occurrence of the damage or discovery of the leakage for the purpose of preventing or minimizing the escape;

Article V

Article III shall not apply to the discharge of oily mixture from the bilges of a ship during the period of twelve months following the date on which the present Convention comes into force for the relevant territory in accordance with paragraph (1) of Article II.

Article VI

(1) Any contravention of Articles III and IX shall be an offence punishable under the law of the relevant territory in respect of the ship in accordance with paragraph (1) of Article II.

(2) The penalties which may be imposed under the law of any of the territories of a Contracting Government in respect of the unlawful discharge from a ship of oil or oily mixture outside the territorial sea of that territory shall be adequate in severity to discourage any such unlawful discharge and shall not be less than the penalties which may be imposed under the law of that territory in respect of the same infringements within the territorial sea.

(3) Each Contracting Government shall report to the Organization the penalties actually imposed for each infringement.

Article VII

(1) As from a date twelve months after the present Convention comes into force for the relevant territory in respect of a ship in accordance with paragraph (1) of Article II, such a ship shall be required to be so fitted as to prevent, as far as reasonable and practicable, the escape of oil into bilges, unless effective means are provided to ensure that the oil in the bilges is not discharged in contravention of this Convention.

(2) Carrying water ballast in oil fuel tanks shall be avoided if possible.

Article VIII

(1) Each Contracting Government shall take all appropriate steps to promote the provision of facilities as follows:

    (a) according to the needs of ships using them, ports shall be provided with facilities adequate for the reception, without causing undue delay to ships, of such residues and oily mixtures as would remain for disposal from ships other than tankers if the bulk of the water had been separated from the mixture;

    (b) oil loading terminals shall be provided with facilities adequate for the reception of such residues and oily mixtures as would similarly remain for disposal by tankers;

    (c) ship repair ports shall be provided with facilities adequate for the reception of such residues and oily mixtures as would similarly remain for disposal by all ships entering for repairs.

(2) Each Contracting Government shall determine which are the ports and oil loading terminals in its territories suitable for the purposes of sub-paragraphs (a), (b) and (c) of paragraph (1) of this Article.

(3) As regards paragraph (1) of this Article, each Contracting Government shall report to the Organization, for transmission to the Contracting Government concerned, all cases where the facilities are alleged to be inadequate.

Article IX

(1) Of the ships to which the present Convention applies, every ship which uses oil fuel and every tanker shall be provided with an oil record book, whether as part of the ship's official log book or otherwise, in the form specified in the Annex to the Convention.

(2) The oil record book shall be completed on each occasion, on a tank-to-tank basis, whenever any of the following operations take place in the ship:

(a) *for tankers:*
  (i) loading of oil cargo;
  (ii) transfer of oil cargo during voyage;
  (iii) discharge of oil cargo;
  (iv) ballasting of cargo tanks;
  (v) cleaning of cargo tanks;
  (vi) discharge of dirty ballast;
  (vii) discharge of water from slop-tanks;
  (viii) disposal of residues;
  (ix) discharge overboard of bilge water containing oil which has accumulated in machinery spaces whilst in port, and the routine discharge at sea of bilge water containing oil unless the latter has been entered in the appropriate log book.

(b) *for ships other than tankers;*
  (i) ballasting or cleaning of bunker fuel tanks;
  (ii) discharge of dirty ballast or cleaning water from tanks referred to under (i) of this sub-paragraph;
  (iii) disposal of residues;

(iv) discharge overboard of bilge water containing oil which has accumulated in machinery spaces whilst in port, and the routine discharge at sea of bilge water containing oil unless the latter has been entered in the appropriate log book.

In the event of such discharge or escape of oil or oily mixture as is referred to in Article IV, a statement shall be made in the oil record book of the circumstances of, and the reason for, the discharge or escape.

(3) Each operation described in paragraph (2) of this Article shall be fully recorded without delay in the oil record book so that all the entries in the book appropriate to that operation are completed. Each page of the book shall be signed by the officer or officers in charge of the operations concerned and, when the ship is manned, by the master of the ship. The written entries in the oil record book shall be in an official language of the relevant territory in respect of the ship in accordance with paragraph (1) of Article II, or in English or French.

(4) Oil record books shall be kept in such a place as to be readily available for inspection at all reasonable times, and, except in the case of unmanned ships under tow, shall be kept on board the ship. They shall be preserved for a period of two years after the last entry has been made.

In resource conservation the nations have agreed to the regulations contained in "Fishing and Conservation of the Living Resources of the High Seas."

The States Parties to this Convention,
Considering that the development of modern techniques for the exploitation of the living resources of the sea, increasing man's ability to meet the need of the world's expanding population for food, has exposed some of these resources to the danger of being over-exploited,
Considering also that the nature of the problems involved in the conservation of the living resources of the high seas is such that there is a clear necessity that they be solved, whenever possible, on the basis of international co-operation through the concerted action of all the States concerned,
Have agreed as follows:

Article 1

1. All States have the right for their nationals to engage in fishing on the high seas, subject (*a*) to their treaty obligations, (*b*) to the interests and rights of coastal States as provided for in this Convention, (*c*) to the provisions contained in the following Articles concerning conservation of the living resources of the high seas.
2. All States have the duty to adopt, or to co-operate with other States in adopting, such measures for their respective nationals as may be necessary for the conservation of the living resources of the high seas.

Article 2

As employed in this Convention, the expression 'conservation of the living resources of the high seas' means the aggregate of the measures rendering possible the optimum sustainable yield from those resources so as to secure a maximum supply of food and other marine products. Conservation programmes should be formulated with a view to securing in the first place a supply of food for human consumption.

Article 3

A State whose nationals are engaged in fishing any stock or stocks of fish or other living marine resources in any area of the high seas where the nationals of other States are not thus engaged shall adopt, for its own nationals, measures in that area when necessary for the purpose of the conservation of the living resources affected.

Article 4

1. If the nationals of two or more States are engaged in fishing the same stock or stocks of fish or other living marine resources in any area or areas of the high seas, these States shall, at the request of any of them, enter into negotiations with a view to prescribing by agreement for their nationals the necessary measures for the conservation of the living resources affected.

2. If the States concerned do not reach agreement within twelve months, any of the parties may initiate the procedure contemplated by Article 9.

Article 5

1. If, subsequent to the adoption of the measures referred

to in Articles 3 and 4, nationals of other States engage in fishing the same stock or stocks of fish or other living marine resources in any area or areas of the high seas, the other States shall apply the measures, which shall not be discriminatory in form or in fact, to their own nationals not later than seven months after the date on which the measures shall have been notified to the Director-General of the Food and Agriculture Organization of the United Nations. The Director-General shall notify such measures to any State which so requests and, in any case, to any State specified by the State initiating the measure.

2. If these other States do not accept the measures so adopted and if no agreement can be reached within twelve months, any of the interested parties may initiate the procedure contemplated by Article 9. Subject to paragraph 2 of Article 10, the measures adopted shall remain obligatory pending the decision of the special commission.

Article 6

1. A coastal State has a special interest in the maintenance of the productivity of the living resources in any area of the high seas adjacent to its territorial sea.

2. A coastal State is entitled to take part on an equal footing in any system of research and regulation for purposes of conservation of the living resources of the high seas in that area, even though its nationals do not carry on fishing there.

3. A State whose nationals are engaged in fishing in any area of the high seas adjacent to the territorial sea of a

State shall, at the request of that coastal State, enter into negotiations with a view to prescribing by agreement the measures necessary for the conservation of the living resources of the high seas in that area.

4. A State whose nationals are engaged in fishing in any area of the high seas adjacent to the territorial sea of a coastal State shall not enforce conservation measures in that area which are opposed to those which have been adopted by the coastal State, but may enter into negotiations with the coastal State with a view to prescribing by agreement the measures necessary for the conservation of the living resources of the high seas in that area.

5. If the States concerned do not reach agreement with respect to conservation measures within twelve months, any of the parties may initiate the procedure contemplated by Article 9.

Article 7

1. Having regard to the provisions of paragraph 1 of Article 6, any coastal State may, with a view to the maintenance of the productivity of the living resources of the sea, adopt unilateral measures of conservation appropriate to any stock of fish or other marine resources in any area of the high seas adjacent to its territorial sea, provided that negotiations to that effect with the other States concerned have not led to an agreement within six months.

2. The measures which the coastal State adopts under the previous paragraph shall be valid as to other States only if the following requirements are fulfilled:

(a) That there is a need for urgent application of conservation measures in the light of the existing knowledge of the fishery;

(b) That the measures adopted are based on appropriate scientific findings;

(c) That such measures do not discriminate in form or in fact against foreign fishermen.

3. These measures shall remain in force pending the settlement, in accordance with the relevant provisions of this Convention, of any disagreement as to their validity.

4. If the measures are not accepted by the other States concerned, any of the parties may initiate the procedure contemplated by Article 9. Subject to paragraph 2 of Article 10, the measures adopted shall remain obligatory pending the decision of the special commission.

5. The principles of geographical demarcation as defined in Article 12 of the Convention on the Territorial Sea and the Contiguous Zone shall be adopted when coasts of different States are involved.

Article 8

1. Any State which, even if its nationals are not engaged in fishing in an area of the high seas not adjacent to its coast, has a special interest in the conservation of the living resources of the high seas in that area, may request the State or States whose nationals are engaged in fishing there to take the necessary measures of conservation under Articles 3 and 4 respectively, at the same time mentioning the scientific reasons which in its opinion make such

measures necessary, and indicating its special interest.
2. If no agreement is reached within twelve months, such State may initiate the procedure contemplated by Article 9.

Article 9

1. Any dispute which may arise between States under Articles 4, 5, 6, 7, and 8 shall, at the request of any of the parties, be submitted for settlement to a special commis-·sion of five members, unless the parties agree to seek a solution by another method of peaceful settlement, as provided for in Article 33 of the Charter of the United Nations.

2. The members of the commission, one of whom shall be designated as chairman, shall be named by agreement between the States in dispute within three months of the request for settlement in accordance with the provisions of this Article. Failing agreement they shall, upon the request of any State party, be named by the Secretary-General of the United Nations, within a further three-month period, in consultation with the States in dispute and with the President of the International Court of Justice and the Director-General of the Food and Agriculture Organization of the United Nations, from amongst well-qualified persons being nationals of States not involved in the dispute and specializing in legal, administrative or scientific questions relating to fisheries, depending upon the nature of the dispute to be settled. Any vacancy arising after the original appointment shall be filled in the same manner as provided for the initial selection.

3. Any State party to proceedings under these Articles

shall have the right to name one of its nationals to the special commission, with the right to participate fully in the proceedings on the same footing as a member of the commission, but without the right to vote or to take part in the writing of the commission's decision.

4. The commission shall determine its own procedure, assuring each party to the proceedings a full opportunity to be heard and to present its case. It shall also determine how the costs and expenses shall be divided between the parties to the dispute, failing agreement by the parties on this matter.

5. The special commission shall render its decision within a period of five months from the time it is appointed unless it decides, in case of necessity, to extend the time limit for a period not exceeding three months.

6. The special commission shall, in reaching its decisions, adhere to these Articles and to any special agreements between the disputing parties regarding settlement of the dispute.

7. Decisions of the commission shall be by majority vote.

Article 10

1. The special commission shall, in disputes arising under Article 7, apply the criteria listed in paragraph 2 of that Article. In disputes under Articles 4, 5, 6 and 8, the commission shall apply the following criteria, according to the issues involved in the dispute:

   (a) Common to the determination of disputes arising under Articles 4, 5 and 6 are the requirements:

   (i) That scientific findings demonstrate the necessity of conservation measures;

  (ii) That the specific measures are based on scientific findings and are practicable; and

  (iii) That the measures do not discriminate, in form or in fact, against fishermen of other States;

 (b) Applicable to the determination of disputes arising under Article 8 is the requirement that scientific findings demonstrate the necessity for conservation measures, or that the conservation programme is adequate, as the case may be.

2. The special commission may decide that pending its award the measures in dispute shall not be applied, provided that, in the case of disputes under Article 7, the measures shall only be suspended when it is apparent to the commission on the basis of *prima facie* evidence that the need for the urgent application of such measures does not exist.

Article 11

The decisions of the special commission shall be binding on the States concerned and the provisions of paragraph 2 of Article 94 of the Charter of the United Nations shall be applicable to those decisions. If the decisions are accompanied by any recommendations, they shall receive the greatest possible consideration.

Article 12

1. If the factual basis of the award of the special commission is altered by substantial changes in the conditions of the stock or stocks of fish or other living marine resources or in methods of fishing, any of the States concerned may

request the other States to enter into negotiations with a view to prescribing by agreement the necessary modifications in the measures of conservation.

2. If no agreement is reached within a reasonable period of time, any of the States concerned may again resort to the procedure contemplated by Article 9 provided that at least two years have elapsed from the original award.

Article 13

1. The regulation of fisheries conducted by means of equipment embedded in the floor of the sea in areas of the high seas adjacent to the territorial sea of a State may be undertaken by that State where such fisheries have long been maintained and conducted by its nationals, provided that non-nationals are permitted to participate in such activities on an equal footing with nationals except in areas where such fisheries have by long usage been exclusively enjoyed by such nationals. Such regulations will not, however, affect the general status of the areas as high seas.

2. In this Article, the expression 'fisheries conducted by means of equipment embedded in the floor of the sea' means those fisheries using gear with supporting members embedded in the sea floor, constructed on a site and left there to operate permanently or, if removed, restored each season on the same site.

Article 14

In Articles 1, 3, 4, 5, 6 and 8, the terms 'nationals' means fishing boats or craft of any size having the nationality of the State concerned, according to the law of that State, irrespective of the nationality of the members of their crews.

Article 15

This Convention shall, until 31 October 1958, be open for signature by all States Members of the United Nations or of any of the specialized agencies, and by any other State invited by the General Assembly of the United Nations to become a Party to the Convention.

Article 16

This Convention is subject to ratification. The instruments of ratification shall be deposited with the Secretary-General of the United Nations.

Article 17

This Convention shall be open for accession by any States belonging to any of the categories mentioned in Article 15. The instruments of accession shall be deposited with the Secretary-General of the United Nations.

Article 18

1. This Convention shall come into force on the thirtieth day following the date of deposit of the twenty-second instrument of ratification or accession with the Secretary-General of the United Nations.
2. For each State ratifying or acceding to the Convention after the deposit of the twenty-second instrument of ratification or accession, the Convention shall enter into force

on the thirtieth day after deposit by such State of its instrument of ratification or accession.

Article 19

1. At the time of signature, ratification or accession, any State may make reservations to articles of the Convention other than to Articles 6, 7, 9, 10, 11 and 12.
2. Any contracting State making a reservation in accordance with the preceding paragraph may at any time withdraw the reservation by a communication to that effect addressed to the Secretary-General of the United Nations.

Article 20

1. After the expiration of a period of five years from the date on which this Convention shall enter into force, a request for the revision of this Convention may be made at any time by any contracting party by means of a notification in writing addressed to the Secretary-General of the United Nations.
2. The General Assembly of the United Nations shall decide upon the steps, if any, to be taken in respect of such request.

Article 21

The Secretary-General of the United Nations shall inform all States Members of the United Nations and the other States referred to in Article 15:

(a) Of signatures to this Convention and of the deposit of instruments of ratification or accession, in accordance with Articles 15, 16 and 17;

(b) Of the date on which this Convention will come into force, in accordance with Article 18;

(c) Of requests for revision in accordance with Article 20;

(d) Of reservations to this Convention, in accordance with Article 19.

Article 22

The original of this Convention, of which the Chinese, English, French, Russian, and Spanish texts are equally authentic, shall be deposited with the Secretary-General of the United Nations, who shall send certified copies thereof to all States referred to in Article 15.

In Witness Whereof the undersigned plenipotentiaries, being duly authorized thereto by their respective governments, have signed this Convention.

Done at Geneva, this twenty-ninth day of April one thousand nine hundred and fifty-eight.

Further legal regulations in the area of wildlife conservation exist for the hunting and killing of seals and whales in the 1957 Washington International Convention on Conservation of North Pacific Fur Seals and the 1946 Washington International Convention for the Regulation of Whaling. The whaling convention establishes a commission to do research on maintaining the whale population and establishes the following regulations for whalers.

SCHEDULE

1. (*a*) There shall be maintained on each factory ship at least two inspectors of whaling for the purpose of maintaining twenty-four hour inspection. These inspectors shall be appointed and paid by the Government having jurisdiction over the factory ship.

(*b*) adequate inspection shall be maintained at each land station. The inspectors serving at each land station shall be appointed and paid by the Government having jurisdiction over the land station.

2. It is forbidden to take or kill gray whales or right whales, except when the meat and products of such whales are to be used exclusively for local consumption by the aborigines.

3. It is forbidden to take or kill calves or suckling whales or female whales which are accompanied by calves or suckling whales.

4. It is forbidden to use a factory ship or a whale catcher attached thereto for the purpose of taking or treating baleen whales in any of the following areas:

(*a*) In the waters north of 66° North Latitude except that from 159° East Longitude eastward as far as 140° West Longitude the taking or killing of baleen whales by a factory ship or whale catcher shall be permitted between 66° North Latitude and 72° North Latitude;

(*b*) in the Atlantic Ocean and its dependent waters north of 40° South Latitude;

(c) in the Pacific Ocean and its dependent waters east of 150° West Longitude between 40° South Latitude and 35° North Latitude;

(d) in the Pacific Ocean and its dependent waters west of 150° West Lonqitude between 40° South Latitude and 20° North Latitude;

(e) in the Indian Ocean and its dependent waters north of 40° South Latitude.

5. It is forbidden to use a factory ship or a whale catcher attached thereto for the purpose of taking or treating baleen whales in the waters south of 40° South Latitude from 70° West Longitude westward as far as 160° West Longitude.

6. It is forbidden to use a factory ship or a whale catcher attached thereto for the purpose of taking or treating humpback whales in any waters south of 40° South Latitude.

7. (a) It is forbidden to use a factory ship or a whale catcher attached thereto for the purpose of taking or treating baleen whales in any waters south of 40° South Latitude, except during the period from December 15 to April 1 following, both days inclusive.

(b) Notwithstanding the above prohibition of treatment during a closed season, the treatment of whales which have been taken during the open season may be completed after the end of the open season.

8. (a) The number of baleen whales taken during the open season caught in any waters south of 40° South Latitude by whale catchers attached to fac-

tory ships under the jurisdiction of the Contracting Governments shall not exceed sixteen thousand blue-whale units.

(b) For the purposes of subparagraph (a) of this paragraph, blue-whale units shall be calculated on the basis that one blue whale equals:

    (1) two fin whales or

    (2) two and a half humpback whales or

    (3) six sei whales.

(c) Notification shall be given in accordance with the provisions of Article VII of the Convention, within two days after the end of each calendar week, of data on the number of blue-whale units taken in any waters south of 40° South Latitude by all whale catchers attached to factory ships under the jurisdiction of each Contracting Government.

(d) If it should appear that the maximum catch of whales permitted by subparagraph (a) of this paragraph may be reached before April 1 of any year, the Commission, or such other body as the Commission may designate, shall determine, on the basis of the data provided, the date on which the maximum catch of whales shall be deemed to have been reached and shall notify each Contracting Government of that date not less than two weeks in advance thereof. The taking of baleen whales by whale catchers attached to factory ships shall be illegal in any waters south of 40° South Latitude after the date so determined.

(e) Notification shall be given in accordance with the provisions of Article VII of the Convention of each factory ship intending to engage in whaling operations in any waters south of 40° South Latitude.

9. It is forbidden to take or kill any blue, fin, sei, humpback, or sperm whales below the following lengths:

(a) blue whales	70 feet (21.3 meters)
(b) fin whales	55 feet (16.8 meters)
(c) sei whales	40 feet (12.2 meters)
(d) humpback whales	35 feet (10.7 meters)
(e) sperm whales	35 feet (10.7 meters)

except that blue whales of not less than 65 feet (19.8 meters), fin whales of not less than 50 feet (15.2 meters), and sei whales of not less than 35 feet (10.7 meters) in length may be taken for delivery to land stations provided that the meat of such whales is to be used for local consumption as human or animal food.

Whales must be measured when at rest on deck or platform, as accurately as possible by means of a steel tape measure fitted at the zero end with a spiked handle which can be stuck into the deck planking abreast of one end of the whale. The tape measure shall be stretched in a straight line parallel with the whale's body and read abreast the other end of the whale. The ends of the whale, for measurement purposes, shall be the point of the upper jaw and the notch between the tail flukes. Measurements, after being accurately read on the tape measure, shall be logged to the nearest foot: that is to say, any whale between 75' 6" and 76' 6" shall be logged as 76', and any whale between 76' 6" and 77' 6" shall be logged as 77'. The measurement of any whale which falls on an exact half foot shall be logged at the next half foot, e.g. 76' 6" precisely, shall be logged as 77'.

10. It is forbidden to use a land station or a whale catcher attached thereto for the purpose of taking or treating baleen whales in any area or in any waters for more than six months in any period of twelve months, such period of six months to be continuous.

11. It is forbidden to use a factory ship, which has been used during a season in any waters south of 40° South Latitude for the purpose of treating baleen whales, in any other area for the same purpose within a period of one year from the termination of that season.

12. (a) All whales taken shall be delivered to the factory ship or land station and all parts of such whales shall be processed by boiling or otherwise, except the internal organs, whale bone and flippers of all whales, the meat of sperm whales and of parts of whales intended for human food or feeding animals.

(b) Complete treatment of the carcasses of "Dauhval" and of whales used as fenders will not be required in cases where the meat or bone of such whales is in bad condition.

13. The taking of whales for delivery to a factory ship shall be so regulated or restricted by the master or person in charge of the factory ship that no whale carcass (except of a whale used as a fender) shall remain in the sea for a longer period than thirty-three hours from the time of killing to the time when it is taken up on to the deck of the factory ship for treatment. All whale catchers engaged in taking whales must report by radio to the factory ship the time when each whale is caught.

14. Gunners and crews of factory ships, land sta-

tions, and whale catchers shall be engaged on such terms that their remuneration shall depend to a considerable extent upon such factors as the species, size, and yield of whales taken, and not merely upon the number of the whales taken. No bonus or other remuneration shall be paid to the gunners or crews of whale catchers in respect of the taking of milkfilled or lactating whales.

15. Copies of all official laws and regulations relating to whales and whaling and changes in such laws and regulations shall be transmitted to the Commission.

16. Notification shall be given in accordance with the provisions of Article VII of the Convention with regard to all factory ships and land stations of statistical information (a) concerning the number of whales of each species taken, the number thereof lost, and the number treated at each factory ship or land station, and (b) as to the aggregate amounts of oil of each grade and quantities of meal, fertilizer (guano), and other products derived from them, together with (c) particulars with respect to each whale treated in the factory ship or land station as to the date and approximate latitude and longitude of taking, the species and sex of the whale, its length and, if it contains a foetus, the length and sex, if ascertainable, of the foetus. The data referred to in (a) and (c) above shall be verified at the time of the tally and there shall also be notification to the Commission of any information which may be collected or obtained concerning the calving grounds and migration routes of whales.

In communicating this information there shall be specified:

   (a) the name and gross tonnage of each factory

ship;

  (b) the number and aggregate gross tonnage of the whale catchers;

  (c) a list of the land stations which were in operation during the period concerned.

Economic Regulation

International laws relating to the regulation of international financial and trading activities derive from such agreements and organizations as the following.

■ *International Monetary Fund*—This body establishes regulations on the extent to which member nations may change their exchange rates. IMF has 103 members; Yugoslavia is the only Communist state.

■ *General Agreement on Trade and Tariffs*—This agreement among nations requires import quotas be eliminated, tariffs not be raised, and tariffs that are lowered for the goods of one country must be lowered for the same goods from all countries—the most-favored-nation principle. However, this principle is being abandoned because of pressure from the underdeveloped nations.

■ *International Wheat Agreement*—This agreement among 10 wheat-exporting and 38 wheat-importing nations states that wheat will be sold within a certain price range and that the importing countries will purchase a certain proportion of their wheat from member exporters. Similar agreements exist for sugar, coffee, and tin.

CONFLICT RESOLUTION

Methods of conflict resolution may be divided into three categories: peaceful means, coercive means short of war, and war. Legal relationships among nations under the law of war differ from those that exist during peacetime and so will be discussed in Chapter 4.

Resolving conflicts peacefully among nations encompasses the following types of activities.

1. Negotiation. States that are the parties to the conflict meet together to seek accommodation and reconciliation.

2. Good offices. A third party acts as a conveyor of messages between the parties to the conflict. This third party is strictly neutral and not allowed to make any proposals or express any opinions about the dispute.

3. Mediation. A third party presents proposed solutions as a means of assisting disputing states in finding accommodation. This third-party effort is not obligatory, and the proposals are not binding on either disputing state.

4. Commission of inquiry. A neutral third party formally investigates the facts of a dispute. This effort facilitates accommodation in situations when the disputing parties do not agree on the facts of a dispute and allows a cooling-off period.

5. Commission of conciliation. A third party investigates and ascertains the facts of a dispute

and then proposes a nonbinding recommended solution.

6. Arbitration. A third party formulates a solution, which is then binding on the disputing states. Both parties must voluntarily agree to accept the arbitration effort and the arbiter's decision or solution. In turn, the arbiter must respect existing rules of international law or any specific rules laid down in the *compromis*—the agreement by which the dispute is submitted to arbitration.

7. Adjudication. A permanent international court resolves a dispute according to international law. The advantages of adjudication are the increased prestige of a permanent court and the possibility of building a body of consistent case law. Today, adjudication is provided through the International Court of Justice.

International law recognizes two general types of coercive means short of war for resolving international disputes. *Rétorsions de droit* are legal acts carried out in an unfriendly manner. Such acts could include rupture of diplomatic relations, discriminatory tariff rates, and discriminatory treatment of aliens. *Reprisals* are acts of coercion undertaken in response to illegal acts against a nation. They are of short duration and carry no intention to escalate them in severity or scope to the point of war. The legal conditions for reprisals were laid down in the 1928 *Naulilaa* case, an arbitral decision on Germany's actions against Portugal.

Naulilaa Incident

*Portugal–Germany, Arbitral Decision of 31 July 1928
Concerning the Responsibility of Germany for
Damage Caused in the Portuguese Colonies
of South Africa*

[*By the Court: Alois de Meuron, Robert Fazy, Robert Guex.*] . . . D.1. The most recent doctrine, notably the German doctrine, defines reprisals in these terms: Reprisals are an act of self-help (*propre justice, Selbst-hilfehandlung*) of the injured state, in retaliation for an unredressed act of the offending state contrary to international law. They have for object to suspend momentarily, in the relations between the two states, the observance of such or such a rule of international law. They are limited by the rules of humanity and good faith applicable in the relations of state to state. They will be illegal unless a previous act in violation of international law has furnished the justification (*motif*).

(e) Even if the arbitrators accepted the accusation that the Portugese authorities had committed an act contrary to international law, justifying, in principle, reprisals, the German contention would nevertheless be rejected for two other reasons, either of them decisive:

(1) Reprisals are not licit except when they have been preceded by a request for redress (*sommation*) which has been unavailing. Employment of force is not justified in effect, except by its character of necessity. *Cf.* Fauchille, *Traité*, I, Part 3, No. 978. But it is impossible to

consider as a demand from state to state the communication by the authorities of the offending state to each other of the news of the pretended offense. ... There was, therefore, on the part of the authorities of South-West Africa, recourse to force without previous attempt to obtain satisfaction by legal means—which constitutes a further reason for denying the legitimacy of the reprisals resorted to.

(2) The necessity of a proportionality between the reprisal and the offense appears to be recognized in the German reply. Even if one admits that international law does not require that reprisals be measured approximately by the offense, one must certainly consider as excessive, and consequently illicit, reprisals out of all proportion to the act which has motivated them. In the present case ... there was an evident disproportion between the incident of Naulilaa and the six acts of reprisal which have followed it.

The arbitrators thus arrive at the conclusion that the German aggressions of October, November, and December, 1914, at the frontier of Angola cannot be considered licit or justified by the incident of Naulilaa or later acts of the Portuguese authorities, there being a lack of sufficient justification, of previous request for redress, and of an admissible proportion between the alleged offense and the reprisals resorted to. ...

For these reasons, Germany must make reparation for the damage caused by the aggressions. ...

The forms of reprisals are varied. The following are some identifiable forms.

1. Embargo—seizure of an offending state's ships and property present in the injured state.

2. Boycott—an organized refusal to purchase goods from the offending state. If such an effort is without active governmental involvement, the effort is outside the real international law.

3. Pacific blockade—prevention of the arrival or departure of a nation's ships in its own or another state's ports. Pacific blockade does not operate against third states and so is not a war measure—hence the word *pacific*. If third-party states are blocked, the blockade becomes an act of war, and a state of war exists. During the Cuban Missile Crisis of 1962 President Kennedy proclaimed his intention of preventing Russian ships from delivering cargo to Cuban ports, but he called that action the establishment of a "quarantine" rather than a blockade. The legal implications of that polite fiction are not yet clear, and future events must reveal whether that-blockade was illegal, initiated a new form of reprisal, or destroyed the law of blockades.

4. Invasion and occupation—entering and occupying a portion of the offending state's territory. An example is the 1914 U.S. occupation of Vera Cruz in response to the jailing of three American soldiers.

The United Nations Charter prohibits the use of force as a reprisal. The implications and limitations of that prohibition will be discussed in Chapter 4.

IV
The Law
of
WAR

LEGAL NATURE OF WAR

Traditionally international law has regarded war as a legitimate form of self-help as long as it was conducted within the rules of the laws of war and neutrality. By doing so international law recognized the principle of national sovereignty and independence as well as the absence of a supranational judicial and police system to provide highly reliable protection to individual nations. Thus nations convened at the Hague Peace Conference in 1899 and 1907 not to outlaw war but to codify the rules within which it was to be conducted.

The devastation wrought by World War I and the feeling that the world in the second decade of the 20th century was too interdependent for any future war to be profitable for victor or vanquished led political leaders in some nations to believe that it was the right time to legally prohibit war. The result was the 1928 Pact of Paris, whose relevant articles specified the following.

Article 1.

The High Contracting Parties solemnly declare in the names of their respective peoples that they condemn recourse to war for the solution of international controversies, and renounce it as an instrument of national policy in their relations with one another.

Article 2.

The High Contracting Parties agree that the settlement or solution of all disputes or conflicts of whatever nature or of whatever origin they may be, which may arise among them, shall never be sought except by pacific means.

Resolved to prevent another World War II, world leaders in 1948 designed an international organization that would allow the nations to peacefully resolve international conflicts and to preserve order by collectively opposing any future Hitler. Secure in the belief that they had designed such an organization, the leaders thought it would therefore be possible to legally prohibit warfare to the nations; hence they wrote into Article II of the U.N. Charter the following requirements.

3. All Members shall settle their international disputes by

peaceful means in such a manner that international peace and security, and justice, are not endangered.

4. All Members shall refrain in their international relations from the threat or use of force against the territorial integrity or political independence of any state, or in any other manner inconsistent with the Purposes of the United Nations.

Not only war but also the use of force, such as reprisals, is prohibited. Is war, then, illegal? The Charter permits the United Nations to conduct war against an aggressor, and it permits nations to use force, individually or collectively, in self-defense against an armed attack until the United Nations can respond to that armed attack. Aside from those two contingencies the Charter's framers undoubtedly intended to outlaw war on the model of the two world wars, but the Charter's system of peace and peace enforcement was stillborn, killed by new developments unforeseen at the time.

First, cooperation among the Great Powers broke down, causing the paralysis in the Security Council and division of much of the world into armed alliance systems tied to the Great Powers. Second, such new concerns as anticolonialism and opposition to white-supremacy regimes were taken by the new nations of the non-West to be legitimate reasons for the use of force. Third, new types of war were developed. Insurgency wars clandestinely abetted by outside powers make identification of an aggressor difficult to determine and document. The potential for nuclear war with intercontinental ballistic missiles makes collective operations against a nuclear power suicide for both the aggressor and the United Nations forces, and collective operations against a client state of a nuclear power dangerous in the extreme. In the years since establishment of the United Nations, wars and the use of force have not been uncommon in the world, a fact that may be reconciled in several ways with the wording of the U.N. Charter. One may assume that:

1. The Charter clearly prohibits recourse to force except as specifically stated, and any other use of force is an international delict.

2. The concept of self-defense may be broadened to include action against an insurgency and its sponsor, or against some other perceived threat, and the purposes of the United Nations can be interpreted to include support of national liberation movements. But wars, as framers of the Charter understood them, remain legally prohibited.

3. Notwithstanding the specific provision of the Charter that a state's right to undertake measures of self-defense is permissible only "until the Security Council has taken measures necessary to maintain international peace and security," the framers must have intended for the nations to retain reserve or implied powers of self-defense when the U.N. system would not work.

4. The legal prohibition against war is dead, null and void, because of the obvious practice of the

nations in continuing to resort to war and the use of force. Hence the traditional law of war continues operative.

Whichever alternative one chooses, wars will remain, either in accordance with U.N. provisions or in spite of them; thus sound reason exists for concern with the laws of war. Yet, if a nation violates the U.N. proscriptions against war what chance is there that such a nation will respect the laws of war? An answer is that *both* war *and* its restraint are important to the nations. The law of war remains potentially a workable field of international law because the states derive mutual benefit from mutual observation, and because reprisals can be undertaken to enforce compliance.

COMMENCEMENT OF WAR

The Hague Conference of 1907 adopted Convention III Relative To The Opening of Hostilities.

Article I

The Contracting Powers recognize that hostilities between themselves must not commence without previous and explicit warning, in the form either of a declaration of war, giving reasons, or of an ultimatum with conditional declaration of war.

Article II

The existence of a state of war must be notified to the

neutral Powers without delay, and shall not take effect in regard to them until after the receipt of a notification. . . .

IDENTITY OF LOCALE AND PARTICIPANTS

The locale of the war encompasses those sections of the world in which the belligerents may carry on hostile actions against each other. No place outside the locale may be converted into a theater of operations. War zones and defense zones are unilateral extensions of belligerent rights into the high seas, which are normally free to neutral shipping.

Recognition of participants in a war is an important matter, for those legally recognized as participants have *belligerent rights:* to establish blockades, to search neutral ships for contraband, to be treated as prisoners of war rather than as criminals when captured, and to use acts of force that normally would be illegal. The following are types of participants.

1. Regular forces. The determination of who is included in the regular forces of a nation's military is a matter of domestic law. Such members as doctors, nurses, and chaplains are considered noncombatants but when captured are entitled to treatment as prisoners of war under the Hague and Geneva regulations.

2. Irregular forces. Until the late 19th century irregular forces such as partisans, guerrillas, and underground were not part of a nation's formal military establishment and, lacking status as legal participants, could be treated as criminals without the

rights of prisoners of war. Such forces, however, have become increasingly a normal type of military group. The 1907 Hague Conference and the 1949 Geneva Conference attempted to extend legal status to such groups, but the conditions these forces must meet to be granted that legal status would destroy their effectiveness in today's guerrilla wars. The conditions for members of an irregular force, according to the 1907 Hague Convention IV are: (*a*) be commanded by a person responsible for his subordinates; (*b*) have a fixed distinctive emblem recognizable at a distance; (*c*) carry arms openly; and (*d*) conduct operations in accordance with the laws and customs of war.

3. Private enemy citizens. Article 2 of that same convention states:

The inhabitants of a territory which has not been occupied, who, on the approach of the enemy, spontaneously take up arms to resist the invading troops without having had time to organize themselves in accordance with Article 1, shall be regarded as belligerents *if they carry arms openly and* if they respect the laws and customs of war [italics added].

4. Foreign volunteers. No current legal status exists for "volunteers" such as those from China involved in the Korean War and those the Soviet Union threatened to send at the time of the 1956 Suez Crisis.

5. Crews of merchant vessels. If an enemy

vessel is captured and does not resist, the crew is interned; if it resists, the crew receives prisoner-of-war treatment. Crew members of a merchant ship that initiates an attack can be treated as war criminals.

LAW OF MILITARY OPERATIONS

Article 22 of the Hague Convention IV Respecting the Laws and Customs of War on Land states: "The right of belligerents to adopt means of injuring the enemy is not unlimited." Limitations involve the types of weapons, types of military operations, and treatment of captured enemy territory, property, and prisoners.

Types of Weapons

The Hague Convention outlawed poison or poisoned weapons and arms, projectives, or materials calculated to cause unnecessary suffering; the use of expanding bullets is illegal through customary law. The Geneva Protocol of 1925 prohibited the use in war of "asphyxiating, poisonous or other gases, and of all analogous liquids, materials or devices. . . ." No specific rule against atomic and nuclear weapons has been adopted.

Types of Operations

Reprinted below are articles relevant to the conduct of military operations from various conventions adopted at the 1907 Hague Peace Conference. These conventions relate to operations on land, the sea, and from the air.

Section II. Hostilities

Chapter I. Means of Injuring the Enemy, Sieges, and Bombardments

Article 22. The right of belligerents to adopt means of injuring the enemy is not unlimited.

Article 23. In addition to the prohibitions provided by special Conventions, it is especially forbidden

- (a) To employ poison or poisoned weapons;
- (b) To kill or wound treacherously individuals belonging to the hostile nation or army;
- (c) To kill or wound an enemy who, having laid down his arms, or having no longer means of defence, has surrendered at discretion;
- (d) To declare that no quarter will be given;
- (e) To employ arms, projectiles, or material calculated to cause unnecessary suffering;
- (f) To make improper use of a flag of truce, of the national flag or of the military insignia and uniform of the enemy, as well as the distinctive badges of the Geneva Convention;
- (g) To destroy or seize the enemy's property, unless such destruction or seizure be imperatively demanded by the necessities of war;
- (h) To declare abolished, suspended, or inadmissible in a court of law the rights and actions of the nationals of the hostile party.

A belligerent is likewise forbidden to compel the nationals of the hostile party to take part in the operations of war directed against their own country, even if they were in the belligerent's service before the commencement of the war.

Article 24. Ruses of war and the employment of measures necessary for obtaining information about the enemy and the country are considered permissible.

Article 25. The attack or bombardment, by whatever means, of towns, villages, dwellings, or buildings which are undefended is prohibited.

Article 26. The officer in command of an attacking force must, before commencing a bombardment, except in cases of assault, do all in his power to warn the authorities.

Article 27. In sieges and bombardments all necessary steps must be taken to spare, as far as possible, buildings dedicated to religion, art, science, or charitable purposes, historic monuments, hospitals, and places where the sick and wounded are collected, provided they are not being used at the time for military purposes.
It is the duty of the besieged to indicate the presence of such buildings or places by distinctive and visible signs, which shall be notified to the enemy before hand.

Article 28. The pillage of a town or place, even when taken by assault, is prohibited.

Chapter II. Spies

Article 29. A person can only be considered a spy when, acting clandestinely or on false pretences, he obtains or endeavors to obtain information in the zone of operations of a belligerent, with the intention of communicating it to the hostile party.

Thus, soldiers not wearing a disguise who have penetrated into the zone of operations of the hostile army, for the purpose of obtaining information, are not considered spies. Similarly, the following are not considered spies: Soldiers and civilians, carrying out their mission openly, intrusted with the delivery of dispatches intended either for their own army or for the enemy's army. To this class belong likewise persons sent in balloons for the purpose of carrying dispatches and, generally, of maintaining communications between the different parts of an army or a territory.

Article 30. A spy taken in the act shall not be punished without previous trial.

Article 31. A spy who, after rejoining the army to which he belongs is subsequently captured by the enemy, is treated as a prisoner of war and incurs no responsibility for his previous acts of espionage.

CHAPTER III. Flags of Truce

Article 32. A person is regarded as a parlementaire who has been authorized by one of the belligerents to enter into communication with the other, and who advances bearing a white flag. He has a right to inviolability, as well as the trumpeter, bugler or drummer, the flagbearer and interpreter who may accompany him.

Article 33. The commander to whom a parlementaire is sent is not in all cases obliged to receive him.

He may take all the necessary steps to prevent the parlementaire taking advantage of his mission to obtain information.

In case of abuse, he has the right to detain the parlementaire temporarily.

Article 34. The parlementaire loses his rights of inviolability if it is proved in a clear and incontestable manner that he has taken advantage of his privileged position to provoke or commit an act of treason.

Convention VII Relating to the Conversion of Merchant Ships into War-Ships

His Majesty the German Emperor, King of Prussia; [etc.]:

Whereas it is desirable, in view of the incorporation in time of war of merchant ships in the fighting fleet, to define the conditions subject to which this operation may be effected;

Whereas, however, the contracting Powers have been unable to come to an agreement on the question whether the conversion of a merchant ship into a war-ship may take place upon the high seas, it is understood that the question of the place where such conversion is effected remains outside the scope of this agreement and is in no way affected by the following rules;

Being desirous of concluding a Convention to this effect, have appointed the following as their plenipotentiaries: [Here follow the names of plenipotentiaries.]
Who, after having deposited their full powers, found in good and due form, have agreed upon the following provisions:

Article 1

A merchant ship converted into a war-ship cannot have the rights and duties accruing to such vessels unless it is placed under the direct authority, immediate control, and responsibility of the Power whose flag it flies.

Article 2

Merchant ships converted into war-ships must bear the external marks which distinguish the war-ships of their nationality.

Article 3

The commander must be in the service of the State and duly commissioned by the competent authorities. His name must figure on the list of the officers of the fighting fleet.

Convention IX Relating to Bombardment By Naval Forces in Time of War

Article 3

After due notice has been given, the bombardment of undefended ports, towns, villages, dwellings, or buildings may be commenced, if the local authorities, after a formal summons has been made to them, decline to comply with requisitions for provisions or supplies necessary for the immediate use of the naval force before the place in question.

These requisitions shall be in proportion to the resources of the place. They shall only be demanded in the name of the commander of the said naval force, and they shall, as far as possible, be paid for in cash; if not, they shall be evidenced by receipts.

Article 4

Undefended ports, towns, villages, dwellings, or buildings may not be bombarded on account of failure to pay money contributions.

Chapter II. General Provisions

Article 5

In bombardments by naval forces all the necessary measures must be taken by the commander to spare as far as possible sacred edifices, buildings used for artistic, scientific, or charitable purposes, historic monuments, hospitals, and places where the sick or wounded are collected, on the understanding that they are not used at the same time for military purposes.

It is the duty of the inhabitants to indicate such monuments, edifices, or places by visible signs, which shall consist of large, stiff rectangular panels divided diagonally into two colored triangular portions, the upper portion black, the lower portion white.

Article 6

If the military situation permits, the commander of the attacking naval force, before commencing the bombardment, must do his utmost to warn the authorities.

Article 7

A town or place, even when taken by storm, may not be pillaged.

Chapter III. Final Provisions

Article 8

The provisions of the present Convention do not apply except between contracting Powers, and then only if all the belligerents are parties to the Convention.

Convention VIII Relative to the Laying of Automatic Submarine Contact Mines

Article 1

It is forbidden—
1. To lay unanchored automatic contact mines, except when they are so constructed as to become harmless one hour at most after the person who laid them ceases to control them;
2. To lay anchored automatic contact mines which do not become harmless as soon as they have broken loose from their moorings;

3. To use torpedoes which do not become harmless when they have missed their mark.

Article 2

It is forbidden to lay automatic contact mines off the coast and ports of the enemy, with the sole object of intercepting commercial shipping.

Article 3

When anchored automatic contact mines are employed, every possible precaution must be taken for the security of peaceful shipping.

The belligerents undertake to do their utmost to render these mines harmless within a limited time, and, should they cease to be under surveillance, to notify the danger zones as soon as military exigencies permit, by a notice addressed to ship owners, which must also be communicated to the Governments through the diplomatic channel.

Article 4

Neutral Powers which lay automatic contact mines off their coasts must observe the same rules and take the same precautions as are imposed on belligerents.

The neutral Power must inform ship owners, by a notice issued in advance, where automatic contact mines have been laid. This notice must be communicated at once to the Governments through the diplomatic channel.

Article 5

At the close of the war, the contracting Powers undertake to do their utmost to remove the mines which they have laid, each Power removing its own mines.

As regards anchored automatic contact mines laid by one of the belligerents off the coast of the other, their position must be notified to the other party by the Power which laid them, and each Power must proceed with the least possible delay to remove the mines in its own waters.

Article 6

The contracting Powers which do not at present own perfected mines of the pattern contemplated in the present Convention, and which, consequently, could not at present carry out the rules laid down in Articles 1 and 3, undertake to convert the *matériel* of their mines as soon as possible, so as to bring it into conformity with the foregoing requirements.

Article 7

The provisions of the present Convention do not apply except between contracting Powers, and then only if all the belligerents are parties to the Convention.

TREATMENT OF CAPTURED ENEMY TERRITORY, PROPERTY, AND PRISONERS

Territory that an enemy occupies during the course

of a war cannot be annexed or set up as an independent state. The occupying power must maintain order but also respect local law to the extent possible in the circumstances. The occupying power may collect taxes for local use and may requisition certain supplies or services, but it cannot force the inhabitants to take up arms against their own country. General devastation of occupied property, including pillage and the destruction of religious, scientific, and art works, is forbidden. Treatment of enemy persons is covered in Article 23, (c, d, and h) of the Hague Convention IV. Treatment of prisoners of war has long been the subject of international concern and agreements. Following are some general provisions of the 1949 Geneva Convention.

Geneva Convention Relative to the Treatment of Prisoners of War of August 12, 1949

The undersigned Plenipotentiaries of the Governments represented at the Diplomatic Conference held at Geneva from April 21 to August 12, 1949, for the purpose of revising the Convention concluded at Geneva on July 27, 1929, relative to the Treatment of Prisoners of War, have agreed as follows:

Article 1. The High Contracting Parties undertake to respect and to ensure respect for the present Convention in all circumstances.

Article 2. In addition to the provisions which shall be implemented in peace time, the present Convention shall apply to all cases of declared war or of any other armed conflict which may arise between two or more of the High Contracting Parties, even if the state of war is not recognized by one of them.

The Convention shall also apply to all cases of partial or total occupation of the territory of a High Contracting Party, even if the said occupation meets with no armed resistance.

Although one of the Powers in conflict may not be a party to the present Convention, the Powers who are parties thereto shall remain bound by it in their mutual relations. They shall furthermore be bound by the Convention in relation to the said Power, if the latter accepts and applies the provisions thereof.

Article 4. A. Prisoners of war, in the sense of the present Convention, are persons belonging to one of the following categories, who have fallen into the power of the enemy:

(1) Members of the armed forces of a Party to the conflict, as well as members of militias or volunteer corps forming part of such armed forces.

(2) Members of other militias and members of other volunteer corps, including those of organized resistance movements, belonging to a Party to the conflict and operating in or outside their own territory, even if this territory is occupied, provided that such militias or volunteer corps, including such organized resistance movements, fulfill the following conditions:

(a) that of being commanded by a person responsible for his subordinates;

(b) that of having a fixed distinctive sign recognizable at a distance;

(c) that of carrying arms openly;

(d) that of conducting their operations in accordance with the laws and customs of war.

(3) Members of regular armed forces who profess allegiance to a government or an authority not recognized by the Detaining Power.

(4) Persons who accompany the armed forces without actually being members thereof, such as civilian members of military aircraft crews, war correspondents, supply contractors, members of labour units or of services responsible for the welfare of the armed forces, provided that they have received authorization from the armed forces which they accompany, who shall provide them for that purpose with an identity card similar to the annexed model.

(5) Members of crews, including masters, pilots and apprentices, of the merchant marine and the crews of civil aircraft of the Parties to the conflict, who do not benefit by more favourable treatment under any other provisions of international law.

(6) Inhabitants of a non-occupied territory, who on the approach of the enemy spontaneously take up arms to resist the invading forces, without having had time to form themselves into regular armed units, provided they carry arms openly and respect the laws and customs of war.

B. The following shall likewise be treated as prisoners of war under the present Convention:

(1) Persons belonging, or having belonged, to the armed forces of the occupied country, if the occupying

Power considers it necessary by reason of such allegiance to intern them, even though it has originally liberated them while hostilities were going on outside the territory it occupies, in particular where such persons have made an unsuccessful attempt to rejoin the armed forces to which they belong and which are engaged in combat, or where they fail to comply with a summons made to them with a view to internment.

(2) The persons belonging to one of the categories enumerated in the present Article, who have been received by neutral or non-belligerent Powers on their territory and whom these Powers are required to intern under international law, without prejudice to any more favourable treatment which these Powers may choose to give and with the exception of Articles 8, 10, 15, 30, fifth paragraph, 58–67, 92, 126 and, where diplomatic relations exist between the Parties to the conflict and the neutral or non-belligerent Power concerned, those Articles concerning the Protecting Power. Where such diplomatic relations exist, the Parties to a conflict on whom these persons depend shall be allowed to perform towards them the functions of a Protecting Power as provided in the present Convention, without prejudice to the functions which these Parties normally exercise in conformity with diplomatic and consular usage and treaties.

C. This Article shall in no way affect the status of medical personnel and chaplains as provided for in Article 33 of the present Convention.

Article 7. Prisoners of war may in no circumstances renounce in part or in entirety the rights secured to them by the present Convention, and by the special agreements referred to in the foregoing Article, if such there be.

Article 12. Prisoners of war are in the hands of the enemy Power, but not of the individuals or military units who have captured them. Irrespective of the individual responsibilities that may exist, the Detaining Power is responsible for the treatment given them.

Prisoners of war may only be transferred by the Detaining Power to a Power which is a party to the Convention and after the Detaining Power has satisfied itself of the willingness and ability of such transferee Power to apply the Convention. When prisoners of war are transferred under such circumstances, responsibility for the application of the Convention rests on the Power accepting them while they are in its custody.

Nevertheless, if that Power fails to carry out the provisions of the Convention in any important respect, the Power by whom the prisoners of war were transferred shall, upon being notified by the Protecting Power, take effective measures to correct the situation or shall request the return of the prisoners of war. Such requests must be complied with.

Article 13. Prisoners of war must at all times be humanely treated. Any unlawful act or omission by the Detaining Power causing death or seriously endangering the health of a prisoner of war in its custody is prohibited, and will be regarded as a serious breach of the present Convention. In particular, no prisoner of war may be subjected to physical mutilation or to medical or scientific experiments of any kind which are not justified by the medical, dental or hospital treatment of the prisoner concerned and carried out in his interest.

Likewise, prisoners of war must at all times be protected, particularly against acts of violence or intimidation and against insults and public curiosity.

Measures of reprisal against prisoners of war are prohibited.

Article 14. Prisoners of war are entitled in all circumstances to respect for their persons and their honour.

Women shall be treated with all the regard due to their sex and shall in all cases benefit by treatment as favourable as that granted to men.

Prisoners of war shall retain the full civil capacity which they enjoyed at the time of their capture. The Detaining Power may not restrict the exercise, either within or without its own territory, of the rights such capacity confers except insofar as the captivity requires.

Article 15. The Power detaining prisoners of war shall be bound to provide free of charge for their maintenance and for the medical attention required by their state of health.

Article 16. Taking into consideration the provisions of the present Convention relating to rank and sex, and subject to any privileged treatment which may be accorded to them by reason of their state of health, age or professional qualifications, all prisoners of war shall be treated alike by the Detaining Power, without any adverse distinction based on race, nationality, religious belief or political opinions, or any other distinction founded on similar criteria.

Other provisions of this convention relate to the premises for internment, food and clothing, sanitary and medical measures, religious activities, labor of prisoners, communication with family, requests and complaints to detaining authorities, discipline and punishment, escape, and reparation.

TERMINATION OF WARFARE

The formal termination of war brings back into effect the law of peace; hence a peace treaty at the end of a war has been necessary to signal the resumption of peace. However, the increasing use of insurgency wars and United Nations involvement in ending some conflicts have led to an undermining of the peace treaty as a legal symbol. Methods of terminating hostilities include the following.

1. Cessation of hostilities. The acts of violence are simply ended, with no political settlement and no legal implications.

2. Truce. Hostilities cease temporarily for a specific purpose, such as observance of a special holiday or burial of the dead after a battle. A truce is of short duration and can cover all or only a specific portion of the locale.

3. Cease-fire. Acts of violence are ended by formal agreement. An American court held that the 1956 Suez War ended when the cease-fire agreement took effect.[3]

4. Armistice. Agreement is reached to end hostilities and begin negotiations for a peace settlement.

A serious breach of the armistice on one side is grounds for the other side's withdrawal from it. Under traditional international law an armistice did not legally end the war. However, the 1949 armistice agreement between Israel and four Arab states and the 1953 Korean armistice agreement have not been replaced by treaties of peace; so while it can be maintained that the state of war and therefore the law of war continue in effect in such situations, that view is increasingly unworkable and may be outdated.

5. Peace treaty. A treaty specifies the postwar conditions and relationships between the former belligerents, reviving or abrogating treaties in force before the hostilities, and signaling the resumption of peace.

6. Subjugation. A belligerent is conquered and destroyed as a sovereign and independent state, its government abolished, and its population effectively controlled. Such destruction of a nation brings a state of peace into existence.

LAW OF NEUTRALITY

A belligerent's need to prevent outside help from reaching its enemy and the need of states not involved in a conflict to be unharmed, unharassed, and unhampered by that conflict in their international affairs led to development of the concept and law of neutrality. Neutrality is a state's abstention from participating in a conflict or aiding a belligerent, and the duty of belligerents to refrain from violating the territory, seizing the possession, or hampering the peaceful commerce of the neutral states.

Article 16 of the Covenant of the League of Nations designated that a war in violation of the League was a war against all the members of the League, thereby abolishing neutrality for League members. The United Nations Charter allows neutrality until such time as the Security Council may call on members to take action against an aggressor.

A neutral state has certain obligations: (1) to enforce its neutrality against violations by one of the belligerents so that the other belligerent will not be disadvantaged; (2) to refrain from providing aid to any of the belligerents; (3) to prevent belligerent acts on its territory and belligerent use of its territory. In return the neutral state has the right to freely use the high seas and to trade with belligerents in nonmilitary goods.

A belligerent also has certain obligations: (1) to respect the freedom of the seas; (2) to make any blockade effective and applicable only to enemy territory or territory under enemy control; (3) to compensate a neutral for any damage resulting from a reprisal against an enemy; (4) to refrain from making use of a neutral's territory. The belligerent has the right to visit a neutral's ship and search for contraband, which is material of military use being supplied to the enemy in violation of the laws of neutrality.

V

CONCLUSIONS

The nations have developed a corpus of international law to solidify order and stability in world affairs and to facilitate mutual efforts for mutual benefit. International law develops when nations find sufficient harmony of interests among themselves to formalize relationships and activities in legal form—that is, when political conditions in the international system are favorable to cooperation and legislation. Being dependent on favorable political conditions, and in the absence of central political organs that can undertake authoritative action to stimulate favorable political conditions, international law embodies variations in adherence and variations in development.

The relevance to actual state practice of the 1899 and 1907 Hague Conferences in the present international system when compared to the current effectiveness of the Geneva Conventions on the Law of the Sea and the Test Ban Treaty reflects the variations in adherence that exist in different segments of international law. Some rules of law have been rendered dead by state practice and have not been replaced. New scientific developments that allow new forms of state activity not contemplated by the earlier rules of law have rendered some rules obsolete. Some new political developments have so politicized some previously regulated activity that the regulations are now dead. But at the same time new issues, such as space exploration, have become subject to international legislation. Older issues, such as the law of treaties and diplomats, recently have been subjected to legal codification. The result is uneven effectiveness within the body structure of international law.

The degree of development of the law also has varied. The United Nations adopted a Universal Declaration on Human Rights in 1949. A Convention on Political Rights and a Convention on Economic and Cultural Rights have been drafted and opened for ratification since 1966. Neither has obtained enough ratifications to come into effect; but if and when they do, the function of promotion of human rights can be added to the functions of international law outlined in Chapter 3. In Europe, however, a European Convention on Human Rights, which provides specification of rights and two organs for enforcement, has been in effect since 1959. Similarly, among the inter-American republics there exists a strong OAS Convention to Prevent and Punish the Acts of Terrorism Taking the Form of Crimes Against Persons and Related Extortion That are of International Significance, 1971. In short, in development variation exists within the body of law at the international level and between the world level and various regional areas.

These variations result from the prevailing degree of political and economic solidarity and technical development among the nations. The laws of war were more applicable, for example, among 19th century nations and armies than among those of the second half of the 20th century. The law of environment and resource protection would not have been considered important before the 20th century. Similarly, the disparity in motivations and policies among the nations prevents conclusion of tough antiterrorist legislation at the present time.

Based on these variations one can postulate three categories of law in terms of the political importance of the subject matter.[4] *The law of the political framework* defines the nature of international society and its major participants and alignments, the state and its equality and independence, the role of consent in international legislation, the major alliance systems and international organizations, the conditions on the use of force, and the procedures for settling disputes. This constitutional-type law is the most political, and its topics carry the highest stakes in the international competition among the nations. The *law of reciprocity* governs the mutual relations of nations in such areas as diplomatic procedures and breadth of territorial sea and their more politically sensitive cooperative efforts, such as economic regulation. The *law of community* covers issues not directly linked with the competition for power and advantage, such as the law of the environment, aircraft seizures, suppression of the drug traffic, and other more scientific and cultural areas.

International law in the contemporary period is beset by challenges that arise from the current divisions in ideals and goals, disparity in development and potential futures, and variations in security and power among the nations of the world, but their discussion is beyond the scope and space of this book.[5] The future development of international law, however, will depend on how those challenges are overcome. If the world can heal its divisions and pacify its revolutionaries and armed prophets, the outlook for the law will be bright. For there will be no lack of issues ripe for international legal regulations and control as the world grows increasingly interdependent, technological, and conscious of its responsibilities to the underdeveloped of the world.

Notes

1. Named after Señor Genaro Estrada, foreign minister of Mexico, who on September 27, 1930, issued a declaration that stated that Mexico would no longer recognize new governments since such recognition implied a judgment on the right of foreign nations to accept, maintain, or replace their governments or authorities.

2. Named after Señor Carlos R. Tobar, secretary of foreign affairs of Ecuador, who on March 15, 1907, stated that recognition should be withheld from governments established by revolution against constitutional regimes.

3. Raymond Aron, *Peace and War* (New York: Frederick A. Praeger, 1967), p. 182.

4. The following division of the law is based on Stanley Hoffmann's categories in "International Systems and International Law," *The State of War*, ed. Stanley Hoffmann (New York: Frederick A. Praeger, 1965), pp. 97-98; Wolfgang Friedman's triary division of the law into international law of coexistence, international law of cooperation—universal concerns, and international law of cooperation—re-

gional groupings, which appears in his *The Changing Structure of International Law* (New York: Columbia University Press, 1964), pp. 60-71; and on Georg Schwarzenbarger's three categories that he calls the law of power, law of reciprocity, and law of coordination, set forth in his article "Jus pacis ac belli," *American Journal of International Law*, 37:460-79, July, 1943.

5. For discussions of such challenges, see Hoffmann, *op. cit.*, pp. 108-22; Richard Falk, *The Status of Law in International Society* (Princeton, N.J.: Princeton University Press, 1970).

Bibliography

This short bibliography is intended to provide listings of major texts, casebooks and significant scholarship on various topics of international law.

Bassiouni, M. Cherif and Ved P. Nanda, eds. *A Treatise on International Criminal Law.* Volume I: *Crime and Punishment.* Volume II: *Jurisdiction and Cooperation.* Springfield, Illinois: Charles C. Thomas, 1973.

Bishop, William. *International Law: Cases and Materials.* 3rd Ed. Boston: Little, Brown and Company, 1971.

Briggs, Herbert. *The Law of Nations: Cases, Documents, and Notes.* 2nd Ed. New York: Appleton-Century-Crofts, 1952.

Brownlie, Ian. *Basic Documents in International Law.* 2nd Ed. Oxford: Clarendon Press, 1972.

Corbett, Percy E. *Law and Society in the Relations of States*. New York: Harcourt Brace Jovanovich, Inc.

D'Amato, Anthony A. *The Concept of Custom in International Law*. Ithaca, N.Y.: Cornell University Press, 1973.

Deutsch, Karl and Stanley Hoffmann, eds. *The Relevance of International Law*. Garden City, N.Y.: Doubleday & Co., 1971.

De Visscher, Charles. *Theory and Reality in Public International Law* Revised Ed. Translated by P.E. Corbett. Princeton: Princeton University Press, 1968.

Elias, T.O. *Africa and the Development of International Law*. Dobbs Ferry, N.Y.: Oceana Publications, 1970.

Falk, Richard. *Legal Order in a Violent World*. Princeton: Princeton University Press, 1968.

————. *The Status of Law in International Society*. Princeton: Princeton University Press, 1970.

————. *This Endangered Planet*. New York: Random House, 1971.

————. Ed. *The International Law of Civil War*. Baltimore: Johns Hopkins University Press, 1969 to 1972.

————. Ed. *The Vietnam War and International Law*. 3 volumes. Princeton: Princeton University Press, 1968, 1969, 1972.

————. and Cyril Black. *The Future of the International Legal Order*. 4 volumes. Princeton: Princeton University Press, 1969 to 1972.

————. and Saul H. Mendlovitz. Eds. *The Strategy of World Order*. Volume II: *International Law*. New York: World Law Fund, 1966.

Friedmann, Wolfgang. *The Changing Structure of International Law*. New York: Columbia University Press, 1964.

————. *The Future of the Oceans*. New York: Braziller, 1971.

Gould, Wesley L. and Michael Barkun. *International Law and the Social Sciences*. Princeton: Princeton University Press, 1970.

Gross, Leo. *International Law in the Twentieth Century*. New York: Appleton-Century-Crofts, 1969.

Hargrove, John Lawrence. *Law, Institutions and the Global Environment*. Dobbs Ferry, N.Y.: Oceana Publications, 1972.

Higgins, A.P. and C.J. Colombos. *The International Law of the Sea*. 4th Ed. New York: Longmans, Green & Co., 1959.

Higgins, Rosilyn. *The Development of International Law through the Political Organs of the United Nations*. New York: Oxford University Press, 1963.

Jenks, C. Wilfred. *The Common Law of Mankind*. London: Stevens, 1958.

Jessup, Phillip C. *A Modern Law of Nations.* New York: The Macmillan Company, 1948.

———. *Transnational Law.* New Haven: Yale University Press, 1956.

———. and H.J. Taubenfeld. *Controls for Outer Space and the Antarctic Analogy.* New York: Columbia University Press, 1959.

Kaplan, Morton and Nicholas deB. Katzenbach. *The Political Foundations of International Law.* New York: John Wiley & Sons, 1961.

Kelsen, Hans. *The Law of the United Nations.* London: Stevens, 1950.

———. *Principles of International Law.* 2nd Ed. Revised and edited by Robert W. Tucker. New York: Holt, Rinehard & Winston, 1966.

Kunz, Joseph. *The Changing Law of Nations.* Columbus, Ohio: Ohio State University Press, 1968.

Lauterpact, Hersh. *The Development of International Law by the International Court.* New York: Frederick A. Praeger, 1958.

Leech, Noyes E.,Covey T. Oliver and Joseph Modeste Sweeney. *The International Legal System: Cases and Materials.* Mineola, N.Y.: The Foundation Press, Inc.,1973.

McDougal, Myres and Florentine P. Feliciano. *Law and Minimum World Public Order: The Legal Regulation of International Coercion.* New Haven: Yale University Press, 1961.

McDougal, Myres and William T. Burke. *Public Order of the Oceans: Contemporary International Law of the Sea.* New Haven: Yale University Press, 1962.

McDougal, Myres, et. al. *Studies in World Public Order.* New Haven: Yale University Press, 1960.

————. *Law and Public Order in Space.* New Haven: Yale University Press, 1963.

————. Interpretation of Agreements and World Public Order: Principles of Content and Procedure. New Haven: Yale University Press, 1967.

McNair, Lord and A.D. Watts. *The Legal Effects of War.* New York: Cambridge University Press, 1967.

Mangone, Gerard. *The Elements of International Law.* Revised Ed. Homewood, Illinois: The Dorsey Press, 1967.

Mendlovitz, Saul H., ed. *Legal and Political Problems of World Order.* New York: World Law Fund, 1962.

Nussbaum, A. *A Concise History of the Law of Nations.* Revised Ed. New York: The Macmillan Company, 1954.

O'Brien, William V., ed. *The New Nations in International Law and Diplomacy.* New York: Frederick A. Praeger, 1965.

Scheinman, Lawrence and David Wilkinson. *International Law and Political Crisis: An Analytic Casebook.* Boston: Little, Brown and Company, 1968.

Sigh, N. *Nuclear Weapons and International Law.* New York: Frederick A. Praeger, 1959.

Stone, Julius, *Aggression and World Order.* Berkeley: University of California Press, 1958.

————. *Legal Controls of International Conflict.* Revised Ed. London: Stevens, 1959.

Tung, William L. *International Law in an Organizing World.* New York: Thomas A. Crowell, 1968.

Von Glahn, Gerhard. *Law Among Nations: An Introduction to Public International Law.* New York: The Macmillan Company, 1965.

Wright, Quincy. *The Role of International Law in the Elimination of War.* Manchester: Manchester University Press, 1961.

Index

EATON RAPIDS
HIGH SCHOOL LIBRARY

HIGH SCHOOL LIBRARY

Pocket Edition

JACKSON'S HALLMARKS

POCKET EDITION JACKSON'S HALLMARKS

ENGLISH, SCOTTISH, IRISH
SILVER & GOLD MARKS
FROM 1300 TO THE PRESENT DAY

edited by Ian Pickford

ANTIQUE COLLECTORS' CLUB

© Antique Collectors' Club 1991
World copyright reserved
First published in hardback 1991
Reprinted 1991, 1992
First published in paperback 1992
Reprinted 1993

Hardback ISBN 1 85149 128 7

Paperback ISBN 1 85149 169 4

Published for the Antique Collectors' Club
by the Antique Collectors' Club Ltd.

All rights reserved. No part of this publication may be reproduced, stored in a
retrieval system, or transmitted in any form or by any means electronic,
mechanical, photocopying, recording or otherwise, without the prior permission of
the publisher.

British Library Cataloguing in Publication Data:
A catalogue record for this book is available from the British Library

Printed in England by the Antique Collectors' Club Ltd.
5 Church Street, Woodbridge, Suffolk

Antique Collectors' Club

The Antique Collectors' Club was formed in 1966 and now has a five figure membership spread throughout the world. It publishes the only independently run monthly antiques magazine *Antique Collecting* which caters for those collectors who are interested in widening their knowledge of antiques, both by greater awareness of quality and by discussion of the factors which influence the price that is likely to be asked. The Antique Collectors' Club pioneered the provision of information on prices for collectors and the magazine still leads in the provision of detailed articles on a variety of subjects.

It was in response to the enormous demand for information on "what to pay" that the price guide series was introduced in 1968 with the first edition of *The Price Guide to Antique Furniture* (completely revised 1978 and 1989), a book which broke new ground by illustrating the more common types of antique furniture, the sort that collectors could buy in shops and at auctions rather than the rare museum pieces which had previously been used (and still to a large extent are used) to make up the limited amount of illustrations in books published by commercial publishers. Many other price guides have followed, all copiously illustrated, and greatly appreciated by collectors for the valuable information they contain, quite apart from prices. The Antique Collectors' Club also publishes other books on antiques, including horology and art reference works, and a full book list is available.

Club membership, which is open to all collectors, costs £19.50 per annum. Members receive free of charge *Antique Collecting,* the Club's magazine (published ten times a year), which contains well-illustrated articles dealing with the practical aspects of collecting not normally dealt with by magazines. Prices, features of value, investment potential, fakes and forgeries are all given prominence in the magazine.

Among other facilities available to members are private buying and selling facilities, the longest list of "For Sales" of any antiques magazine, an annual ceramics conference and the opportunity to meet other collectors at their local antique collectors' clubs. There are over eighty in Britain and more than a dozen overseas. Members may also buy the Club's publications at special pre-publication prices.

As its motto implies, the Club is an amateur organisation designed to help collectors get the most out of their hobby: it is informal and friendly and gives enormous enjoyment to all concerned.

For Collectors — By Collectors — About Collecting

The Antique Collectors' Club, 5 Church Street, Woodbridge, Suffolk

Contents

Acknowledgements

My thanks must go to Henry Fothringham, Michael McAleer, the late Kurt Ticher, Timothy Kent, G.N. Barrett, Canon Maurice Ridgway, Martin Gubbins and Dr. Margaret Gill.

I am indebted to the Wardens of the Worshipful Company of Goldsmiths for their permission to quote from their records; also to Miss Susan Hare, Past Librarian of the Worshipful Company of Goldsmiths, and to David Beasley, Librarian.

Additional thanks should go to David W. Evans, Deputy Warden, Dr. Frank William Bennett, past Deputy Warden and Mr. David Barnes Dalladay, past Assistant Deputy Warden of the Worshipful Company of Goldsmiths for their assistance in the updating of the London hallmarks.

Particular thanks must go to Mr. Arthur Grimwade, Mr. John Culme, Mr. Anthony Dove, Mr. Brand Inglis, Mr. John Cooper, the Assay Master of Sheffield; Mr. David Johnson, and Molly Pearce, Keeper of Applied Arts, Weston Park Museum, Sheffield, for their advice on Sheffield; Mr. Jeremy Pearson and Mr. Richard Rendel for their help in the West Country (Exeter).

In addition Captain R. Le Bas of the Dublin Assay Office, Mr. Brian Beet, Ann Bennett, the Guardians of Birmingham Assay Office, the Birmingham University Field Archaeology Unit, Mr. Geoffrey Corbett, Mr. H.L. Douch, Mr. Robin Emmerson, Mr. John Forbes, Mrs. Phillipa Glanville, Mr. Richard Gray, the Laing Art Gallery, the Manchester City Art Galleries, Catherine Ross of the Laing Art Gallery, members of the NADFAS Church Recorders, the late Charles Oman, Mr. Michael Newman, The Shrewsbury Museum, Mr. Eric Smith, Mr. Peter Waldron, Mr. Donald Wilson and Mr. Richard Vander all receive acknowledgement for help given.

Ian Pickford, 1991

Preface

The object in producing this pocket edition of *Jackson's* has been to provide the information most likely to be needed when travelling, in a form that is both quick and easy to use.

Complete cycles of silver marks are given for all the important assay offices, with footnotes where necessary showing variations for gold, platinum, Britannia standard, import marks, etc.

For the smaller centres a selection of marks has been chosen in each case to give the most important variations likely to be found.

After the cycles of marks of each assay office a selection of makers' marks is given. These marks include not only the famous and important or interesting makers' names, but also the most prolific manufacturers and retailers, thus providing a good chance of finding a particular maker's mark in this section.

Since the vast majority of pieces to be found are from the 18th century and later, the makers' marks have, with only a few exceptions, been chosen from the post-1697 period.

In addition to the mark/marks of a maker, the period in which he/she was working has also been given in general terms, e.g. early 18th century or second quarter 19th century ('early 18th C' or '2nd ¼ 19th C'), as exact years of commencement, or more often cessation of work have not always been known.

The comments, where given, after a particular maker are to indicate such things as type of work produced (e.g. spoonmaker), how important that maker may be, whether prolific or rare, possible confusion with other makers, and any particular points to look for, e.g. a connection with an important designer.

Should any more detailed explanation, further variation of hallmarks, or makers' marks not given, be required, then reference to the main volume of *Jackson's* will, of course, be necessary.

Ian Pickford
1991

Understanding Hallmarks

Probably the easiest way to understand the hallmarking system in Britain is to examine its development in London and then observe how it was applied elsewhere.

The system is an ancient one. The first known statute governing standards was in 1238, although there were certainly controls on the workers in precious metals prior to this.

At this stage (in the 13th century) there were no official marks as such. Makers would, however, sometimes engrave their name and perhaps place of working on the piece. The Dolgelly chalice is a good example. Made in about 1250 it is engraved underneath 'NICOL'VS ME FECIT DE HER FORDIE', i.e. 'Nicholas of Hereford made me'.

The end of the 13th century saw the introduction of a marking system. Current research indicates that the reasons for it were to assist customs officials in preventing the export of silver from England (see *Jackson's,* pp.19-21).

The mark introduced in 1300 was a leopard's head. This mark was to be struck on silver of the standard of coinage or better, and gold of the touch of Paris (19.2 carats) or better, throughout the realm.

It is interesting to notice that both gold and silver were to receive the same mark and that it was to be used throughout the country, not just in London.

Using the standard of coinage (sterling, i.e. 92.5% silver content) for silver was important, since it allowed the ready interchange of goldsmiths' work (silver vessels, etc.) into coins and vice versa as the economic situation, either personal or national, required.

All known examples of leopards' head marks up to 1478 are in circular punches, the very earliest (c.1300-60) being plain circular (Figure 1) and those after about 1360 in a beaded, circular punch (Figure 2).

Figure 1

To help prevent the forgery of leopards' head marks, which were being struck on substandard wares by unscrupulous goldsmiths, a statute was passed in 1363. By this statute every master goldsmith was to have a mark of his own by which his work could be recognised. These early makers' marks were all symbols, for it was only with the spread of literacy that initials started to appear in the late 15th to early 16th century. Clearly then two marks were struck on a piece of silver or gold from 1363 onwards (see Figure 2).

Figure 2

For about the next century the system would appear to have worked well as it was not until 1478 that a further mark was added. This is what is referred to today as the date letter, which was introduced as the result of unscrupulous touch wardens (the men responsible for testing and marking silver and gold), in the second half of the 15th century, striking the leopard's head, for a financial consideration, on work which they knew to be below standard. This was easy for them to do at this time since the testing and marking were carried out in the goldsmiths' own shops. Apart from defrauding the customers there was the more serious long term effect (as happened also in the early 14th century), of these substandard wares being accepted from their marks as standard by the Mint and converted directly into coin. Ultimately this would lead to a loss of confidence in the currency and the dire national economic problems that would follow.

To stop this happening, important changes took place in 1478. First, the touch wardens were required to work in an office in the Goldsmiths' Hall. All goldsmiths then had to take their work to the Hall to have it marked (hence Hall Marks). Secondly, the leopard's head was given a crown and thirdly, a new mark — the date letter — was introduced (see Figure 3).

Figure 3

Originally this third mark was not to indicate the year in which the piece was tested, as it is today, but was the Assay Master's mark by which he could be identified should a properly marked piece be found to be below standard.

The Assay Master was sworn in annually in May. Since

the alphabetical letter by which he was identified moved on to the next letter, regardless of whether the same man was appointed, it is easy to see how these letters were later regarded as date letters.

The three marks of leopard's head, maker's mark and date letter remained the only marks in London from 1478 until 1544, when a fourth, the lion passant, was added to the system (Figure 4).

Figure 4

This, probably the most famous of all English marks, often referred to as the 'Sterling Lion', was added, not as a protection against fraud, but to show the Royal control that the Assay Office came under for a short period and which was retained thereafter.

What may be regarded as the Established System of marking sterling standard silver, was thus in operation from 1544 onwards. There was no further change to the system until the end of the 17th century. This change, the introduction of the Britannia standard in 1697, was radical, and resulted from the need to protect the coinage from being melted down to produce objects. The standard for silver was raised from 92.5% to 95.84% minimum silver content, whilst the silver coinage was retained at 92.5%, which meant that silver from coins could not be used for goldsmiths' work without refining, thus protecting it.

To demonstrate that this new standard was in force all the marks were changed (see Figure 5). The figure of Britannia replaced the sterling lion (hence Britannia standard) the lion's head erased replaced the crowned leopard's head. A new cycle of date letters was started just over a year earlier

Figure 5

than would normally have been the case and new makers'
marks were registered, now the first two letters of the
goldsmith's surname rather than his initials. (Note: Gold
was not affected by this change and continued to be marked
with the crowned leopard's head and lion passant guardant.)

In 1720 sterling was reintroduced as an alternative to the
Britannia standard. Although the two standards have been
in force from 1720 to the present day, little Britannia
standard will be found between about 1735 and the end of
the 19th century.

The year 1784 saw the introduction of a new but
temporary mark, which was the duty mark, and was struck
on silver to show that duty to pay for the American War of
Independence had been paid. The mark chosen was the
monarch's head and this will be found with successive heads
struck on pieces up to 1890 (see Figure 6). Thus from 1784

Figure 6

to 1890 five marks will be found on a piece of London silver;
this then reverts to four marks from 1890 to the present day.

There have been no really important changes to the
marking of silver since 1890. Jubilee marks will be found in
1934-5 (Figure 7) and in 1977 (Figure 9). A coronation mark
will be found in 1952-3 (Figure 8). These are, however,
voluntary additional marks and not true hallmarks.

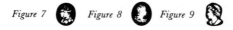

Figure 7   *Figure 8*   *Figure 9*

Distinct gold marking develops from the introduction of
18 carat gold in 1798. From 1300 up to this date it should
be remembered that gold was marked in the same way as
sterling standard silver (leaving aside the 1697-1720 period).

The 1973 Hallmarking Act which came into effect in 1975
brought about a number of changes. The most important of
these was the introduction of platinum into the system. It
has been given the distinct mark of an orb and cross within
a pentagon (Figure 10).

By this same Act all Assay Offices now use the same date
letter which represents a calendar year. The use of the lion's

Figure 10

head erased was also dropped from Britannia standard marking.

ENGLISH PROVINCIAL MARKS

Provincial marking in England may be divided into three periods:

  (1) Prior to 1697
  (2) 1697-1701-2
  (3) 1701-2 to the present day

1. Prior to 1697

Many centres used marks. These range from the use of makers' marks only (often struck more than once on a piece), in some of the smaller centres, to proper cycles of marks, including the use of date letters found in major centres such as York.

2. 1697-1701-2

The Act introducing Britannia standard in 1697 unfortunately omitted any provision for marking in the provinces. It was therefore technically illegal for any of these centres to mark silver. The provinces appear to have ignored this, choosing rather to alter the character of the marks they were then using to make them less easily recognisable. (This causes great problems in identifying these marks today.)

3. 1701-2 to the present day

After the bungled Act of Parliament which had technically excluded the provinces from marking in 1697, a further Act was passed by which those centres which had a mint operating could also have an Assay Office. By this act from 1701 onwards Exeter, Bristol, Norwich, Chester, and York could all mark silver.

  Unfortunately, this second act was a further bungle since it included Bristol and Norwich, neither of which could justify at this time the need for an Assay Office, and excluded Newcastle, which was then one of the most important provincial centres. A further Act was then passed specifically for Newcastle which was, as a result, able to mark from 1702 onwards. From that date all the minor centres were required to send items for marking to the official Assay Office in their area.

The marks required for the major centres were effectively the same as those used in London with the addition of a town mark. The actual shapes of punches, styles of letters, and cycles differ from those in London but the general character is the same.

In time all provincial centres stopped using the leopard's head; the last was in 1883.

SCOTLAND

Edinburgh
By an enactment of 1457 gold and silver of the required standard (20 carats for gold and 91.66% minimum silver content for silver) were to be marked with the deacon's mark and the maker's mark.

The Deacon was the chief office bearer of the craft within the town; he would normally be a working goldsmith and as such would use his 'maker's mark' as his Deacon's mark, when in office. Thus a marked piece of this early date (of which none is known) would have been marked with what would have the appearance of two makers' marks.

In 1485 the town mark was added to the above and from that date until 1681 three marks were struck on a piece (see Figure 11).

Figure 11

Exact dating of Edinburgh pieces to a particular year during this period can only occasionally be achieved due to Deacons being appointed for a number of years over a span of years.

1681 saw two important changes: first the introduction of cycles of date letters which continue to the present day, and secondly the replacement of the Deacon's mark by the Assay Master's mark.

The Assay Master would be a working goldsmith and, as with the Deacons before him, would use his maker's mark for this purpose. Pieces therefore continued to be struck with what appear to be two makers' marks together with the town mark and now with the addition of a date letter (Figure 12).

Figure 12

The Act of 1696 which introduced Britannia Standard to England was, of course, before the Act of Union and therefore was not applied in Scotland. However, the Act by which Sterling standard was reintroduced in 1720 was after the Act of Union. Scots goldsmiths, as a result of this Act, had to raise their standard to sterling. This did not, however, lead to any changes to any marks in Scotland.

In 1759 the thistle mark replaced the Assay Master's mark (see Figure 13); it in turn was replaced by a lion rampant in 1975. Otherwise from the second half of the 18th century onwards duty marks and optional marks follow what has been given for London.

Figure 13

Scots Provincial

Scotland is particularly rich in the number of centres which marked silver. Since the marks were produced by the silversmiths themselves there are no hard and fast rules to follow. The vast majority of pieces to be found date from the late 18th and early 19th centuries. During this period it was quite usual for a maker to stamp his own mark twice on the piece, together with his own town mark. Town marks divide into two groups, those which are an abbreviation of the name of the town and those based on the heraldry of the town.

The above are, however, very broad generalisations, exceptions to which will easily be found.

(Note: Some Indian Colonial marks may easily be mistaken for Scottish Provincial.)

IRELAND

Dublin

In 1605 it was decreed by the Dublin City Council that silver of the correct standard (coin) was to be marked with a lion, a harp and a castle together with a maker's mark.

To date no silver has been found bearing these marks.

By a new Charter of 1637 silver and gold was to be marked with a crowned harp (the King's standard mark) and a maker's mark. A year later a date letter was added to the above and it is from 1638 on that examples survive of Dublin hallmarks.

Figure 14

The above use of three marks (Figure 14) continued until 1730-1 when, to show that duty had been paid, the Hibernia mark was added thus giving four marks (Figure 15).

Figure 15

In 1807 Hibernia was replaced as a duty mark by the monarch's head (similar to that already in use in England and Scotland); it was not dropped but continued to be stamped as the 'town mark' of Dublin, providing until 1890, when the monarch's head was dropped, five marks (Figure 16).

Figure 16

(Note: Britannia standard never applied in Ireland. Hibernia punches can easily be mistaken for Britannia.)

Irish Provincial

Cork and Limerick both used similar styles of marks. During the late 17th to early 18th century a castle/castle turret mark, often repeated twice, was used in both. (A ship mark if found was only used in Cork.) With the castle mark, a maker's mark will also be found which is often struck twice.

From the early 18th century to the early 19th century the word 'Sterling' (in full) was adopted by both centres and used with makers' marks which, as earlier, were often repeated twice.

With the similarity of marks in these two centres, distinguishing one from the other is best done by reference to the makers' marks (see *Jackson's,* pp.710-26). The majority of pieces from these two centres are from Cork; other Irish Provincial silver is only rarely found.

(Note: The word 'Sterling' is stamped on vast quantities of North American silver.)

GOLD MARKS

Gold and silver were, when of the required standard, struck with the same marks as each other until 1798. (The exception to this being the period 1697 to June 1720 during the compulsory Britannia standard for silver.)

The introduction of 18 carat gold in 1798 saw, for the first time, truly distinctive gold marking; 22 carat continued to be struck with the same marks as sterling standard silver until 1844.

However, in 1816 the assay master's note book records "Impressions of the Sun to be used from and after 29 of May 1816 on the 22 carat standard". This rare mark was struck in addition to the sterling standard type marks, and continued in use until the introduction of the crown and twenty-two (separate) punches in 1844.* Because of the demand for cheaper gold watch cases in America, 1854 saw the addition of 15, 12 and 9 carat to the standards for gold. The marks for these lower standards are quite distinct from the established 22 and 18 carats.

The 15 and 12 carat standards were used for the last time in 1932 when 14 carat was introduced.

No changes in standard have occurred since 1932 and so from 1933 to the present day, we have the four standards of 22, 18, 14 and 9 carats.

* This applies to London only.

PLATINUM MARKS

The 1973 hallmarking act brought for the first time platinum within the hallmarking system. A standard of 950 parts per thousand was introduced. The mark chosen was an orb and cross within a pentagon (used by all four assay offices) and the first pieces were marked in London on 2nd January 1975.

IMPORT MARKS

Imported plate was required in 1842 to be submitted for assay and marking before being sold in England, Scotland or Ireland (an exception was made of pre-1800 plate). There was no provision, however, in this act for an import mark, the current marks of the assay office to which the piece had been submitted being stamped.

It was by the Act of 1867 that an extra mark of F in an oval punch was required to be struck on imported wares of the correct standard.

The whole system was radically reformed by "The Hall-marking of Foreign Plate Act, 1904". By this act quite distinct import marks were introduced, Phoebus (the Sun) being used as the mark for London* (a square punch for gold and an oval punch for silver). Numerical punches were introduced for the standards. The current date letter was also struck.

Problems arose over the use of the sun mark (due to existing trade marks) as a result of which it was changed by Order in Council (11th May 1906) to the sign of the constellation Leo. The first Leo marks were actually produced with Leo upside down. Apart from the alterations in gold standards in 1932 and the addition of platinum and change in the style of the numerical punches in 1975, the system of import marks has remained the same to the present day.

* London is taken here as the example.

CONVENTION HALLMARKS

The United Kingdom, together with Austria, Denmark, Finland, Ireland, Norway, Portugal, Sweden and Switzerland have ratified the International Hallmarking Convention (the United Kingdom in 1976). By this convention special marks are legally recognised as approved hallmarks by the United Kingdom. Imported pieces bearing these marks do not, therefore, have to be submitted for import marking.

The convention marks struck in London comprise the Leopard's Head, the Common Control Mark, The Fineness mark (numerals showing the standard in parts per thousand) and the Sponsor's (i.e. maker's) mark.

It is possible for imported wares to be submitted for convention hallmarks. In this case the appropriate import mark replaces the leopard's head.

CHAPTER I

London

Cycles of Hallmarks

THE LEOPARD'S HEAD MARK
DATE ANTERIOR TO 1478
(The ascribed dates are approximate)

DATE	MARK
1300	
1300-50	
1350	
1400	
1450	
1470	

CYCLE I

	LEOPARD'S HEAD CROWNED	DATE LETTER
EDW.IV 1478-79		
1479-80	⬡	**B**
1480-81	⬡	**C**
1481-82	⬡	**D**
1482-83		
RICH.III 1483-84		
1484-85		
HEN.VII 1485-86		
1486-87		
1487-88		
1488-89	"	**U**
1489-90	"	**M**
1490-91	"	**N**
1491-92	"	**O**
1492-93		
1493-94	"	**Q**
1494-95	"	**R**
1495-96		**S**
1496-97	⬡	**T**
1497-98		

CYCLE II

	LEOPARD'S HEAD CROWNED	DATE LETTER
1498-99	⬡	**a**
1499-1500	"	**b**
1500-1	"	**c**
1501-2	"	**d**
1502-3		
1503-4	"	**f**
1504-5	"	**g**
1505-6		
1506-7	⬡	**i**
1507-8	"	**k**
1508-9	⬡	**l**
HEN.VIII 1509-10	⬡	**m**
1510-11	"	**n**
1511-12	"	**o**
1512-13	"	**p**
1513-14	⬡	**q**
1514-15	"	**r**
1515-16	⬡	**s**
1516-17	"	**t**
1517-18	"	**u**

CYCLE III

	LEOPARD'S HEAD CROWNED	DATE LETTER
1518-19	🦁	A
1519-20	🦁	B
1520-21	🦁	C
1521-22	"	D
1522-23	"	E
1523-24	"	F
1524-25	"	G
1525-26	"	h
1526-27		
1527-28	"	K
1528-29	"	l
1529-30	"	M
1530-31	"	N
1531-32	🦁	O
1532-33	"	P
1533-34	"	Q
1534-35	"	R
1535-36	"	S
1536-37	"	T
1537-38	"	V

CYCLE IV

	LEOPARD'S HEAD CROWNED	DATE LETTER	LION PASSANT FROM 1544
1538-39	🦁	A	
1539-40	🦁	B	
1540-41	"	C	
1541-42	"	D	
1542-43		E	
1543-44	"	F	
1544-45*	"	G	🦁
1545-46	🦁	H	🦁
1546-47	"	I	"
EDW.VI 1547-48	"	K	
1548-49	"	L	🦁
1549-50	"	M	"
1550-51 †	🦁	N	🦁
1551-52	"	O	🦁
	"	O	
1552-53	"	P	🦁
MARY 1553-54	"	Q	"
1554-55	"	R	"
1555-56	"	S	"
1556-57	"	T	"
1557-58	"	V	🦁

* Variation: 🦁 G

† There is a variant of the lion passant in a shaped shield.

CYCLE V

	LEOPARD'S HEAD CROWNED	DATE LETTER	LION PASSANT
ELIZ.I 1558-60		a	
1559-60	"	b	"
1560 to 6 Jan.1561	"	C	"
7 Jan. 1561- May 1561	"	d	"
June 1561-62	"	d	
1562-63		e	"
1563-64	"	f	"
1564-65	"	g	"
1565-66	"	h	"
1566-67	"	i	"
1567-68	"	k k	"
1568-69	"	l	"
1569-70	"	m	"
1570-71	"	n	"
1571-72	"	o	"
1572-73	"	p	"
1573-74	"	q	
1574-75	"	r	"
1575-76	"	s	"
1576-77	"	t	"
1577-78	"	u	"

CYCLE VI

	LEOPARD'S HEAD CROWNED	DATE LETTER	LION PASSANT
1578-79		A	
1579-80	"	B	"
1580-81	"	C	"
1581-82	"	D	"
1582-83	"	E	"
1583-84	"	F	"
	"	G	"
1584-85	"	G	"
1585-86	"	H	"
1586-87	"	I	"
1587-88	"	K	"
1588-89	"	L	"
1589-90	"	M	"
1590-91	"	N	"
1591-92	"	O	"
1592-93		P	
1593-94	"	Q	"
1594-95	"	R	
1595-96	"	S	"
1596-97	"	T	"
1597-98	"	V	"

CYCLE VII

	LEOPARD'S HEAD CROWNED	DATE LETTER	LION PASSANT
1598-99			
1599-1600	"		
1600-1	"		"
1601-2	"		
1602-3	"		"
JAS.I 1603-4	"		"
1604-5	"		
1605-6	"		"
1606-7	"		
1607-8	"		"
1608-9	"		"
1609-10	"		"
1610-11	"		
1611-12	"		"
1612-13	"		"
1613-14	"		"
1614-15	"		"
1615-16	"		"
1616-17	"		"
1617-18	"		"

CYCLE VIII

	LEOPARD'S HEAD CROWNED	DATE LETTER	LION PASSANT
1618-19			
1619-20	"		"
1620-21	"		"
1621-22	"		"
1622-23	"		"
1623-24	"		"
1624-25	"		"
CHAS.I 1625-26	"		"
1626-27	"		"
1627-28	"		"
1628-29	"		"
1629-30	"		"
1630-31	"		"
1631-32	"		"
1632-33	"		"
1633-34	"		"
1634-35	"		"
1635-36	"		"
1636-37	"		"
1637-38	"		"

CYCLE IX

	LEOPARD'S HEAD CROWNED	DATE LETTER	LION PASSANT
1638-39			
1639-40	"		"
1640-41	"		"
1641-42	"		"
1642-43	"		"
1643-44	"		"
1644-45	"		"
1645-46	"		"
1646-47	"		"
1647-48			
1648-49	"		"
COMWTH. 1649-50	"		"
1650-51	"		"
1651-52	"		"
1652-53	"		"
1653-54	"		"
1654-55	"		"
1655-56	"		"
1656-57	"		"
1657-58	"		"

CYCLE X

	LEOPARD'S HEAD CROWNED	DATE LETTER	LION PASSANT
1658-59			
1659 Up to 12 July 1660	"		"
CHAS.II From 13 July 1660 to 27 June 1661	"		"
From 28 June 1661-62	"		"
1662-63	"		
1663-64	"		"
1664-65	"		"
1665-66	"		"
1666-67	"		"
1667-68	"		"
1668-69			
1669-70	"		"
1670-71	"		"
1671-72	"		"
1672-73	"		"
1673-74	"		"
1674-75	"		"
1675-76	"		"
1676-77	"		"
1677-78	"		"

CYCLE XI*

	LEOPARD'S HEAD CROWNED	DATE LETTER	LION PASSANT
1678-79		a	
1679-80	"	b	
1680-81		c	
1681-82	"	d	"
1682-83	"	e	"
1683-84	"	f	"
1684-85	"	g	"
JAS.II 1685-86	"	h	"
1686-87	"	i	"
1687-88	"	k	"
1688-89	"	l	"
WM.& MY. 1689-90		m	
1690-91	"	n	"
1691-92	"	o	"
1692-93	"	p	"
1693-94	"	q	"
1694-95	"	r	"
WM.III 1695-96	"	s	"
20 May 1696 to 27 March 1697	"	t	"

* Cycles XI-XXVI
Marks reproduced courtesy of the Worshipful Company of Goldsmiths
┆ (Only Britannia standard in force)

CYCLE XII

SILVER ┆			
	BRITANNIA	DATE LETTER	LION'S HEAD ERASED
27 March to 28 May 1697		a	
1697-98	"	B	"
1698-99	"	C	"
1699-1700	"	D	"
1700-1	"	E	"
1701-2	"	F	"
ANNE 1702-3	"	G	"
1703-4	"	H	"
1704-5	"	I	"
1705-6	"	K	"
1706-7	"	L	"
1707-8	"	M	"
1708-9	"	N	"
1709-10	"	O	"
1710-11	"	P	"
1711-12	"	Q	"
1712-13	"	R	"
1713-14	"	S	"
GEO.I 1714-15	"	T	"
1715-16	"	V	"

GOLD (22ct.)			
	LEOPARD'S HEAD CROWNED	DATE LETTER	LION PASSANT
Date as Above		As Above	

CYCLE XIII

BRITANNIA STANDARD			
	BRITANNIA	DATE LETTER	LION'S HEAD ERASED
1716-17	🐾	A	🦁
1717-18	"	B	"
1718-19	"	C	"
1719-20	"	D	"
1720-21	"	E	"
1721-22	"	F	"
1722-23	"	G	"
1723-24	"	H	"
1724-25	"	I	"
1725-26	"	K	"
1726-27	"	L	"
GEO.II 1727-28	"	M	"
1728-29	"	N	"
1729-30	"	O	"
1730-31	"	P	"
1731-32	"	Q	"
1732-33	"	R	"
1733-34	"	S	"
1734-35	"	T	"
1735-36	"	V	"

GOLD			
	LEOPARD'S HEAD CROWNED	DATE LETTER	LION PASSANT
1716-17	👑	A	🦁
1717-18	"	B	"
1718-19	"	C	"
1719-20	"	D	"

STERLING STANDARD SILVER & GOLD (22ct)
(Until 1720, only Britannia Standard in force)

	LEOPARD'S HEAD CROWNED	DATE LETTER	LION PASSANT
1720-21	👑	E	🦁
	👑	"	"
1721-22	"	F	🦁
1722-23	"	G	"
1723-24	"	H	"
1724-25	👑	I	🦁
1725-26	"	K	"
1726-27	👑	L	🦁
GEO.II 1727-28	"	M	"
1728-29	"	N	"
1729-30	👑	O	🦁
1730-31	"	P	"
1731-32	"	Q	"
1732-33	"	R	"
1733-34	"	S	"
1734-35	"	T	"
1735-36	"	V	"

CYCLE XIV

STERLING STANDARD SILVER & GOLD (22ct)			
	LEOPARD'S HEAD CROWNED	DATE LETTER	LION PASSANT
1736-37	🛡	a	🦁
1737-38	"	b	"
1738-39*	"	c	"
1739-40	"	d	"
	🛡	d	🦁
1740-41	"	e	"
1741-42	"	f	"
1742-43	"	g	"
1743-44	"	h	"
1744-45	"	i	"
1745-46	"	k	"
1746-47	"	l	"
1747-48	"	m	"
1748-49	"	n	"
1749-50	"	o	"
1750-51	"	p	"
1751-52*	"	q	"
1752-53	"	r	"
1753-54	"	s	"
1754-55	"	t	"
1755-56	"	u	"

BRITANNIA STANDARD SILVER			
	BRITANNIA	DATE LETTER	LION'S HEAD ERASED
Date as Above	🛡	As Above	🦁

CYCLE XV

STERLING STANDARD SILVER & GOLD (22ct)			
	LEOPARD'S HEAD CROWNED	DATE LETTER	LION PASSANT
1756-57	🛡	A	🦁
1757-58	"	B	"
1758-59*	"	C	"
1759-60*	"	D	"
GEO.III 1760-61	"	E	"
1761-62	"	F	"
1762-63	"	G	"
1763-64	"	H	"
1764-65	"	J	"
1765-66	"	K	"
1766-67	"	L	"
1767-68	"	M	"
1768-69	"	N	"
1769-70	"	O	"
1770-71	"	P	"
1771-72	"	Q	"
1772-73	"	R	"
1773-74	"	S	"
1774-75	"	T	"
1775-76	"	U	"

BRITANNIA STANDARD SILVER			
	BRITANNIA	DATE LETTER	LION'S HEAD ERASED
Date as Above	🛡	As Above	🦁

CYCLE XVI

STERLING STANDARD SILVER & GOLD (22ct)			
	LEOPARD'S HEAD CROWNED	DATE LETTER	LION PASSANT	
1776-77	🏴	**a**	🦁	
1777-78	"	**b**	"	
1778-79	"	**c**	"	
1779-80	"	**d**	"	
1780-81	"	**e**	"	
1781-82	"	**f**	"	
1782-83	"	**g**	"	
1783-84	"	**h**	"	
Up to 30 Nov.1784	"	**i**	"	
				DUTY MARK
From 1 Dec. 1784-85*	"	"	"	👑
1785-86*	"	**k**	"	"
1786-87	"	**l**	"	👤
1787-88	"	**m**	"	"
1788-89	"	**n**	"	"
1789-90	"	**o**	"	"
1790-91	"	**p**	"	"
1791-92	"	**q**	"	"
1792-93	"	**r**	"	"
1793-94	"	**s**	"	"
1794-95	"	**t**	"	"
1795-96	"	**u**	"	"
BRITANNIA STANDARD SILVER			
	BRITANNIA	DATE LETTER	LION'S HEAD ERASED
Date as Above	🦁	As Above	🦁

CYCLE XVII

STERLING STANDARD SILVER & GOLD (22ct)			
	LEOPARD'S HEAD CROWNED	DATE LETTER	LION PASSANT*	DUTY MARK
1796-97	🦁	**A**	🦁	👤
Up to 5 July 1797	"	**B**	"	"
6 July 1797 to 28 May 1798	"	"	"	👤
1798-99	"	**C**	"	👤
1799-1800	"	**D**	"	"
1800-1	"	**E**	"	"
1801-2	"	**F**	"	"
1802-3	"	**G**	"	"
1803-4	"	**H**	"	"
Up to 10 Oct.1804	"	**I**	"	"
11 Oct. 1804 to 28 May 1805	"	"	"	👤
1805-6	"	**K**	"	👤
1806-7	"	**L**	"	"
1807-8	"	**M**	"	"
1808-9	"	**N**	"	"
1809-10	"	**O**	"	"
1810-11	"	**P**	"	"
1811-12	"	**Q**	"	"
1812-13	"	**R**	"	"
1813-14	"	**S**	"	"
1814-15	"	**T**	"	"
Up to 13 June 1815	"	**U**	"	"
14 June to 31 Aug. 1815	"	"	"	👤
1 Sept. 1815 to 28 May 1816	"	"	"	👤

BRITANNIA STANDARD			
	BRITANNIA	DATE LETTER	LION'S HEAD ERASED	DUTY MARK
Date as Left	🏛	As Left	🦁	👤

GOLD (18ct.) 1798 on			
	LEOPARD'S HEAD ERASED	DATE LETTER	CROWN † + 18	DUTY MARK
Date as Left	🦁	As Left	👑18	👤

† An alternative for the Crown + 18   👑 **18**

CYCLE XVIII

BRITANNIA STANDARD SILVER

	BRITANNIA	DATE LETTER	LION'S HEAD ERASED	DUTY MARK
Date as Right		As Right		

GOLD (18ct.)

	LEOPARD'S HEAD CROWNED	DATE LETTER	CROWN † + 18	DUTY MARK
Date as Right		As Right		

† An alternative for the Crown + 18

§ Added 1816-1843 for 22ct. gold.

STERLING STANDARD SILVER & GOLD (22ct)

	LEOPARD'S HEAD	DATE LETTER	LION* PASSANT	DUTY MARK
1816-17§		a		
1817-18	"	b	"	"
1818-19	"	c	"	"
1819-20	"	d	"	"
GEO.IV 1820-21	"	e	"	"
1821-22	"	f	"	"
		"		
1822-23	"	g	"	"
1823-24	"	h	"	"
1824-25	"	i	"	"
1825-26		k	"	"
1826-27		l	"	"
1827-28	"	m	"	"
1828-29	"	n	"	"
1829-30	"	o	"	"
WM.IV 1830-31	"	p	"	"
1831-32	"	q	"	"
1832-33	"	r	"	"
1833-34	"	s	"	"
1834-35	"	t	"	
1835-36	"	u	"	"

CYCLE XIX

STERLING STANDARD SILVER & GOLD (22ct)			
	LEOPARD'S HEAD	DATE LETTER	LION PASSANT	DUTY MARK
1836-37	🦁	𝕬	🦁	👑
VICT. 29th May to 20th June 1837	"	𝕭	"	"
21st June 1837 to 28th May 1838	🦁	"	🦁	👑
1838-39	"	𝕮	"	"
1839-40	"	𝕯	"	👑
1840-41	🦁	𝕰	🦁	👑
1841-42	"	𝕱	"	"
1842-43	"	𝕲	"	"
1843-44	"	𝕳	"	"
1844-45	"	𝕴	"	"
1845-46	"	𝕵	"	"
1846-47	"	𝕷	"	"
1847-48	"	𝕸	"	"
1848-49	"	𝕹	"	"
1849-50	"	𝕺	"	"
1850-51	"	𝕻	"	"
1851-52	"	𝕼	"	"
1852-53	"	𝕽	"	"
1853-54	"	𝕾	"	"
1854-55	"	𝕿	"	"
1855-56	"	𝖀	"	"

BRITANNIA STANDARD SILVER			
	BRITANNIA	DATE LETTER	LION'S HEAD ERASED	DUTY MARK
Date as Left	🛡️	As Left	🦁	👑

GOLD (22ct.) 1844 ONWARDS			
	LEOPARD'S HEAD	DATE LETTER	CROWN + 22	DUTY MARK
Date as Left	🦁	𝕴	👑22	👑

GOLD (18ct.)			
	LEOPARD'S HEAD	DATE LETTER	CROWN† + 18	DUTY MARK
Date as Left	🦁	As Left	👑18	👑

FROM 1854

GOLD (15ct.)			
	LEOPARD'S HEAD	DATE LETTER	CARAT MARK	DUTY MARK
Date as Left	🦁	𝕌	15	·625	👑

GOLD (12ct.)			
	LEOPARD'S HEAD	DATE LETTER	CARAT MARK	DUTY MARK
Date as Left	🦁	𝕌	12	·5	👑

GOLD (9ct.)			
	LEOPARD'S HEAD	DATE LETTER	CARAT MARK	DUTY MARK
Date as Left	🦁	𝕌	9	·375	👑

† Variation: 👑 18

CYCLE XX

BRITANNIA STANDARD SILVER*

	LION'S HEAD ERASED	DATE LETTER	BRIT-ANNIA	DUTY MARK
Date as Right	🦁	As Right	🛡	👑

GOLD (22ct.)*

	LEOPARD'S HEAD	DATE LETTER	CROWN + 22	DUTY MARK
Date as Right	🦁	𝖆	👑22	👑

GOLD (18ct.)*

	LEOPARD'S HEAD	DATE LETTER	CROWN + 18	DUTY MARK
Date as Right	🦁	𝖆	👑18	👑

GOLD (15ct.)*

	LEOPARD'S HEAD	DATE LETTER	CARAT MARK	DUTY MARK
Date as Right	🦁	𝖆	15·625	👑

GOLD (12ct.)*

	LEOPARD'S HEAD	DATE LETTER	CARAT MARK	DUTY MARK
Date as Right	🦁	𝖆	12·5	👑

GOLD (9ct.)*

	LEOPARD'S HEAD	DATE LETTER	CARAT MARK	DUTY MARK
Date as Right	🦁	𝖆	9·375	👑

STERLING STANDARD SILVER*

	LEOPARD'S HEAD	DATE LETTER	LION PASSANT	DUTY MARK
1856-57	🦁	𝖆	🦁	👑
1857-58	"	𝖇	"	"
1858-59	"	𝖈	"	"
1859-60	"	𝖉	"	"
1860-61	"	𝖊	"	"
1861-62	"	𝖋	"	"
1862-63	"	𝖌	"	"
1863-64	"	𝖍	"	"
1864-65	"	𝖎	"	"
1865-66	"	𝖐	"	"
1866-67	"	𝖑	"	"
1867-68	"	𝖒	"	"
1868-69	"	𝖓	"	"
1869-70	"	𝖔	"	"
1870-71	"	𝖕	"	"
1871-72	"	𝖖	"	"
1872-73	"	𝖗	"	"
1873-74	"	𝖘	"	"
1874-75	"	𝖙	"	"
1875-76	"	𝖚	"	"

Ⓕ was struck on imported wares in addition to the marks shown, from 1867-1904.

CYCLE XXI

STERLING STANDARD SILVER*

	LEOPARD'S HEAD	DATE LETTER	LION PASSANT	DUTY† MARK
1876-77		A		
1877-78	"	B	"	"
1878-79	"	C	"	"
1879-80	"	D	"	"
1880-81	"	E	"	"
1881-82	"	F	"	"
1882-83	"	G	"	"
1883-84	"	H	"	"
1884-85	"	I	"	"
1885-86	"	K	"	"
1886-87	"	L	"	"
1887-88	"	M	"	"
1888-89	"	N	"	"
1889-1st May 1890	"	O	"	"
2nd May 1890 28th May 1890	"	"	"	
June 1890-91	"	P	"	
1891-92	"	Q	"	
1892-93	"	R	"	
1893-94	"	S	"	
1894-95	"	T	"	
1895-96	"	U	"	

BRITANNIA STANDARD SILVER*

	LION'S HEAD	DATE LETTER	BRIT-ANNIA	DUTY† MARK
Date as Left		A		

GOLD (22ct.)*

	LEOPARD'S HEAD	DATE LETTER	CROWN + 22	DUTY† MARK
Date as Left		A		22	

GOLD (18ct.)*

	LEOPARD'S HEAD	DATE LETTER	CROWN + 18	DUTY† MARK
Date as Left		A	18	

GOLD (15ct.)*

	LEOPARD'S HEAD	DATE LETTER	CARAT MARK	DUTY† MARK
Date as Left		A	15	·625	

GOLD (12ct.)*

	LEOPARD'S HEAD	DATE LETTER	CARAT MARK	DUTY† MARK
Date as Left		A	12	·5	

GOLD (9ct.)*

	LEOPARD'S HEAD	DATE LETTER	CARAT MARK	DUTY† MARK
Date as Left		A	9	·375	

* was struck on imported wares in addition to the marks shown, from 1867-1904.

† Duty Mark only to 1890.

CYCLE XXII

BRITANNIA STANDARD SILVER*

	LION'S HEAD ERASED	DATE LETTER	BRIT- ANNIA
Date as Right	🦁	As Right	🔶

GOLD (22ct.)*

	LEOPARD'S HEAD ‡	CROWN + 22	DATE LETTER
Date as Right	🦁	👑22	**a**

GOLD (18ct.)*

	LEOPARD'S HEAD ‡	CROWN + 18 ‡	DATE LETTER
Date as Right	🦁	👑18	**a**

GOLD (15ct.)*

	LEOPARD'S HEAD	CARAT MARK	DATE LETTER
Date as Right	🦁	·625	**a**

GOLD (12ct.)*

	LEOPARD'S HEAD	CARAT MARK	DATE LETTER
Date as Right	🦁	·5	**a**

GOLD (9ct.)*

	LEOPARD'S HEAD	CARAT MARK	DATE LETTER
Date as Right	🦁	·375	**a**

STERLING STANDARD SILVER*

	LEOPARD'S HEAD	DATE LETTER	LION PASSANT
1896-97	🦁	**a**	🦁
1897-98	"	**b**	"
1898-99	"	**c**	"
1899-1900	"	**d**	"
1900-1	"	**e**	"
EDW.VII 1901-2	"	**f**	"
1902-3	"	**g**	"
1903-4	"	**h**	"
1904-5	"	**i**	"
1905-6	"	**k**	"
1906-7	"	**l**	"
1907-8	"	**m**	"
1908-9	"	**n**	"
1909-10	"	**o**	"
GEO.V 1910-11	"	**p**	"
1911-12	"	**q**	"
1912-13	"	**r**	"
1913-14	"	**s**	"
1914-15	"	**t**	"
1915-16	"	**u**	"

* was struck on imported wares in addition to the marks shown from 1867-1904.

‡ 🦁 replaces previous Leopard's Head shown, from 1897-98.

‡ Alternative mark up to 1904. From 1904 onwards only separate punches Crown and 18 used.

CYCLE XXII (continued)

IMPORTED WARES		
1904-1905 ☀	1906 on ☮	
Silver (Britannia)	9584	𝐢
" (Sterling)	925	𝐢
Gold 22ct.	⊠ ·916	𝐢
" 18ct.	⊠ ·75	𝐢
" 15ct.	⊠ ·625	𝐢
" 12ct.	⬦ ·5	𝐢
" 9ct.	⬦ ·375	𝐢

CYCLE XXIII**

BRITANNIA STANDARD SILVER

	LION'S HEAD ERASED	BRIT-ANNIA	DATE LETTER
Date as Right			As Right

GOLD (22ct.)

	LEOPARD'S HEAD	CARAT MARK	DATE LETTER
Date as Right		22	

GOLD (18ct.)

	LEOPARD'S HEAD	CARAT MARK	DATE LETTER
Date as Right		18	

GOLD (15ct.) up to 1932 †

	LEOPARD'S HEAD	CARAT MARK	DATE LETTER
Date as Right		·625	

GOLD (12ct.) up to 1932 †

	LEOPARD'S HEAD	CARAT MARK	DATE LETTER
Date as Right		·5	

GOLD (9ct.)

	LEOPARD'S HEAD	CARAT MARK	DATE LETTER
Date as Right		·375	

STERLING STANDARD SILVER

	LEOPARD'S HEAD	LION PASSANT	DATE LETTER
1916-17			a
1917-18	"	"	b
1918-19	"	"	c
1919-20	"	"	d
1920-21	"	"	e
1921-22	"	"	f
1922-23	"	"	g
1923-24			h
1924-25	"	"	i
1925-26	"	"	k
1926-27	"	"	l
1927-28	"	"	m
1928-29	"	"	n
1929-30	"	"	o
1930-31	"	"	p
1931-32	"	"	q
1932-33	"	"	r
1933-34	"	"	s
*1934-35	"	"	t
*1935-36	"	"	u

GOLD (14ct.) from 1932 †

	LEOPARD'S HEAD	CARAT MARK	DATE LETTER
Date as Right		·585	r

 * Jubilee mark. This was a voluntary mark used in these years.

† 12ct. and 15ct. gold were discontinued in 1932-33 and replaced by a single standard, 14ct. gold.

** For import marks Cycle XXIII see p.42.

CYCLE XXIV**

STERLING STANDARD SILVER		
	LEOPARD'S HEAD	LION PASSANT	DATE LETTER
EDW.VII 1936-37			**A**
GEO.VI 1937-38	"	"	**B**
1938-39	"	"	**C**
1939-40	"	"	**D**
1940-41	"	"	**E**
1941-42	"	"	**F**
1942-43	"	"	**G**
1943-44	"	"	**H**
1944-45	"	"	**I**
1945-46	"	"	**K**
1946-47	"	"	**L**
1947-48	"	"	**M**
1948-49	"	"	**N**
1949-50	"	"	**O**
1950-51	"	"	**P**
1951-52	"	"	**Q**
ELIZ.II 1952-53*	"	"	**R**
1953-54*	"	"	**S**
1954-55	"	"	**T**
1955-56	"	"	**U**

BRITANNIA STANDARD SILVER		
	LION'S HEAD ERASED	BRIT-ANNIA	DATE LETTER
Date as Left			As Left

GOLD (22ct.)		
	LEOPARD'S HEAD	CARAT MARK	DATE LETTER
Date as Left		22	**A**

GOLD (18ct.)		
	LEOPARD'S HEAD	CARAT MARK	DATE LETTER
Date as Left		18	**A**

GOLD (14ct.)		
	LEOPARD'S HEAD	CARAT MARK	DATE LETTER
Date as Left		·585	**A**

GOLD (9ct.)		
	LEOPARD'S HEAD	CARAT MARK	DATE LETTER
Date as Left		·375	**A**

*   A coronation mark was also used in these years as an optional additional mark.

**   For import marks Cycle XXIV see p.42.

CYCLE XXV**

BRITANNIA STANDARD SILVER		
LION'S HEAD ERASED	BRIT-ANNIA	DATE LETTER
Date as Right		As Right

GOLD (22ct.)		
LEOPARD'S HEAD	CARAT MARK	DATE LETTER
Date as Right	22	

GOLD (18ct.)		
LEOPARD'S HEAD	CARAT MARK	DATE LETTER
Date as Right	18	

GOLD (14ct.)		
LEOPARD'S HEAD	CARAT MARK	DATE LETTER
Date as Right	·585	

GOLD (9ct.)		
LEOPARD'S HEAD	CARAT MARK	DATE LETTER
Date as Right	·375	

** For import marks Cycle XXV see p.42.

	STERLING STANDARD SILVER		
	LEOPARD'S HEAD	LION PASSANT	DATE LETTER
1956-57			a
1957-58	"	"	b
1958-59	"	"	c
1959-60	"	"	d
1960-61	"	"	e
1961-62	"	"	f
1962-63	"	"	g
1963-64	"	"	h
1964-65	"	"	i
1965-66	"	"	k
1966-67	"	"	l
1967-68	"	"	m
1968-69	"	"	n
1969-70	"	"	o
1970-71	"	"	p
1971-72	"	"	q
1972-73	"	"	r
1973-74	"	"	s
Up to 31 Dec.1974	"	"	t

** For import marks Cycle XXV see p.42.

CYCLES XXIII, XXIV & XXV

MARKS ON IMPORTED WARES

	IMPORT MARK †	CARAT MARK	DATE LETTER
Silver (Britannia)		9584	a
Silver (Sterling)		925	a
Gold 22ct.		916	a
" 18ct.		75	a
" 15ct.*		625	a
" 12ct.*		·5	a
" 9ct.		375	a

MARKS ON IMPORTED WARES*
(From 1932)

	IMPORT MARK †	CARAT MARK	DATE LETTER
Gold 14ct.		585	r

*   12ct. and 15ct. gold were discontinued in 1932-33 and replaced by a single standard, 14ct. gold.

†   From 1950 on the import (Leo) mark is struck the other way up.

CYCLE XXVI

STERLING STANDARD SILVER

	LEOPARD'S HEAD	LION PASSANT	DATE LETTER
1975			𝒜
1976	"	"	ℬ
1977*	"	"	𝒞
1978	"	"	𝒟
1979	"	"	ℰ
1980	"	"	ℱ
1981	"	"	𝒢
1982	"	"	ℋ
1983	"	"	𝒥
1984	"	"	𝒦
1985	"	"	ℒ
1986	"	"	ℳ
1987	"	"	𝒩
1988	"	"	𝒪
1989	"	"	𝒫
1990	"	"	𝒬
1991	"	"	ℛ

BRITANNIA STANDARD SILVER

	LEOPARD'S HEAD	BRIT-ANNIA	DATE LETTER
Date as Above			𝒜

PLATINUM

	LEOPARD'S HEAD	PLATINUM MARK	DATE LETTER
Date as Above			𝒜

GOLD

	LEOPARD'S HEAD	CARAT MARK		DATE LETTER
22ct.			916	𝒜
18ct.			750	𝒜
14ct.			585	𝒜
9ct.			375	𝒜

* Silver Jubilee mark (optional)

CYCLE XXVI (continued)

IMPORT MARKS		
	IMPORT MARK	CARAT MARK	DATE LETTER
Silver (Britannia)	⬡	958	𝒜
Silver (Sterling)	⬡	925	𝒜
Gold 22ct.	⬡	916	𝒜
" 18ct.	⬡	750	𝒜
" 14ct.	⬡	585	𝒜
" 9ct.	⬡	375	𝒜
Platinum	⬡	950	𝒜

CONVENTION HALLMARKS

PRECIOUS METAL	LEOPARD'S HEAD	COMMON CONTROL MARK	FINENESS MARK
Gold 18ct.		750	750
14ct.	"	585	585
9ct.	"	375	375
Silver (Sterling)	"	925	925
Platinum	"	950	950

ON IMPORTED WARES

PRECIOUS METAL	IMPORT MARK	COMMON CONTROL MARK	FINENESS MARK
Gold 18ct.		750	750
14ct.	"	585	585
9ct.	"	375	375
Silver (Sterling)		925	925
Platinum		950	950

Marks reproduced courtesy The Worshipful Company of Goldsmiths.

MARK	MAKER	PERIOD	COMMENTS
A&CoLᵗᵈ	Asprey & Co Ltd	This mark early 20th C on	Justifiably famous for the quality of its products
AB	Abraham Buteux - post 1721 sterling mark	2nd ¼ 18th C	Fine Huguenot maker
AB GB	Alice & George Burrows	Early 19th C	Good, run-of-the-mill makers
A	Adie Brothers Ltd	20th C	Prolific makers
A·B·S	A B Savory	2nd ¼ 19th C	Large 19th C firm
A·C	Ann Chesterman	Last ¼ 18th C	Mainly small pieces of holloware
AC	Augustine Courtauld	1st ½ 18th C	Fine Huguenot maker, quite prolific
AC	" "	" "	
A·C	Alexander Crichton	Late 19th/20th C	Usually very fine copies of earlier pieces
AC Cᵒ	The Alexander Clark Co Ltd	1st ½ 19th C	Prolific manufacturers
AC MCᵒ	The Alexander Clark Manufacturing Co		
AD	Alfred Dunhill	20th C	Usually smokers' accessories
AF	Alexander Field	Late 18th/Early 19th C	Run-of-the-mill work (do not confuse with Andrew Fogelberg)
A·F	Andrew Fogelberg	2nd ½ 18th C	Very important and interesting work (do not confuse this mark with that of Alexander Field, whose work is quite inferior. The period of overlap is 1780-93, during which period Fogelberg was in partner-ship with Gilbert, using the AF SG mark)
A·F S·G / AF SG	Andrew Fogelberg & Stephen Gilbert	Last ¼ 18th C	Very important and interesting work
AL / AL	Thomas Allen	Late 17th/Early 18th C	Spoon maker
A·L / AL	Aug. Le Sage	2nd ½ 18th C	Important maker

MARK	MAKER	PERIOD	COMMENTS
AP	Abraham Portal	3rd ¼ 18th C	Apprentice to Paul de Lamerie but shows none of his master's flair. He was more interested in drama!
	Peter Archambo I	1st ½ 18th C	Important Huguenot
	Hugh Arnett & Edward Pocock	c.2nd ¼ 18th C	Wide range, a lot of flatware
	The Artificer's Guild Ltd	1st ½ 20th C	Interesting art metalwork
	Adey, Joseph & Albert Savory	Mid 19th C	Large 19th c family firm
	Anne Tanqueray	2nd ¼ 18th C	Probably the greatest of all women silversmiths
	Ayme Videau	2nd ¼ 18th C	Fine Huguenot maker of particularly good coffee pots
	" "	" "	
A·Z·J·Z	Arthur Zimmerman & John Zimmerman	Late 19th/Early 20th C	Prolific manufacturers of cigarette cases, boxes, vesta cases, etc.
Ba	Thomas Bamford	c.2nd ¼ 18th C	Prolific maker of good, run-of-the-mill casters
BA	Joseph Barbut	1st ¼ 18th C	Spoon maker
BA	Richard Bayley	1st ½ 18th C	Prolific maker of good holloware
BD	Burrage Davenport	2nd ½ 18th C	Good, run-of-the-mill work
BE	Benjamin Bentley	Late 17th/Early 18th C	Spoon maker
BG	Benjamin Godfrey	2nd ¼ 18th C	A very fine goldsmith
P·G	" "	" "	
BS	" "	" "	
B.H.M	Berthold Hermann Muller	Late 19th/Early 20th C	Importer of vast quantities of silver from Germany, based on earlier work (much collected today)
BI	Joseph Bird	Late 17th/Early 18th C	Mostly good candlesticks
IBi	" "	" "	
BM	Berthold Muller	Late 19th/Early 20th C	Importer of vast quantities of silver from Germany, based on earlier work (much collected today)
BM	" "	" "	

MARK	MAKER	PERIOD	COMMENTS
	John Bodington	Late 17th/Early 18th C	Very fine English work. One of the best English goldsmiths of the period
	Jonathan Bradley	Late 17th/Early 18thC	Spoon maker
	Benjamin Smith	1st ¼ 19th C	Important maker (part of Rundell, Bridge & Rundell)
	Benjamin & James Smith	Early 19th C	Highly important (worked for Rundell, Bridge & Rundell)
	Abraham Buteux	2nd ¼ 18th C	Fine Huguenot maker
	Benjamin Watts - post 1720 sterling mark	Late 17th/Early 18th C	Mostly spoons
	Carrington & Co	20th C	Retailers, often fine reproductions
	Collingwood & Co	20th C	Retailers
	Charles Padgett & Walter Padgett	Early 20th C	Became Padgett & Braham; very large producer today
	Lawrence Coles	Late 17th/Early 18th C	Spoon maker
	Charles Asprey	Mid 19th C	Justifiably famous for the quality of its products
	Charles Asprey & Charles Asprey jun	End 19th C	
	Charles Asprey & George Asprey	Late 19th/Early 20th C	
	Christopher Canner I	Late 17th/Early 18th C	Many casters
	Charles Aldridge & Henry Green	2nd ½ 18th C	Good, run-of-the-mill work
	Charles Belk	Late 19th/Early 20th C	Manufacturer
	Charles Bellassyse	Mid 18th C	Good maker
	Charles Boyton	Mid 19th C	Spoon maker
	" "	2nd ½ 19th C	Spoon maker and manufacturer of a wide range
	" "	End 19th C	
	Charles Boyton & Son	20th C	

MARK	MAKER	PERIOD	COMMENTS
	Christopher Canner - post 1720 sterling mark	Late 17th/Early 18th C	Many casters
	Charles Eley	2nd ¼ 19th C	Spoon maker
	Charles Fabergé	Early 20th C	London branch of the famous Peter Carl Fabergé of St. Petersburg
	Charles Thomas Fox	1st ½ 19th C	Member of an important 19th C family of goldsmiths
	" "	" "	
	Crispin Fuller	1st ¼ 19th C	Run-of-the-mill maker
	Charles Frederick Hancock	2nd ½ 19th C	Important makers and retailers
	" "	" "	
	" "	" "	
	Hancocks & Co	Late 19th C & on	
	" "	" "	
	Carlo Giuliano	2nd ½ 19th C	Important jeweller
	Carlo Joseph Giuliano & Arthur Alphonse Giuliano	Late 19th/Early 20th C	Important jewellers
	Wm Charnelhouse	Early 18th C	Often found on spoons
	John Chartier	Late 17th/Early 18th C	Very important Huguenot
	" "	" "	
	Christian Hillan	2nd ¼ 18th C	A very fine maker
	Charles Hougham	Last ¼ 18th C	Usually spoons and buckles
	Charles Kandler	Mid 18th C	Highly important, one of the all-time greats

MARK	MAKER	PERIOD	COMMENTS
CK	Charles Kandler II	Last ¼ 18th C	Do not confuse with the highly important Charles Frederick Kandler
CL	Jos Clare	1st ¼ 18th C	Good prolific maker, wide range
CL	Nicholas Clausen	1st ¼ 18th C	Important and interesting maker. Work is difficult to find
CL	David Clayton	Late 17th/Early 18th C	Specialist toy and miniature maker. Very collectable
CL	Jonah Clifton	Early 18th C	Good holloware
C·M	Charles Mappin	Late 19th C	Manufacturer
Co	Matt Cooper	Early 18th C	Mostly fine candlesticks
CO	Robert Cooper	Late 17th/Early 18th C	Made pieces for Samuel Pepys. Good English maker
CO	Edward Cornock	1st ¼ 18th C	Mostly small salvers, spoon trays and tobacco boxes
CO	John Corporon	1st ¼ 18th C	Very fine Huguenot work, but difficult to find
CO	Augustus Courtauld	1st ½ 18th C	Quite prolific. Fine Huguenot maker
CR	Paul Crespin	Mid 18th C	Highly important, and serious rival to Paul de Lamerie, certainly his equal
CR	" "	" "	
CR	" "	" "	
CR A	Charles Robert Ashbee	Late 19th/Early 20th C	Very important Arts & Crafts
CR GS	Charles Reily & George Storer	2nd ¼ 19th C	Very fine small work
CR WS	Charles Rawlings & William Summers	Mid 19th C	Fine and very collectable small work
CS✱FS	Cornelius Desormeaux Saunders & James Francis Hollings Shepherd	Late 19th/Early 20th C	Prolific manufacturers of small work and jewellery
CS FS	Cornelius Saunders & Frank Shepherd	Late 19th/Early 20th C	Prolific manufacturers of small work and jewellery

MARK	MAKER	PERIOD	COMMENTS
CSH	Charles Stuart Harris	2nd ½ 19th C	Spoon maker
CSH	" "	" "	
C.S H	" "	Late 19th/Early 20th C	Prolific maker of a very wide range, usually very fine copies of earlier pieces
C.S &S	C S Harris & Sons Ltd	Late 19th/Early 20th C	
C.S H & S	" "	" "	
CTF GF	Charles Thomas Fox & George Fox	Mid 19th C	Important makers
CV	Louys Cuny	1st ¼ 18th C	Very fine Huguenot
C W	Charles Wright	3rd ¼ 18th C	Good standard holloware
D&J W	D & J Wellby Ltd	2nd ½ 19th C/c.20th C	Mostly fine copies of early pieces
DA	Isaac Dalton	1st ¼ 18th C	Spoon maker
DA	Wm Darker	1st ½ 18th C	Good general maker, quite prolific
DA	Isaac Davenport	Late 17th/Early 18th C	Spoon maker
DC	David Clayton - post 1720 sterling mark	Late 17th/Early 18th C	Specialist toy/miniature maker. Very collectable
DH	David Hennell	Mid 18th C	Specialist and prolific maker of salts
DH	" "	" "	
D·H	" "	" "	
R D·H H	D & R Hennell	3rd ¼ 18th C	Mostly salts
DI	Isaac Dighton	Late 17th/Early 18th C	Good English work of the period
DM	Dorothy Mills	Mid 18th C	Good, usually small pieces
DP	Daniel Piers	Mid 18th C	Fine maker
DP	" "	" "	

MARK	MAKER	PERIOD	COMMENTS
	Digby Scott & Benjamin Smith	Early 19th C	Highly important (worked for Rundell, Bridge & Rundell)
	Digby Scott, Benjamin Smith & James Smith		
	Daniel Smith & Robert Sharp	2nd ½ 18th C	Important makers. Made some of the finest silver of the period
	" "	" "	
	" "	Last ¼ 18th C	
	David Tanqueray - post 1720 sterling mark	1st ¼ 18th C	Very fine Huguenot work associated with his father-in-law, David Willaume
	Duncan Urquhart & Naphtali Hart	Late 18th/Early 19th C	Run-of-the-mill tea services
	David Willaume - post 1720 sterling mark	Late 17th/Early 18th C	Very important Huguenot
	David Willaume II	2nd ¼ 18th C	Important Huguenot
	" "	" "	
	Daniel & John Wellby	2nd ½ 19th C/c.20th C	Mostly fine copies of early pieces
	" "	" "	
	" "	" "	
	Elkington & Co Ltd (of Birmingham)	Mid 19th/20th C	Major manufacturer whose work ranges from the very ordinary to very important designs; the quality is always superb
	" "	" "	
	John East	Late 17th/Early 18th C	Good English maker
	Edward Aldridge	Mid 18th C	Good, run-of-the-mill maker, mostly pierced work, baskets, etc.
	Edward Aldridge & Co	3rd ¼ 18th C	
	Edward Aldridge & John Stamper		

MARK	MAKER	PERIOD	COMMENTS
	Elizabeth Buteux	2nd ¼ 18th C	One of the best women silversmiths
	Edward, Edward jun, John & William Barnard	2nd ¼ 19th C	Major manufacturers
	Edward Barnard & John Barnard	Mid 19th C	
	" "	" "	
	Edward, John & William Barnard	" "	
	Edward Barnard & Sons Ltd	Early 20th C	
	Ebenezer Coker	Mid 18th C	Specialist in spoons, salvers and candlesticks (often confused with Elias Cachart, look at loops at end of letters: Cachart loops back through, Coker does not)
	" "	" "	
	Edw Cornock - post 1723 sterling mark	1st ¼ 18th C	Mostly small salvers, spoon trays and tobacco boxes
	Elizabeth Eaton	Mid 19th C	Specialist spoon maker
	" "	" "	
	Elizabeth Eaton & John Eaton	" "	
	Edward Farrell	1st ½ 19th C	Very interesting maker, producing important if at times eccentric (today very valuable) pieces
	Edward Feline	Late 1st ¼/2nd ¼ 18th C	Fine work, many good coffee pots
	" "	" "	
	Elizabeth Godfrey	Mid 18th C	One of the best women silversmiths (formerly Elizabeth Buteux, see entry)
	Edward Hutton (Wm Hutton & Sons)	2nd ½ 19th C/20th C	Large Sheffield manufacturers
	Elizabeth Jackson (later Oldfield)	Mid 18th C	Specialist spoon maker
	Edward Ker Reid	2nd ½ 19th C	Good general work
	Elizabeth Morley	Late 18th C	Small pieces

MARK	MAKER	PERIOD	COMMENTS
EM JM	Edward Mappin & Joseph C Mappin	2nd ½ 19th C	Large Sheffield manufacturers
E O	Elizabeth Oldfield (formerly Jackson)	3rd ¼ 18th C	Specialist spoon maker
ER	Elizabeth Roker	Last ¼ 18th C	Spoon maker
E R	Emick Romer	3rd ¼ 18th C	Interesting maker who often made epergnes
E T	Elizabeth Tookey	3rd ¼ 18th C	Spoon maker
E·T	" "	" "	
E·V	Edward Vincent	1st ½ 18th C	Very fine English craftsman, who could be naughty; he was into duty dodging after 1720 in a big way: be careful
&V	" "	" "	
E·Wl	Edward Wakelin	3rd ¼ 18th C	Very important maker
EW	Edward Wood	2nd ¼ 18th C	Specialist salt maker
EW	" "	" "	
F	Wm Fawdery - pre-1697 and post 1720 sterling mark	Late 17th/Early 18th C	Good English work
FA	William Fawdery	" "	
FA	Wm Fawdery	" "	
FA	" "	" "	
FA	John Fawdery	1st ¼ 18th C	Good holloware
FA	Thos Farren	1st ½ 18th C	Very fine maker
F·B N·D	Francis Butty & Nich Dumee	3rd ¼ 18th C	Good makers
F.B.T	Francis Boone Thomas (F B Thomas & Co)	2nd ½ 19th C/1st ½ 20th C	Bond Street retailer (always fine quality pieces)
FC	Fras Crump	Mid 18th C	Good maker of fairly standard holloware
F·C	" "	" "	
FC	" "	" "	

MARK	MAKER	PERIOD	COMMENTS
F E	Frederick Elkington	Mid 19th/20th C	Major manufacturers whose work ranges from the very ordinary to very important designs; the quality is always superb
FG	Francis Garthorne – pre-1697 and post 1721 sterling mark	Late 17th/Early 18th C	Competent English work of the period
F H	Fras Higgins I	1st ½ 19th C	Important 19th C spoon maker
F H	Francis Higgins	Mid 19th C	Specialist spoon maker
FH	" "	" "	
fh	" "	" "	
FH	" "	2nd ½ 19th/Early 20th C	
FH	" "	" "	
F.H&S LTD	F Higgins & Son Ltd	Early 20th C	
FK	Charles Frederick Kandler	Mid 18th C	Highly important, one of the all-time greats
FK	" "	" "	
FK	Fred Knopfell	3rd ¼ 18th C	Very interesting former journeyman of Paul de Lamerie
FL	Wm Fleming	c.1st ¼ 18th C	Very prolific, particularly peppers, saucepans and mugs
FN	Francis Nelme	c.2nd ¼ 18th C	Important, but over-shadowed by his father
FN	" "	" "	
FO	Thos Folkingham	c.1st ¼ 18th C	Wide range of fine silver
FS	Fras Stamp	Last ¼ 18th C	Good maker
FW	Fuller White	Mid 18th C	Good, run-of-the-mill holloware
FW	" "	" "	

MARK	MAKER	PERIOD	COMMENTS
	Fuller White & John Fray	Mid 18th C	Good holloware
	Goldsmiths & Silver-smiths Co Ltd	20th C	Very large retailers of jewellery and silver
	" "	" "	
	" "	" "	
	Daniel Garnier	Late 17th/Early 18th C	Important Huguenot
	George W Adams (Chawner & Co)	Mid 19th C	Chawners were the most important mid 19th C firm of spoon makers
	George Angell	Mid 19th C	Important maker
	" "	" "	
	William Gamble	Late 17th/Early 18th C	Competent English maker - Hogarth was apprenticed to his son
	Geo Garthorne	Late 17th/Early 18th C	Competent English work of the period
	George Burrows	2nd ½ 18th C	Usually spoons
	George Cowles	Late 18th C	Good maker
	George Fox	2nd ½ 19th C	Member of the important Fox family
	" "	" "	
	George Gray	Last ¼ 18th C	Often overstruck on the work of Hester Bateman and Peter and Ann Bateman
	George Hindmarsh	Mid 18th C	Specialist salver maker
	" "	" "	
	George Heming & William Chawner	Last ¼ 18th C	Fine makers
	" "	" "	

MARK	MAKER	PERIOD	COMMENTS
	Glover Johnson - post 1720 sterling mark	1st ¼ 18th C	Prolific maker of ordinary casters
	George Greenhill Jones	2nd ¼ 18th C	Mostly casters and sauce-pans
	George Jackson & David Fullerton	Very end 19th/Early 20th C	Wide range, particularly good flatware
	George Lambert	2nd ½ 19th C	Fine maker
	Gilbert Marks	Late 19th/Early 20th C	Important art nouveau work
	George Methuen	Mid 18th C	Specialist in salvers, etc.
	" "	" "	
	Gorham Manu-facturing Co	20th C	Large American manu-facturer with Birmingham factory
	George Maudsley Jackson	Late 19th C	Wide range of particularly good flatware
	George Nathan & Ridley Hayes	Late 19th/Early 20th C	Birmingham manu-facturers
	Meshach Godwin	Late 1st/2nd ¼ 18th C	Mostly run-of-the-mill peppers and other small pieces
	James Gould	Late 1st/2nd ¼ 18th C	Specialist candlestick maker
	William Gould	Mid 18th C	Specialist candlestick maker
	Jas Goodwin	1st ¼ 18th C	Small mugs, peppers, etc.
	George Henry Hart (Guild of Handicraft)	1908 and on	Formed by members of the Guild of Handicraft Ltd after its liquidation (Note: do not confuse with next mark which it resembles. From 1912 on it is George Hart)
	Guild of Handicraft Ltd	1900-1908	Important Arts & Crafts makers under C R Ashbee. (Note: easy to confuse with George Hart's mark above. Date is important and look for the Ltd after the G of H)
	David Greene	1st ¼ 18th C	Specialist candlestick maker

MARK	MAKER	PERIOD	COMMENTS
GR	Henry Greene	Early 18th C	Mostly spoons
GR	Gundry Roode - post 1720 sterling mark	2nd ¼ 18th C	Salts
GRE	George Richards Elkington	Mid 19th/20th C	Major manufacturers whose work ranges from ordinary to very important designs; the quality is always superb
GS	Gabriel Sleath	1st ½ 18th C	Prolific, good English work
GS	" " - post 1720 sterling mark	" "	
GS	" " "	" "	
GS	George Smith III	Last ¼ 18th C	Prolific specialist spoon maker
G S	George Smith IV	Last ¼ 18th C	Prolific spoon maker
GS C	Gabriel Sleath & Fras Crump	Mid 18th C	Good, run-of-the-mill holloware
GS TH	George Smith & Thomas Hayter	Late 18th C	Good, general makers
GS TH	" "	" "	
GS WF	George Smith & William Fearn	Last ¼ 18th C	Prolific spoon makers
GU	Nathaniel Gulliver	2nd ¼ 18th C	Good holloware, particularly coffee pots
GU	George R Unite (of Birmingham)	Late 19th/Early 20th C	Prolific maker of small pieces
GW	George Wickes	Mostly 2nd ¼ 18th C	Very important English goldsmith
GW	" "	" "	
G	" " - post 1721 sterling mark	" "	
GW	George Wintle	1st ¼ 19th C	Spoon maker
GW	" "	" "	
H&Co LD	Heming & Co Ltd (now Bruford & Heming)	20th C	Important retailers of silver and jewellery

MARK	MAKER	PERIOD	COMMENTS
	Hukin & Heath Ltd - 20th C mark	Late 19th/Early 20th C	Most important for their pieces designed by Dr C Dresser
	Hunt & Roskell Ltd	Late 19th C	Major 19th C firm, originates with Paul Storr
	" "	Early 20th C	
	Paul Hanet	1st/2nd ¼ 18th C	Huguenot spoonmaker
	Pierre Harache I	Late 17th C	Extremely important Huguenot
	Holland, Aldwinckle & Slater	Late 19th/Early 20th C	Important manufacturers
	" "	" "	
	Hugh Arnett & Edward Pocock - post 1720 sterling mark	c. 2nd ¼ 18th C	Wide range, a lot of flatware
	Henry Bailey	3rd ¼ 18th C	Standard commercial pieces
	" "	" "	(Note: this mark is often confused with that of Hester Bateman (see entry). The H does not flow with this mark as it does with Hester's)
	Hester Bateman	2nd ½ 18th C	Overrated, overpriced, run-of-the-mill, mass-produced pieces (see also Hy. Bailey re possible confusion with mark)
	" "	" "	
	Henry Brind	Mid 18th C	Good, run-of-the-mill maker
	Henry Chawner	Last ¼ 18th C	Run-of-the-mill maker
	Henry Chawner & Jno Eames	Late 18th C	Good, general work
	" "	" "	
	Henry Greenway	Last ¼ 18th C	A very good maker of particularly fine coffee pots, etc.
	Henry George Murphy	1st ½ 20th C	One of the most interesting Art Deco silversmiths

MARK	MAKER	PERIOD	COMMENTS
H·H	Henry Hebert	2nd ¼ 18th C	Good maker
H·H	" "	" "	
H·H	" "	" "	
H·H	" "	" "	
H·H	" "	" "	
H·H **H·H**	Henry Holland (of Holland, Aldwinckle & Slater) " "	Mid 19th C " "	Important manufacturer
HI V	Saml Hitchcock	1st ¼ 18th C	Spoon maker
H J L	Henry John Lias	Late 19th C	Large manufacturing silversmith
H J L JW	Henry John Lias & James Wakely	Late 19th C	Large manufacturing silversmith
HL	Herbert Charles Lambert (see Lambert & Rawlings)	Early 20th C	Important retailers
HL HL **HL HL**	Henry John Lias & Henry John Lias	Mid 19th C	Large manufacturing silversmith
HN	Hannah Northcote	1st ¼ 19th C	Spoon maker
HN RH	Henry Nutting & Robert Hennell	Early 19th C	Good makers
Ho	Edward Holaday	1st ¼ 18th C	Good English work
HO	Sarah Holaday	Late 1st ¼/2nd ¼ 18th C	Good woman silversmith
H·P **H·P**	Humph Payne - post 1720 sterling mark " "	1st ½ 18th C " "	Good English work, quite prolific
·HS·	Harold Stabler	1st ½ 20th C	Important Art Deco work

MARK	MAKER	PERIOD	COMMENTS
	Henry Vander & Arthur Vander (now C J Vander Ltd)	Early 20th C	Important manufacturing silversmiths
	Henry Wilkinson & Co	Late 19th/Early 20th C	Important Sheffield manufacturers
	James Schruder	Mid 18th C	Very fine maker who produced very interesting rococo
	Chas Jackson	1st ¼ 18th C	Spoon maker
	Joseph Barbut - post 1720 sterling mark	1st ¼ 18th C	Spoon maker
	John Bridge	c. 2nd ¼ 19th C	Important maker (the Bridge of Rundell, Bridge & Rundell)
	" "	" "	
	Isaac Callard	2nd ¼ 18th C	Specialist spoon maker (good quality)
	" "	" "	
	John Carter II	2nd ½ 18th C	Specialist candlestick and salver maker (Note: some of his candlesticks were designed by Robert Adam)
	John Chartier - post 1723 sterling mark	Late 17th/Early 18th C	Very important Huguenot
	Joseph Clare - post 1720 sterling mark	1st ¼ 18th C	Good, prolific maker, wide range
	John Crouch I & Thomas Hannam	2nd ½ 18th C	Very good makers
	Joseph Craddock & William Reid	Early 19th C	Good makers
	Thos Jenkins	Late 17th/Early 18th C	Important English maker
	John Figg	Mid 19th C	Very fine and often interesting work
	James Gould - post 1721 sterling mark	Late 1st/2nd ¼ 18th C	Specialist candlestick maker
	" "	" "	
	John Hunt & Robert Roskell (mid to end 19th C marks)	Late 19th C	Major 19th C firm, originates with Paul Storr

MARK	MAKER	PERIOD	COMMENTS
I·J·K	John James Keith	Mid 19th C	Most prolific maker of church plate
I·K	John Keith	Mid 19th C	
I·K	" "	" "	
I·K R·S	John Keith & Richard Stiff	2nd ½ 19th C	
I·L	John Lambe	Last ¼ 18th C	Spoon maker
IL	Isaac Liger - post 1720 sterling mark	1st ¼ 18th C	Fine Huguenot pieces sometimes engraved by Simon Gribelin, in which case, very important
I·L H·L	John & Henry Lias	1st ½ 19th C	One of the most prolific 19th C family firms
H·L H·L	" "	Mid 19th C	
I·L H·L C·L	John, Henry & Charles Lias	c. 2nd ¼ 19th C	One of the most prolific 19th C family firms
I·M	Jacob Margas - post 1720 sterling mark	1st ¼ 18th C	Good Huguenot
I·M	John Mewburn	Late 18th/Early 19th C	Good general work
I·M	Jno Millington - post 1720 sterling mark	1st ½ 18th C	Spoon maker
I & M I·SH · I·M & I·SH	John Mortimer & John Samuel Hunt	Mid 19th C	Major 19th C firm, originates with Paul Storr
I·M C·K	Jas Murray & Chas Kandler	Mid 18th C	Kandler is highly important, one of the all-time greats. Little is known of Murray
I·O	Glover Johnson	1st ¼ 18th C	Prolific maker of ordinary casters
I·O	George Greenhill Jones	1st ½ 18th C	Mostly small pieces, peppers, cream jugs, etc.
I·P	John Pollock	Mid 18th C	Good, run-of-the-mill maker
I·P	Joseph Preedy	Late 18th/Early 19th C	Good maker
I·P E·W	John Parker & Edward Wakelin	3rd ¼ 18th C	Important makers
I·R	Isaac Ribouleau - post 1720 sterling mark	2nd ¼ 18th C	Fine Huguenot, but difficult to find
I·S	John Hugh le Sage	1st ½ 18th C	Important Huguenot goldsmith

MARK	MAKER	PERIOD	COMMENTS
I·S	John Scofield	Last ¼ 18th C	Very important, particularly his candlesticks, the best of which are the finest of the period
I·S	James Stamp	Early 4th ¼ 18th C	Good holloware, candlesticks, etc. (Note: similar to John Scofield's mark: they overlap for a short period, 1778-1780)
I·SH / **I·SH**	John Samuel Hunt " "	Mid 19th C " "	Major 19th C firm, originates with Paul Storr
I·T	John Tuite	Mostly 2nd ¼ 18th C	Specialist salver maker
I·W R·G	J Wakelin & Robert Garrard	Late 18th/very early 19th C	Important makers
I·W·S W·E	J W Story & W Elliott	Early 19th C	Good makers
I·W W·T	John Wakelin & William Taylor	Last ¼ 18th C	Important makers
I·Y	James Young	2nd ½ 18th C	Good, run-of-the-mill maker
I·Y O·I	James Young & Orlando Jackson	2nd ½ 18th C	Good makers
J·A	Joseph Angell	1st ½ 19th C	Very fine 19th C family of goldsmiths
J·A	" "	Mid 19th C	
J·A I·A	Joseph & John Angell	1st ½ 19th C	
J·A J·A	Joseph Angell sen & Joseph Angell jun	2nd ¼ 19th C	
J·A J·S	John Aldwinckle & James Slater	Late 19th C	Good makers
A·S·H	Joseph, Albert, Horace & Ethelbert Savory	Late 19th C	Large 19th C firm
J·A T·S	John Aldwinckle & Thomas Slater	Late 19th C	Good makers
J·B	John Barbe	Mid 18th C	Good, run-of-the-mill maker

MARK	MAKER	PERIOD	COMMENTS
	Joseph Barbut	1st ¼ 18th C	Spoon maker
	Jes Barkentin (of Barkentin & Krall)	2nd ½ 19th C	Highly important work in 1860s for William Burgess
	James Beebe	Early 19th C	Spoon maker
	Carrington & Co	Late 19th/Early 20th C	Important retailers
	" "	" "	
	John Bodman Carrington (Carrington & Co)		
	James Barclay Hennell	Late 19th C	Good maker
	John Cafe	Mid 18th C	Specialist candlestick maker
	Jacques Cartier	20th C	Famous jeweller
	John Collard Vickery	20th C	Retailers
	John Denzilow	Last ¼ 18th C	Good, run-of-the-mill maker
	James Dixon & Sons - 20th C mark	20th C	Sheffield manufacturers
	John & William Deakin (James Deakin & Sons Ltd)	Late 19th/Early 20th C	Sheffield manufacturers
	John Emes	End 18th/Early 19th C	Wide range of run-of-the-mill work; prolific maker of tea and coffee sets
	" "	" "	
	John, Edward, Walter & John Barnard (Barnard & Sons Ltd)	2nd ½ 19th C	Major manufacturers
	James Garrard	Late 19th C	Important maker
	James Goodwin - post 1721 sterling mark	1st ¼ 18th C	Small mugs, peppers, etc.
	James Gould	Mid 18th C	Specialist candlestick maker
	" "	Late 1st/2nd ¼ 18th C	

MARK	MAKER	PERIOD	COMMENTS
	John Harvey	Mid 18th C	Found particularly on wine labels
	Joseph Heming	Late 19th/Early 20th C	Important retailer of silver and jewellery
	Joseph Heming & Co	Late 19th/Early 20th C	Important retailer of silver and jewellery
	John Lampfert	3rd ¼ 18th C	Specialist spoon maker. Often fine and interesting examples
	John Linnit	Early 19th C	Very good small work
	John Newton Mappin	Late 19th/Early 20th C	Very large Sheffield manufacturers
	" "	" "	
	" "	" "	
	" "	" "	
	" "	" "	
	John Newton Mappin & George Webb	" "	
	John Payne	3rd ¼ 18th C	Good work
	John Pollock	Mid 18th C	Good, run-of-the-mill maker
	John Paul Cooper	20th C	Interesting and important maker
	Joseph Ridge (John Round & Son Ltd)	Late 19th/Early 20th C	Large Sheffield manufacturers
	John Round & Son Ltd	" "	
	John le Sage	1st ½ 18th C	Important Huguenot goldsmith
	James Schruder	Mid 18th C	Very fine maker, who produced very interesting rococo
	John Schuppe	3rd ¼ 18th C	Specialist maker of cow creamers (much sought after)
	John Swift	Mid 18th C	Good tankards and other holloware

MARK	MAKER	PERIOD	COMMENTS
	Joseph & Albert Savory	Mid 19th C	Large 19th C firm
	" "	" "	
	Joseph & Horace Savory	Late 19th C	Large 19th C firm
	John Tuite	Mostly 2nd ¼ 18th C	Specialist salver maker
	John Heath & John Middleton (of Hukin & Heath)	Late 19th/Early 20th C	Most important for their pieces designed by Dr C Dresser
	Joshua Vander	Early 20th C	Important manufacturing silversmith
	John Vander & John Hedges (Tessiers)	Late 19th/Early 20th C	Important manufacturing silversmith
	John James Whiting	Mid 19th C	Spoon maker
	" "	" "	
	James Wintle	2nd ¼ 19th C	Spoon maker
	John Wirgman	Mid 18th C	A fine maker
	John Wren	Late 18th C	Spoon maker
	J W Benson Ltd	Late 19th/Early 20th C	Important firm
	" "	" "	
	James Dixon & Sons	Late 19th/Early 20th C	Large Sheffield manufacturer
	James Wakely & Frank Wheeler	Late 19th/Early 20th C	Large manufacturer
	Hukin & Heath	Late 19th/Early 20th C	(It is this mark which is found on pieces designed for the firm by Dr C Dresser in the 1870s/80s)
	Charles Frederick Kandler	Mid 18th C	Highly important, one of all-time greats
	Chas Kandler & Jas Murray		Little is known of Murray
	Paul de Lamerie	1st ½ 18th C	Highly important, highly sought after, highly priced. Probably the most famous of all 18th C goldsmiths

MARK	MAKER	PERIOD	COMMENTS
	Jno Ladyman	Late 17th/Early 18th C	Specialist spoon maker. Do not confuse this mark with Paul de Lamerie!
	Geo Lambe	1st ¼ 18th C	Spoon maker
	John Laughton II	Late 17th/Early 18th C	Specialist maker of fine candlesticks
LAC	Lionel Alfred Crichton (Crichton Brothers)	20th C	Retailers of usually fine reproductions of early pieces
LC	Louisa Courtauld	3rd ¼ 18th C	Fine and interesting woman silversmith
LC GC	Louisa Courtauld & George Cowles	" "	Fine makers
LC SC	Louisa & Samuel Courtauld	Last ¼ 18th C	Fine makers
	Samuel Lea	1st ¼ 18th C	Good holloware
	Ralph Leeke	Early 18th C	Important English maker
LE	Timothy Ley	Late 17th/Early 18th C	Standard English tankards and mugs
	Louis Hamon	Mid 18th C	Very fine, difficult to find
F L★H B	Lewis Herne & Francis Butty	3rd ¼ 18th C	Good makers
F L★H B	" "	" "	
	Isaac Liger	1st ¼ 18th C	Fine Huguenot pieces sometimes engraved by Simon Gribelin, in which case, very important
LM	Lewis Mettayer - post 1720 sterling mark	1st ½ 18th C	Very important Huguenot
LO	Nathaniel Lock	Late 17th/Early 18th C	Not the best of English work
	Mathew Lofthouse	Early 18th C	Mostly drinking vessels
LO	Seth Lofthouse	1st ¼ 18th C	Competent English work
LU	Wm Lukin	Early 18th C	Some very good pieces, mostly from George I period onwards
LY&Cᵒ	Liberty & Co	Late 19th/Early 20th C	Highly important Art Nouveau pieces designed by Archibald Knox

MARK	MAKER	PERIOD	COMMENTS
MA / MA	Geo Manjoy " " (probably)	Late 17th/Early 18th C " "	Specialist maker of miniatures/toys. Very collectable
MA	Jacob Margas	1st ¼ 18th C	Good Huguenot
MA	Samuel Margas	Late 1st ¼/2nd ¼ 18th C	Good maker with a wide range
Ma	Thos Mason	1st ½ 18th C	Good prolific maker, wide range
MA	Wm Mathew	Late 17th/Early 18th C	Good English work
M·B	Moses Brent	Late 18th/Early 19th C	Prolific knife maker
MC	Mary Chawner	2nd ¼ 19th C	Spoon maker
MC GA	Mary Chawner & George W Adams	1840	Spoon makers
MD / MD	Marmaduke Daintrey " "	Mid 18th C " "	Mostly a specialist spoon maker. Worked later in his life at Hartley Row in Hampshire
Me	Thomas Merry I (probably)	1st ¼ 18th C	Maker of fine candlesticks, tapersticks
ME	Lewis Mettayer	1st ½ 18th C	Important Huguenot work which may be linked with his brother-in-law, David Willaume, to whom he was also apprenticed
MG	Meshach Godwin - post 1722 sterling mark	Late 1st/2nd ¼ 18th C	Mostly run-of-the-mill peppers and other small pieces
MI	John Millington	1st ½ 18th C	Spoon maker
ML	Mathw Lofthouse - post 1720 sterling mark	Early 18th C	Mostly drinking vessels
Mⁿ Wᴮ &	Mappin & Webb Ltd " " - 20th C mark	Late 19th/Early 20th C " "	Very large manufacturers
MO	Thos Morse	1st ¼ 18th C	Mostly good holloware
MP	Mary Pantin	2nd ¼ 18th C	Fine woman silversmith

MARK	MAKER	PERIOD	COMMENTS
	Mary Rood - post 1720 sterling mark	1st ½ 18th C	Salts
	Francis Nelme - post 1722 sterling mark, but used by his father before 1697	c.2nd ¼ 18th C	Important, but over-shadowed by his father
	Bowles Nash	1st ½ 18th C	Mostly good holloware and salvers
	Nathaniel Appleton & Ann Smith	2nd ½ 18th C	Prolific makers of cream jugs
	Nayler Brothers	20th C	Manufacturing silversmiths
	Nicholas Clausen - post 1720 sterling mark	1st ¼ 18th C	Important and interesting maker whose work is difficult to find
	Nich Dumee	Last ¼ 18th C	Good, run-of-the-mill maker
	Anthony Nelme	Late 17th/Early 18th C	Probably the most important English goldsmith of the period
	Nathaniel Gulliver	2nd ¼ 18th C	Good holloware, particularly coffee pots
	Nicholas Sprimont	Mid 18th C	Extremely important, extremely rare, extremely valuable work
	Orlando Jackson	2nd ½ 18th C	Good maker
	" "	" "	
	Ollivant & Botsford	Late 19th/Early 20th C	Manchester retailers
	Chas Overing	Late 17th/Early 18th C	Good large pieces
	Benjamin Pyne - pre-1679 & post 1720 sterling mark	Late 17th/Early 18th C	Important English gold-smith of the period
	Peter Archambo I - post 1720 sterling mark	1st ½ 18th C	Important Huguenot
	" "	" "	
	Simon Pantin	Early 18th C	Very good Huguenot
	" "	" "	
	Wm Paradise	1st ½ 18th C	Mostly good mugs and tankards

MARK	MAKER	PERIOD	COMMENTS
	Thomas Parr I	Late 17th/Early 18th C	Mostly good English holloware
	Humph Payne	1st ½ 18th C	Good English maker, quite prolific
	" "	" "	
	Peter Archambo II & Peter Meure	3rd ¼ 18th C	Fine makers
	Peter & Ann Bateman	Late 18th C	Prolific, run-of-the-mill manufacturers
	Peter, Ann & William Bateman	Early 19th C	Prolific, general run-of-the-mill work
	Peter & Jonathan Bateman	1790	Much sought by Bateman collectors; mark used for less than six months
	Peter & William Bateman	Early 19th C	Prolific, run-of-the-mill makers
	Paul Callard	3rd ¼ 18th C	Mostly spoons
	Paul Crespin	Mid 18th C	Highly important and serious rival to Paul de Lamerie, certainly his equal
	" "	" "	
	" " - post 1720 sterling mark	" "	
	William Petley	1st ¼ 18th C	Spoon maker
	Phillips Garden	Mid 18th C	Fine technician; acquired and used Paul de Lamerie's casting patterns after 1752 (these pieces are much sought after)
	" "	" "	
	" "	" "	
	" "	" "	
	Pierre Gillois	2nd ½ 18th C	Specialist caddy maker
	Paul Hanet - post 1721 sterling mark	1st/2nd ¼ 18th C	Huguenot spoon maker
	Pézé Pilleau	Late 1st/2nd ¼ 18th C	Fine Huguenot, who also made false teeth!

MARK	MAKER	PERIOD	COMMENTS
	Paul de Lamerie	1st ½ 18th C	Highly important, highly sought after, highly priced; probably the most famous of all 18th C goldsmiths
	" " - post 1733 sterling mark	" "	
	Pierre Platel	Late 17th/Early 18th C	Extremely important Master of Paul de Lamerie
	Pézé Pilleau	Late 1st/2nd ¼ 18th C	Fine Huguenot, who also made false teeth!
	" " - post 1720 sterling mark	" "	
	Peter Podie	Last ¼ 18th C	Good maker
	Philip Rainaud - post 1720 sterling mark	1st ¼ 18th C	Very fine Huguenot work is rare. (Rainaud and Paul de Lamerie were the only apprentices of Pierre Platel)
	Philip Roker II	2nd ¼ 18th C	Specialist spoon maker
	" "	" "	
	Philip Roker III	Last ¼ 18th C	Spoon maker
	Philip Rollos II - post 1720 sterling mark	Late 17th/Early 18th C	Important Huguenot
	Philip Rundell	Early 19th C	Very important maker
	Paul Storr	Late 18th/1st ½ 19th C	Highly important, highly priced (most important work c.1807-20 when with Rundell, Bridge & Rundell; later work is less sought after)
	" "	" "	
	Benjamin Pyne	Late 17th/Early 18th C	Important English goldsmith of the period
	" "	" "	
	Roberts & Belk Ltd	Late 19th/Early 20th C	Sheffield manufacturers
	Alex Roode	Late 17th/Early 18th C	Salts & other plate
	Robert Abercromby	2nd ¼ 18th C	Specialist in good salvers
	" "	" "	

MARK	MAKER	PERIOD	COMMENTS
	Philip Rainaud	1st ¼ 18th C	Very fine Huguenot work is rare (Rainaud and Paul de Lamerie were the only apprentices of Pierre Platel)
	Robert Abercromby & George Hindmarsh	2nd ¼ 18th C	Specialist salver makers
	Richard Bayley	1st ½ 18th C	Prolific maker of good holloware
	Rundell, Bridge & Rundell	1st ¼ 19th C	Highly important makers
	Richard Crossley	Late 18th C	Spoon maker
	Richard Carter, Daniel Smith, Robert Sharp	Last ¼ 18th C	Important makers
	Richard Crossley & George Smith	Early 19th C	Spoon makers
	Rebecca Emes & Edward Barnard	Early 19th C	Very large output of good silver, many tea and coffee sets
	Rebecca & William Emes	1808	Mark only used for 3½ months, good work
	Robert Frederick Fox	Early 20th C	Last member of this important family of goldsmiths
	Robert Garrard I	Early 19th C	Important maker
	Robert Garrard II	Early/Mid 19th C	
	" "	Mid 19th C	
	" "	" "	
	Richard Gosling	Mid 18th C	Specialist spoon maker
	Richard Gurney & Co	Mid 18th C	Usually good, run-of-the-mill holloware
	Richard Gurney & Thomas Cook	" "	
	Robert Hennell II	1st ⅓ 19th C	Good maker

MARK	MAKER	PERIOD	COMMENTS
RH	Robert Hennell	Last ¼ 18th C	Good, general work; some particularly fine pierced coasters
RH	" "	Mid 19th C	Very fine work
RH DH	Robert & David Hennell	Late 18th/Early 19th C	Good, general work
RH DH SH	Robert, David & Samuel Hennell	Early 19th C	Good makers
RH SH	Robert & Samuel Hennell	Early 19th C	Good makers
RI	Isaac Ribouleau	2nd ¼ 18th C	Fine Huguenot, but difficult to find
RI IS	Robert Jones & John Scofield	1776-1778	First work of the important maker John Scofield
RM	Robert Makepeace	Late 18th C	Good maker
RM EH	Martin, Hall & Co Ltd	2nd ½ 19th/Early 20th C	Large Sheffield manufacturers
RM EH	" "	" "	
RM RC	Robert Makepeace & Richard Carter	Last ¼ 18th C	Fine makers
RM TM	Robert & Thomas Makepeace	Late 18th C	Good makers
RN&CR	Omar Ramsden & Alwyn Carr	Late 19th/Early 20th C	The most important work of Ramsden is during this partnership
RO	Philip Roker II	c.2nd ¼ 18th C	Spoon maker
RIO	Philip Rollos II	Early 18th C	Important Huguenot
Ro	Philip Rollos	Late 17th/Early 18th C	Important Huguenot
RO	James Rood	1st ¼ 18th C	Specialist salt maker
RO	Mary Rood	1st ½ 18th C	Salts
R‡P	R Peaston	3rd ¼ 18th C	Often found on casters (run-of-the-mill)

MARK	MAKER	PERIOD	COMMENTS
R·R	Robert Rew	3rd ¼ 18th C	Salver maker
RR / R·R	Richard Rugg " "	3rd ¼ 18th C " "	Salver maker. Both Rew and Rugg worked at the same time and specialised in making salvers (Rew's is the largest of the marks)
R R·A·R I·M·H	Hunt & Roskell - late 19th C mark	Late 19th/Early 20th C	Major 19th C firm, originates with Paul Storr
RS	Robert Sharp	Late 18th C	Important maker
RS / R·S	Richard Sibley " "	1st ½ 19th C " "	A very fine goldsmith
RU	John Ruslen	Late 17th/Early 18th C	One of the best English makers of the period
SA	Stephen Adams	2nd ½ 18th C	Spoon maker
SA	Stephen Adams, jun	Early 19th C	Spoon maker
S·A	John Hugh le Sage	1st ½ 18th C	Important Huguenot goldsmith
SB / S·B	Susanna Barker " "	Last ¼ 18th C " "	Usually small pieces
S·C / S·C	Samuel Courtauld " "	Mid 18th C " "	Fine Huguenot work
Sc	Wm Scarlett	Late 17th/Early 18th C	Specialist spoon maker - beware of forgeries
SC I·C	Sebastian & James Crespell	3rd ¼ 18th C	Prolific makers of plates and dishes
Se	Jas Seabrook	1st ¼ 18th C	Mostly good tapersticks
SG / SG	Sebastian Harry Garrard - 20th C mark " "	Late 19th/Early 20th C 20th C	Important maker
SG	Samuel Godbehere	Last ¼ 18th C	Good, run-of-the-mill maker

MARK	MAKER	PERIOD	COMMENTS
SG EW	Samuel Godbehere & Edward Wigan	Last ¼ 18th C	Good, general makers of usually small pieces, spoons, cream jugs, etc.
SG EW IB	Samuel Godbehere, Edward Wigan & James Boult	„ „	
SH	Samuel Herbert	Mid 18th C	Mostly pierced work, baskets, etc.
SH	Sarah Holaday - post 1725 sterling mark	Late 1st ¼/2nd ¼ 18th C	This mark is often confused with Alice Sheene's, which is earlier and always Britannia standard. Good woman silversmith.
SH	Solomon Hougham	Late 18th/Early 19th C	Run-of-the-mill maker
SH	Alice Sheene	1st ¼ 18th C	Good woman silversmith (do not confuse this mark with Sarah Holaday's, which is later (1725 on))
S H S R IED	Solomon Hougham, Solomon Royes & John East Dix	Early 19th C	Good, run-of-the-mill work
H SH B	Herbert & Co	Mid 18th C	Mostly pierced work, baskets, etc.
H SH B	S. Herbert & Co	„ „	
SI	Francis Singleton	Late 17th/Early 18th C	Competent English work
SJ	Simon Jouet	2nd ¼ 18th C	Fine maker
SJ	„ „	„ „	
SJP	Solomon Joel Phillips	20th C	Mark usually found on very fine copies of early pieces
SL	Simon le Sage	3rd ¼ 18th C	Very fine Huguenot goldsmith
SL	„ „	„ „	
SL	Gabriel Sleath	1st ½ 18th C	Prolific, good English work
SL	„ „	„ „	
SM	Saml Margas - post 1720 sterling mark	Late 1st ¼/2nd ¼ 18th C	Good maker with a wide range

MARK	MAKER	PERIOD	COMMENTS
SM	S Mordan & Co Ltd	Late 19th/Early 20th C	Very collectable small pieces; vast numbers of pencils
SM&Co	" "	" "	
S M &Co	" "	" "	
SP	Simon Pantin - post 1720 sterling mark	Early 18th C	Very good Huguenot
S·P	Simon Pantin II	2nd ¼ 18th C	Good Huguenot goldsmith
Sp	Thos Spackman	Early 18th C	Spoons
S·P	Wm Spackman	1st ¼ 18th C	Good, run-of-the-mill, general work
S·R C·B	Roberts & Belk Ltd - late 19th C mark	Late 19th/Early 20th C	Sheffield manufacturers
S.S	Stephen Smith	2nd ½ 19th C	Very fine silversmith
S.S.	" "	" "	
S.S W·N	Stephen Smith & William Nicholson	Mid 19th C	Very fine silversmiths
S.S W.N	" "	" "	
St	Ambrose Stevenson	1st ¼ 18th C	Wide range
St	Saml Taylor	Mid 18th C	Good holloware
SW	Samuel Welder	Late 1st ¼/2nd ¼ 18th C	Specialist and prolific caster maker
sw	" " - post 1720 sterling mark	1st ¼ 18th C	
SW	Samuel Wintle	Last ¼ 18th C	Spoon maker (many sugar tongs)
SW	Samuel Wood	Mid 18th C	Specialist and prolific caster maker
S.W	" "	" "	
S·W	" "	" "	

MARK	MAKER	PERIOD	COMMENTS
Richard Syng	Late 17th/Early 18th C	Competent, but not great English holloware
Ann Tanqueray	2nd ¼ 18th C	Probably the greatest of all women silversmiths
David Tanqueray	1st ¼ 18th C	Very fine Huguenot work associated with his father-in-law, David Willaume
Thomas Bamford	c.2nd ¼ 18th C	Prolific maker of good, run-of-the-mill casters
Thomas Bradbury & Sons	Late 19th/Early 20th C	Sheffield manufacturers
" "	" "	
" "	" "	
Robert Timbrell & Joseph Bell	1st ¼ 18th C	Good holloware
Thomas Bumfriss & Orlando Jackson	2nd ½ 18th C	Good makers
Thomas Chawner	2nd ½ 18th C	Spoon maker
T Cox Savory	2nd ¼ 19th C	Large 19th C firm
Thomas & William Chawner	3rd ¼ 18th C	Specialist and very fine flatware makers
" "	" "	
" "	" "	
" "	" "	
Thomas Daniel	Last ¼ 18th C	Good, run-of-the-mill maker
" "	" "	
Thomas Dealtry	2nd ½ 18th C	Flatware and knife handles
Thomas Daniel & John Wall	Last ¼ 18th C	Good, run-of-the-mill makers
Thomas Tearle	1st ½ 18th C	Good, run-of-the-mill maker

MARK	MAKER	PERIOD	COMMENTS
	Thomas Farren	1st ½ 18th C	Very fine maker
	" " - post 1720 sterling mark	" "	
	Thos Folkingham - post 1720 sterling mark	1st ¼ 18th C	Wide range of fine silver
	Thomas Gilpin	Mid 18th C	A very fine goldsmith
	Thomas Heming	2nd ½ 18th C	Important maker; Royal goldsmith
	" "	" "	
	" "	" "	
	Thomas & George Hayter	1st ½ 19th C	Mostly spoon makers
	Thomas Hannam & John Crouch	2nd ½ 18th C	Very good makers
	Thomas Hannam & John Crouch (or Carter)	" "	Fine salvers
	Robert Timbrell	Late 17th/Early 18th C	Good English work
	Timothy Ley - pre 1697 and post 1720 sterling mark	Late 17th/Early 18th C	Standard English tankards and mugs
	Thomas Morley	Last ¼ 18th C	Small pieces
	Thomas Northcote	Late 18th C	Spoon maker
	Thomas Northcote & George Bourne	Late 18th/Early 19th C	Good, general work; usually smaller pieces
	Thomas Pitts	2nd ½ 18th C	Specialist in pierced work, epergnes, baskets, etc.
	Thomas Phipps & Edward Robinson	Last ¼ 18th C	Usually very fine boxes, etc., but can be found on large pieces
	" "	Late 18th/Early 19th C	
	Thomas Phipps, Edward Robinson & James Phipps	" "	

MARK	MAKER	PERIOD	COMMENTS
	Thomas, Walter & Henry Holland - late 19th C mark	Late 19th/Early 20th C	Important manufacturers
	Thomas Tearle - post 1720 sterling mark	1st ½ 18th C	Good run-of-the-mill maker
	Thomas Wallis	Last ¼ 18th C	Spoon maker
	″ ″	Late 18th/Early 19th C	
	Thomas Whipham	Mid 18th C	Prolific maker of good holloware, particularly coffee pots, teapots, tankards and mugs
	″ ″	″ ″	
	″ ″	″ ″	
	Thomas Whipham & Charles Wright	2nd ½ 18th C	Prolific makers of holloware, particularly coffee pots, teapots, tankards and mugs
	Edward Vincent	1st ½ 18th C	Very fine English craftsman, who could be naughty; he was into duty dodging after 1720 in a big way: be careful
	Walker & Hall - 20th C mark	20th C	Large Sheffield manufacturer
	Wakely & Wheeler - 20th C mark	20th C	Large manufacturers and silversmiths
	William Abdy	Last ¼ 18th C	Good, run-of-the-mill maker
	Joseph Ward	Late 17th/Early 18th C	Very good English work
	Sam Wastell	Early 18th C	Good English work
	″ ″	″ ″	
	Benjamin Watts	Late 17th/Early 18th C	Mostly spoons
	William Bateman	1st ½ 19th C	Very good (best of the Batemans)
	Walter Brind	2nd ½ 18th C	Prolific maker of good holloware
	″ ″	″ ″	
	William Burwash	Early 19th C	Good maker

MARK	MAKER	PERIOD	COMMENTS
	William Bateman & Daniel Ball	2nd ¼ 19th C	Prolific, general run-of-the-mill work
	" "	" "	
	Walter & John Barnard	Late 19th C	Major manufacturers
	William Burwash & Richard Sibley	1st ¼ 19th C	Very good makers
	William Cafe	3rd ¼ 18th C	Specialist candlestick maker
	William Chawner	1st ¼ 19th C	Prolific spoon maker
	William Comyns & Sons Ltd	2nd ½ 19th/Early 20th C	Large manufacturer
	" "	" "	
	William Cripps	Mid 18th C	Very fine work
	" "	" "	
	Wm Darker - post 1720 sterling mark	1st ½ 18th C	Good general maker, quite prolific
	William Eaton	Late 1st ¼/2nd ¼ 19th C	Spoon maker
	" "	" "	
	William Eley II	2nd ¼ 19th C	Spoon maker
	Robert Eley	Late 18th/Early 19th C	Spoon maker
	Saml Welder	1st ¼ 18th C	Prolific maker of casters
	William, Charles & Henry Eley	c.1824	Spoon makers
	William Eley & William Fearn	Late 18th/Early 19th C	Prolific spoon makers
	William Eley, William Fearn & William Chawner	1st ¼ 19th C	Prolific spoon makers
	William Fearn	2nd ½ 18th C	Prolific spoon maker

MARK	MAKER	PERIOD	COMMENTS
WF	William Fountain	Late 18th/Early 19th C	Good, general work
WF DP	William Fountain & Daniel Pontifex	Late 18th C	Good makers
WF PS	William Frisbee & Paul Storr	1792-3	First work of the highly important Paul Storr
WG	William Gould	Mid 18th C	Specialist candlestick maker
WG	" "	" "	
WG	" "	" "	
WG	William Grundy	Mid 18th C	Good holloware maker
WG	" "	" "	
WG	" "	" "	
WG	" "	" "	
WG	" "	" "	
E WG F	William Grundy & Edward Fernell	Mid 18th C	Good, run-of-the-mill makers
WG JL	William Gibson & John Langman	Late 19th/Early 20th C	Retail jewellers and silversmiths
W.G J.L	" "	" "	
WH	William Holmes	Last ¼ 18th C	Good maker
S⁵ W A L⁵	William Hutton & Sons Ltd	2nd ½ 19th/Early 20th C	Large Sheffield manufacturers
WH ND	William Holmes & Nich Dumee	Last ¼ 18th C	Good makers
W.H.S	Searle & Co	20th C	Retailers
WI	George Wickes	Mostly 2nd ¼ 18th C	Very important English goldsmith
WI	Starling Wilford	2nd ¼ 18th C	Mostly casters
WI	David Willaume	Late 17th/Early 18th C	Very important Huguenot
WI	David Willaume II	2nd ¼ 18th C	Important Huguenot

MARK	MAKER	PERIOD	COMMENTS
WK	William Kidney	Mid 18th C	A fine goldsmith, often underrated
WK	„ „	„ „	
W·J B·J M·B·S	Edward Barnard & Sons Ltd	20th C	Major manufacturers
WP	Wm Peaston	Mid 18th C	Specialist salver maker
W·P	William Plummer	3rd ¼ 18th C	Specialist in pierced work
WP	William Pitts	Last ¼ 18th C	Specialist in pierced work, epergnes, baskets, etc.
W·P I·P	William Pitts & Joseph Preedy	End 18th C	Pierced work, baskets, epergnes, etc.
W·P J·P	W & J Priest	Late 18th C	Standard work
WR&H·	Walker & Hall - late 19th C mark	Late 19th/Early 20th C	Large Sheffield manufacturers
WRS	W R Smily	Mid 19th C	Spoon maker
W·S	William Shaw	3rd ¼ 18th C	Good holloware maker
WS	William Spackman - post 1720 sterling mark	1st ¼ 18th C	Good run-of-the-mill general work
W·S	William Sumner	Early 19th C	Spoon maker
WS C·S	Walter & Charles Sissons	Late 19th C	Sheffield manufacturers
WS G·S	William & George Sissons	3rd ¼ 19th C	
WS RC	William Sumner & Richard Crossley	Last ¼ 18th C	Good, run-of-the-mill makers
W·S P	William Shaw & William Priest	3rd ¼ 18th C	Makers of good holloware
W·T	Walter Thornhill (Thornhill & Co)	19th C	Retailer of very fine pieces
WT RA	William Theobalds & Robert Atkinson	2nd ¼ 19th C	Mostly fine flatware
WV	William Vincent	Last ¼ 18th C	Run-of-the-mill teapots, etc.

Birmingham

Cycles of Hallmarks

CYCLE I

	LION PASSANT	ANCHOR	DATE LETTER	DUTY MARK
1773-74	🦁	⚓	A	
1774-75	"	"	B	
1775-76	"	"	C	
1776-77	"	"	D	
1777-78	"	"	E	
1778-79	"	"	F	
1779-80	"	"	G	
1780-81	"	"	H	
1781-82	"	"	I	
1782-83	"	"	K	
1783-84	"	"	L	
Up to 30 Nov. 1784	"	"	M	
From 1 Dec. 1784-July 1785	"	"	"	👑
1785-86	"	"	N	"
1786-87	"	"	O	👑
1787-88	"	"	P	"
1788-89	"	"	Q	"
1789-90	"	"	R	"
1790-91	"	"	S	"
1791-92	"	"	T	"
1792-93	"	"	U	"
1793-94	"	"	V	"
1794-95	"	"	W	"
1795-96	"	"	X	"
1796-97	"	"	Y	"
1797	"	"	Z	"
1797-98*	"	"	"	👑👑
	"	"	"	👑

CYCLE II

	LION PASSANT	ANCHOR	DATE LETTER	DUTY MARK
1798-99	🦁	⚓	a	👑
1799-1800	"	"	b	"
1800-1 ‡	"	"	c	"
1801-2	"	"	d	"
1802-3	"	"	e	"
1803-4	"	"	f	"
1804-5	"	"	g	"
1805-6	"	"	h	"
1806-7	"	"	i	"
1807-8	"	"	j	"
1808-9	"	"	k	"
1809-10	"	"	l	👑
1810-11	"	"	m	"
1811-12	"	"	n	"
1812-13	"	"	o	👑
1813-14	"	"	p	"
1814-15	"	"	q	"
1815-16	"	"	r	"
1816-17	"	"	s	"
1817-18	"	"	t	"
1818-19	"	"	u	"
1819-20	"	"	v	"
GEO.IV 1820-21	"	"	w	"
1821-22	"	"	x	"
1822-23	"	"	y	"
1823-24	"	"	z	"

* Double duty.

‡ On plate of 1801 to 1811 the King's head mark is frequently found in a stamp of oval shape, and on plate of 1812 to 1825 it is sometimes in a foliated stamp as shown at 1797-98 and 1809-10.

CYCLE III

	LION PASSANT	ANCHOR	DATE LETTER	DUTY MARK
1824-25	🦁	⚓	𝔄	👑
1825-26	"	"	𝔅	"
1826-27	"	"	ℭ	👑
1827-28	"	"	𝔇	"
1828-29	"	"	𝔈	"
1829-30	"	"	𝔉	👑
WM.IV 1830-31	"	"	𝔊	"
1831-32	"	"	𝔥	👑
1832-33	"	"	𝔍	"
1833-34	"	"	𝔎	"
1834-35	"	"	𝔏	👑
1835-36	"	"	𝔐	"
1836-37	"	"	𝔑	"
VICT. 1837-38	"	"	𝔇	"
1838-39*	"	"	𝔓	👑
1839-40	"	"	𝔔	"
1840-41	"	"	𝔑	"
1841-42	"	"	𝔖	"
1842-43	"	"	𝔗	"
1843-44	"	"	𝔘	"
1844-45	"	"	𝔘	"
1845-46	"	"	𝔚	"
1846-47	"	"	𝔵	"
1847-48	"	"	𝔜	"
1848-49	"	"	𝔷	"

CYCLE IV

	LION PASSANT	ANCHOR	DATE LETTER	DUTY MARK
1849-50	🦁	⚓	A	👑
1850-51	"	"	B	"
1851-52	"	"	C	"
1852-53	"	"	D	"
1853-54	"	"	E	"
1854-55	"	"	F	"
1855-56	"	"	G	"
1856-57	"	"	H	"
1857-58	"	"	I	"
1858-59	"	"	J	"
1859-60	"	"	K	"
1860-61	"	"	L	"
1861-62	"	"	M	"
1862-63	"	"	N	"
1863-64	"	"	O	"
1864-65	"	"	P	"
1865-66	"	"	Q	"
1866-67 †	"	"	R	"
1867-68	"	"	S	"
1868-69	"	"	T	"
1869-70	"	"	U	"
1870-71	"	"	V	"
1871-72	"	"	W	"
1872-73	"	"	X	"
1873-74	"	"	Y	"
1874-75	"	"	Z	"

* On plate of the early part of 1838-39 the head of King William is sometimes found stamped, although Queen Victoria succeeded to the throne in 1837.

† 🅕 was struck on imported wares in addition to the marks shown from 1867-1904.

CYCLE V

	LION PASSANT	ANCHOR	DATE LETTER	DUTY MARK
1875-76	🦁	⚓	𝖆	👑
1876-77	"	"	𝖇	"
1877-78	"	"	𝖈	"
1878-79	"	"	𝖉	"
1879-80	"	"	𝖊	"
1880-81	"	"	𝖋	"
1881-82	"	"	𝖌	"
1882-83	"	"	𝖍	"
1883-84	"	"	𝖎	"
1884-85	"	"	𝖐	"
1885-86	"	"	𝖑	"
1886-87	"	"	𝖒	"
1887-88	"	"	𝖓	"
1888-89	"	"	𝖔	"
Up to 1 May 1890	"	"	𝖕	"
2 May to July 1890	"	"	"	
1890-91	"	"	𝖖	
1891-92	"	"	𝖗	
1892-93	"	"	𝖘	
1893-94	"	"	𝖙	
1894-95	"	"	𝖚	
1895-96	"	"	𝖛	
1896-97	"	"	𝖜	
1897-98	"	"	𝖝	
1898-99	"	"	𝖞	
1899-1900	"	"	𝖟	

CYCLE VI

	ANCHOR	LION PASSANT	DATE LETTER
1900-1	⚓	🦁	𝕒
EDW.VII 1901-2	"	"	𝕓
1902-3	"	"	𝕔
1903-4	"	"	𝕕
1904-5	"	"	𝕖
1905-6	"	"	𝕗
1906-7	"	"	𝕘
1907-8	"	"	𝕙
1908-9	"	"	𝕚
1909-10	"	"	𝕜
GEO.V 1910-11	"	"	𝕝
1911-12	"	"	𝕞
1912-13	"	"	𝕟
1913-14	"	"	𝕠
1914-15	"	"	𝕡
1915-16	"	"	𝕢
1916-17	"	"	𝕣
1917-18	"	"	𝕤
1918-19	"	"	𝕥
1919-20	"	"	𝕦
1920-21	"	"	𝕧
1921-22	"	"	𝕨
1922-23	"	"	𝕩
1923-24	"	"	𝕪
1924-25	"	"	𝕫

CYCLE VII

	ANCHOR	LION PASSANT	DATE LETTER
1925-26	⚓	🦁	A
1926-27	"	"	B
1927-28	"	"	C
1928-29	"	"	D
1929-30	"	"	E
1930-31	"	"	F
1931-32	"	"	G
1932-33	"	"	H
1933-34	"	"	J
1934-35*	"	"	K
1935-36*	"	"	L
EDW.VIII 1936-37	"	"	M
GEO.VI 1937-38	"	"	N
1938-39	"	"	O
1939-40	"	"	P
1940-41	"	"	Q
1941-42	"	"	R
1942-43	"	"	S
1943-44	"	"	T
1944-45	"	"	U
1945-46	"	"	V
1946-47	"	"	W
1947-48	"	"	X
1948-49	"	"	Y
1949-50	"	"	Z

CYCLE VIII

	ANCHOR	LION PASSANT	DATE LETTER
1950-51	⚓	🦁	A
1951-52	"	"	B
ELIZ.II 1952-53 ‡	"	"	C
1953-54 ‡	"	"	D
1954-55	"	"	E
1955-56	"	"	F
1956-57	"	"	G
1957-58	"	"	H
1958-59	"	"	J
1959-60	"	"	K
1960-61	"	"	L
1961-62	"	"	M
1962-63	"	"	N
1963-64	"	"	O
1964-65	"	"	P
1965-66	"	"	Q
1966-67	"	"	R
1967-68	"	"	S
1968-69	"	"	T
1969-70	"	"	U
1970-71	"	"	V
1971-72	"	"	W
1972-73	"	"	X
1973-74	⚓	🦁	Y
Up to 31 Dec.1974	⚓	🦁	Z

* There was an optional Silver Jubilee mark for these two years.

‡ There was an optional Coronation mark for these years.

CYCLE IX

	ANCHOR	LION PASSANT	DATE LETTER					
1975	⚓	🦁	𝓐					
1976	"	"	𝓑					
1977*	"	"	𝓒					
1978	"	"	𝓓					
1979	"	"	𝓔					
1980	"	"	𝓕					
1981	"	"	𝓖					
1982	"	"	𝓗					
1983	"	"	𝓘					
1984	"	"	𝓚					
1985	"	"	𝓛					
1986	"	"	𝓜					
1987	"	"	𝓝					
1988	"	"	𝓞					
1989	"	"	𝓟					
1990	"	"	𝓠					
1991	"	"	𝓡					

* There is an optional Silver Jubilee mark for this year.

PLATINUM 1975

	ANCHOR	PLATINUM MARK	DATE LETTER
Date as Above	⊞	⬠	𝓐

GOLD MARKS

Since 1824, gold has been assayed at Birmingham in the same way as at London with the obvious difference of the anchor replacing the leopard's head.

As an example, the range of Birmingham gold marks for 1920-21 is given in the table on the right.

22ct.	👑	22	⚓	V
18ct	"	18	"	".
15ct.	15	·625	"	"
12ct.	12	·5	"	"
9ct.	9	375	"	"

IMPORT MARKS FROM 1904 ON

1904-32

	IMPORTED GOLD				IMPORTED SILVER		
22ct.	△	22 ·916	+ Date letter & sponsor's mark	Britannia	△	·9584	+ Date letter & sponsor's mark
20ct.	"	20 ·833	"	Sterling	"	·925	"
18ct.	"	18 ·75	"				
15ct.	"	15 ·625	"				
12ct.	"	12 ·5	"				
9ct.	"	9 375	"				

1932-74*

	GOLD			SILVER
22ct.	△	22 ·916	+ Date letter & sponsor's mark	(As 1904-32)
18ct.	"	18 ·750	"	
14ct.	"	14 ·585	"	
9ct.	"	9 ·375	"	

From 1975 on

Platinum	△	950	+ Date letter & sponsor's mark
Gold 22ct.	△	916	"
18ct.	"	750	"
14ct.	"	585	"
9ct.	"	375	"
Silver Britannia	△	925	"
Sterling	"	958	"

* In 1932 and from then on 14ct. replaced 15ct. and 12ct.

CONVENTION MARKS (Birmingham) 1976 on

PRECIOUS METAL	ASSAY OFFICE MARK	COMMON CONTROL MARK	FINENESS MARK
Platinum		950	950
Gold 18ct.	"	750	750
14ct.	"	585	585
9ct.	"	375	375
Sterling		925	925

Convention marking on imported wares

PRECIOUS METAL	ASSAY OFFICE MARK	COMMON CONTROL MARK	FINENESS MARK
Platinum	△	950	950
Gold 18ct.	△	750	750
14ct.	"	585	585
9ct.	"	375	375
Silver (Sterling)	△	925	925

MARK	MAKER	PERIOD	COMMENTS
	A & J Zimmerman Ltd	20th C	Manufacturer
	" "	" "	
	Adie Brothers	20th C	Large manufacturers
	Alexander Clark & Co	20th C	Manufacturers
	" "	" "	
	A E Jones	20th C	Manufacturers. Their Art Nouveau is collected although not top flight. More recently pieces designed by Eric Clements for the firm are very interesting
B.C.	Bernard Cuzner	1st ½ 20th C	Interesting work
	Barker Ellis Silver Co	2nd ½ 20th C	Manufacturers
	Birmingham Guild of Handicraft	End 19th/Early 20th C	Interesting Arts and Crafts
B.G.L?	" "	" "	
C&B	Cocks & Bettridge	Early 19th C	Maker of boxes, vinaigrettes, caddy spoons, etc.
C.J.S	Cyril Shiner	20th C	Particularly interesting Art Deco
CT	Charles Thomas	2nd ½ 20th C	Interesting Art Deco
D&F	Deakin & Francis Ltd	20th C	Manufacturers
D & H	Deakin & Harrison	1st ½ 20th C	Manufacturers
D & H	" "	" "	
D&H	" "	" "	
D & S	Deykin & Son	End 19th/Early 20th C	Manufacturers

MARK	MAKER	PERIOD	COMMENTS
	Elkington & Co Ltd	19th C	Quality is always superb. Designs vary from run-of-the-mill commercial to extremely important by people like Morel-Ladueil and Dr C Dresser
	" "	Mid 19th C	
	" "	" "	Important 19th C firm with very wide range
	" "	19th C	
	" "	Late 19th C	
	" "	20th C	
	Elkington Mason & Co	19th C	
ES	Edward Smith	Mid 19th C	Boxes, etc.
FC	Francis Clark	Mid 19th C	Small work
NH	Nathan & Hayes	End 19th/Early 20th C	Manufacturers
GU	George Unite	Late 19th/Early 20th C	Wide range of small pieces
GW	Gervase Wheeler	Mid 19th C	Boxes, etc.
H&H	Hukin & Heath Ltd	Late 19th/Early 20th C	Most important for pieces by them designed by Dr C Dresser (late 1870s and 1880s)
H&H	" "	" "	
H&H	" "	Early 20th C	
H&H	" "	2nd ¼ 20th C	
H&T	Hilliard & Thomason	2nd ½ 19th C	Card cases, caddy spoons, etc.
HM	H. Matthews	Late 19th/Early 20th C	Wide range
IB	John Bettridge	Early 19th C	Boxes, etc.
IS	John Shaw	Late 18th/Early 19th C	Boxes, vinaigrettes
IT	Joseph Taylor	Late 18th/Early 19th C	Prolific maker of small pieces

MARK	MAKER	PERIOD	COMMENTS
JB / **JB**	Joseph Bettridge / " "	2nd ¼ 19th C / " "	Small work
J.B.C &S / **JBC &S Lᵈ** / **J.B.C B**	J B Chatterley & Sons / " " / " "	End 19th/Early 20th C / " " / " "	Manufacturers
J H.&Cᵒ	John Hardman & Co	Mid 19th/Early 20th C	Important Gothic revival pieces designed by A W N Pugin
JL	John Lawrence & Co	Mid 19th/Early 20th C	Small work
JTH / **JHM**	Heath & Middleton	Late 19th C	Most important for pieces designed for them by Dr C Dresser (late 1870s and 1880s)
J.W / **JW**	Joseph Willmore / " "	1st ½ 19th C / " "	Prolific maker of boxes, vinaigrettes, caddy spoons, etc.
L&C	Lea & Clark	Early 19th C	Small work
L&C	W. Lea & Co	Early 19th C	Boxes, vinaigrettes, etc.
L&Cᵒ	Ledsam & Vale	Early 19th C	Boxes, etc.
L&Cᵒ	Liberty & Co	End 19th C/20th C	Important Art Nouveau
LS&Cᵒ	L. Smith & Co	20th C	Manufacturer
LV&W	Ledsam, Vale & Wheeler	2nd ¼ 19th C	Boxes
MB	Matthew Boulton	Late 18th/Early 19th C	Very important maker; wide range
MB IF / **M B I F**	Matthew Boulton & John Fothergill / " "	Late 18th C / " "	
ML / **M** / **ML**	Matthew Linwood / " " / " "	Late 18th/Early 19th C / " " / " "	Boxes, vinaigrettes, caddy spoons, etc.

MARK	MAKER	PERIOD	COMMENTS
N&H	Nathan & Hayes	Late 19th/Early 20th C	Wide range
NM	Nathaniel Mills	Mid 19th C	Famous maker of fine boxes, vinaigrettes, etc.
RW	Robert Welch	2nd ½ 20th C	Important modern designer
RW	" "	" "	
RW	" "	" "	
RW	" "	" "	
SGM	Stanley Morris	Mid/2nd ½ 20th C	Designer/craftsman; interesting work
SP	Samuel Pemberton	Late 18th/Early 19th C	Prolific maker of boxes, vinaigrettes, caddy spoons, etc.
S P	" "	" "	
SP	" "	" "	
SP	" "	" "	
WH&Co	W Hutton & Sons Ltd	20th C	Manufacturer
SW	Silver Workshop	2nd ½ 20th C	Interesting designs
T&P	Taylor & Perry	2nd ¼ 19th C	Boxes, card cases, caddy spoons, etc.
TK&S	Toye Kenning & Spencer	20th C	Prolific makers of regalia, medals, etc.
TS	Thomas Shaw	Late 1st ¼/2nd ¼ 19th C	Boxes, etc.
TW	Thomas Willmore	Late 18th/Early 19th C	Buckle maker
V.B&S	Vale Bros & Sermon	Late 19th/Early 20th C	Manufacturer
Y&W	Yapp & Woodward	Mid 19th C	Boxes, etc.
Z	A & J Zimmerman	20th C	

CHAPTER III
Chester

Cycles of Hallmarks

APPROXIMATE DATE	MARK
1678	
c.1683	
1685	
c.1697-1701	

The above is a selection of early Chester marks. Prior to the mid 17th century makers' marks only appear to have been struck. See *Jackson's* pp.389/390 for full list.

CHESTER HALLMARKS
CYCLE I

DATE	CITY ARMS	CITY CREST	DATE LETTER
1 Feb. 1686-87 -2 June 1690			
2 June 1690-92	"	"	
1692-93 or 1694	"	"	
1693 or 1694-1695	"	"	
1695	"	"	
1696	"	"	
Until 25 March 1697*	"	"	

* Date-letter conjectured.

CYCLE II

	BRIT-ANNIA	LION'S HEAD ERASED	CITY ARMS	DATE LETTER
29 Sept. 1701				A
1702-7 April 1703	"	"	"	B
7 April 1703-4	"	"	"	C
1704-5	"	"	"	D
1705-6	"	"	"	E
1706-7	"	"	"	F
1707-8	"	"	"	G
1708-9	"	"	"	H
1709-10	"	"	"	I
1710-11	"	"	"	K
9 July 1711-9 July 1712	"	"	"	L
1712-13	"	"	"	M
1713-14		"	"	N
1714-15	"	"	"	O
1715-16	"	"	"	P
1716-17	"	"	"	Q
1717-18	"	"	"	R
1718-19	"	"	"	S
1719-1 June 1720	"	"	"	T

	LION PASSANT	LEOPARD'S HEAD	CITY ARMS	DATE LETTER
2 June 1720-9 July 1720				T
9 July 1720-21	"	"	"	U
1721-22	"	"	"	V
1722-23	"	"	"	W
1723-24	"	"	"	X
9 July 1724-25*	"	"	"	Y
1725-26*	"	"		Z

CYCLE III

	LION PASSANT	LEOPARD'S HEAD	CITY ARMS	DATE LETTER
9 July 1726-*† 10 July 1727				A
10 July 1727-*† 9 July 1728	"	"	"	B
9 July 1728-*† 9 July 1729	"	"	"	C
9 July 1729-† 9 July 1730		"	"	D
9 July 1730-† 9 July 1731		"	"	E
9 July 1731-10 July 1732	"		"	F
10 July 1732-9 July 1733	"	"	"	G
9 July 1733-9 July 1734	"	"	"	H
9 July 1734-9 July 1735	"	"	"	I
9 July 1735-9 July 1736	"		"	K
9 July 1736-9 July 1737	"	"	"	L
9 July 1737-10 July 1738	"	"	"	M
10 July 1738-9 July 1739	"	"	"	N
9 July 1739-9 July 1740	"	"	"	O
9 July 1740-§ 9 July 1741	"	"	"	P
9 July 1741-9 July 1742	"	"	"	Q
9 July 1742-‡ 9 July 1743	"	"	"	R
9 July 1743-9 July 1744	"	"	"	S
9 July 1744-9 July 1745	"	"	"	T
9 July 1745-9 July 1746	"	"	"	U
9 July 1746-9 July 1747	"	"	"	V
9 July 1747-9 July 1748	"	"	"	W
9 July 1748-10 July 1749	"	"	"	X
10 July 1749-9 July 1750	"	"	"	Y
9 July 1750-9 July 1751	"	"	"	Z

*   Alternative lion passant 1724-29

§   Alternative City Arms used in 1741

†   Alternative leopard's head 1726-31

‡   A short bodied lion with undipped corners to the punch may be found in 1742.

CYCLE IV

	LION PASSANT	LEOPARD'S HEAD*	CITY ARMS	DATE LETTER
9 July 1751-9 July 1752	[lion]	[leopard]	[arms]	a
9 July 1752-20 July 1753	"	"	"	b
20 July 1753-20 July 1754	"	"	"	c
20 July 1754-21 July 1755	"	"	"	d
21 July 1755-21 July 1756	"	"	"	e
21 July 1756-20 July 1757	"	"	"	f
20 July 1757-§ 20 July 1758	"	"	"	g
20 July 1758-20 July 1759	"	"	"	h
20 July 1759-20 July 1760	"	"	"	i
20 July 1760-20 July 1761	"	"	[arms]	k
20 July 1761-20 July 1762	"	"	"	l
20 July 1762-20 July 1763	[lion]	"	"	m
20 July 1763-20 July 1764	"	"	"	n
20 July 1764-20 July 1765	"	"	"	o
20 July 1765-20 July 1766	"	"	"	p
20 July 1766-20 July 1767	"	"	"	q
20 July 1767-20 July 1768	"	"	"	R
20 July 1768-20 July 1769	"	"	"	S
20 July 1769-20 July 1770	"	"	"	T
20 July 1770-20 July 1771	"	"	"	U
20 July 1771-20 July 1772	"	"	"	V
20 July 1772-20 July 1773	"	"	"	W
20 July 1773-20 July 1774	"	"	"	X
20 July 1774-20 July 1775	"	"	"	Y
20 July 1775-20 July 1776	"	"	"	Z

CYCLE V

	LION PASSANT	LEOPARD'S HEAD*	CITY ARMS	DATE LETTER	DUTY MARK
20 July 1776-20 July 1777	[lion]	[leopard]	[arms]	a	
20 July 1777-20 July 1778	"	"	"	b	
20 July 1778-20 July 1779 †	"	[leopard]	[arms]	c	
20 July 1779-20 July 1780 †	"	"	"	d	
20 July 1780-20 July 1781 †	"	"	"	e	
20 July 1781-20 July 1782 †	[lion]	"	"	f	
20 July 1782-20 July 1783	"	[leopard]	[arms]	g	
20 July 1783-31 Nov. 1784	"	"	"	h	
1 Dec. 1784-28 Jan. 1785 ‡	"	"	"	"	[duty head]
28 Jan. 1785-20 July 1785	"	"	"	i	"
20 July 1785-20 July 1786	"	"	"	k	"
" " "	"	"	"	"	[duty head]
20 July 1786-20 July 1787	"	"	"	l	"
20 July 1787-20 July 1788	"	"	"	m	"
20 July 1788-20 July 1789	"	"	"	n	"
20 July 1789-20 July 1790	"	"	"	o	"
20 July 1790-20 July 1791	"	"	"	p	"
20 July 1791-20 July 1792	"	"	"	q	"
20 July 1792-20 July 1793	"	"	"	r	"
20 July 1793-20 July 1794	"	"	"	s	"
20 July 1794-20 July 1795 **	"	[leopard]	"	t	"
20 July 1795-20 July 1796 **	"	"	"	U	"
20 July 1796-[20 July 1797]	"	"	"	V	"

* The leopard's head punch used 1735-1778 becomes very worn during this period. [symbol]

§ Alternative City Arms used in 1757. [symbol]

† Alternative leopard's head 1778-82. [symbol]

‡ Duty mark incuse.

** Leopard's head as in 1782 may be found.

CYCLE VI

	LION PASSANT	LEOPARD'S HEAD	CITY ARMS	DATE LETTER	DUTY* MARK
[20 July 1797-1798]	(lion)	(leopard)	(city arms)	A	(duty)
[20 July 1798-20 July 1799]	"	"	"	B	"
[20 July 1799-20 July 1800 †]	(lion)	(leopard)	"	C	"
[20 July 1800-20 July 1801 †]	"	"	"	D	"
[20 July 1801-20 July 1802]	"	"	"	E	"
1802-1803	"	"	"	F	"
1803-1804	"	"	"	G	"
1804-1805	"	"	"	H	"
1805-1806	"	"	"	I	"
1806-1807	(lion)	(leopard)	(city arms)	K	"
1807-5 July 1808	"	"	"	L	
5 July 1808-5 July 1809	"	"	"	M	"
5 July 1809-1810	"	(leopard)	(city arms)	N	"
1810-5 July 1811	"	"	"	O	"
5 July 1811-1812	"	"	"	P	"
1812-5 July 1813	"	"	"	Q	"
5 July 1813-5 July 1814	"	"	"	R	"
5 July 1814-1815	"	"	"	S	"
1815-1816	"	"	"	T	"
1816-5 July 1817	"	"	"	U	"
5 July 1817-5 July 1818	"	"	"	V	"

CYCLE VII

	LION PASSANT	LEOPARD'S HEAD	CITY ARMS	DATE LETTER	DUTY* MARK
5 July 1818-7 Sept. 1819	(lion)	(leopard)	(city arms)	A	(duty)
7 Sept. 1819-10 May 1820	(lion)	(leopard)	"	B	"
10 May 1820-8 Nov. 1821	"	"	"	C	"
8 Nov. 1821-5 July 1823 ‡	"	(leopard)	"	D	"
5 July 1823-5 July 1824	"	"	(city arms)	E	"
5 July 1824-5 July 1825§	"	(leopard)	"	F	"
5 July 1825-5 July1826§	"	"	"	G	"
5 July 1826-5 July 1827§	"	"	"	H	"
5 July 1827-5 July 1828§	"	"	"	I	"
5 July 1828-5 July 1829§	"	"	"	K	"
5 July 1829-5 July 1830§	(lion)	"	"	L	"
5 July 1830-5 July 1831§	"	"	"	M	"
5 July 1831-5 July 1832§	"	"	"	N	"
5 July 1832-5 July 1833§	"	"	"	O	"
5 July 1833-5 July 1834	"	"	(city arms)	P	"
5 July 1834-5 July 1835	(lion)	"	"	Q	"
5 July 1835-5 July 1836	"	"	"	R	"
5 July 1836-5 July 1837	"	"	"	S	"
5 July 1837-5 July 1838	"	"	(city arms)	T	(duty)
5 July 1838-5 July 1839	"	"	"	U	"

* Other known duty marks used between 1797-1837.

† The lion passant guardant and leopard's head as used in 1797 may still be found.

‡ Lion also appears in plain rectangular punch in 1821-23. The leopard's head may be found as in 1819. There was also a variant of the city arms.

§ Leopard's head may be found as in 1821.

CYCLE VIII

	LION PASSANT	TOWN MARK	DATE LETTER	DUTY MARK
1839-40	🦁	🛡	𝕬	👑
1840-41	"	"	𝕭	"
1841-42	"	"	𝕮	"
1842-43	"	"	𝕯	"
1843-44	"	"	𝕰	"
1844-45	"	"	𝕱	"
1845-46	"	"	𝕲	"
1846-47	"	"	𝕳	"
1847-48	"	"	𝕴	"
1848-49	"	"	𝕶	"
1849-50	"	"	𝕷	"
1850-51	"	"	𝕸	"
1851-52	"	"	𝕹	"
1852-53	"	"	𝕺	"
1853-54	"	"	𝕻	"
1854-55	"	"	𝕼	"
1855-56	"	"	𝕽	"
1856-57	"	"	𝕾	"
1857-58	"	"	𝕿	"
1858-59	"	"	𝖀	"
1859-60	"	"	𝖁	"
1860-61	"	"	𝖂	"
1861-62	"	"	𝖃	"
1862-63	"	"	𝖄	"
1863-64	"	"	𝖅	"

CYCLE IX

	LION PASSANT	TOWN MARK	DATE LETTER	DUTY MARK
1864-65	🦁	🛡	𝖆	👑
1865-66	"	"	𝖇	"
1866-67*	"	"	𝖈	"
1867-68	"	"	𝖉	"
1868-69	"	"	𝖊	"
1869-70	"	"	𝖋	"
1870-71	"	"	𝖌	"
1871-72	"	"	𝖍	"
1872-73	"	"	𝖎	"
1873-74	"	"	𝖐	"
1874-75	"	"	𝖑	"
1875-76	"	"	𝖒	"
1876-77	"	"	𝖓	"
1877-78	"	"	𝖔	"
1878-79	"	"	𝖕	"
1879-80	"	"	𝖖	"
1880-81	"	"	𝖗	"
1881-82	"	"	𝖘	"
1882-83	"	"	𝖙	"
1883-84	"	"	𝖚	"

* **F** Struck in addition to the above on imported wares 1867-1904.

CYCLE X

	LION PASSANT	TOWN MARK	DATE LETTER	DUTY MARK
1884-85	🦁	🛡	**A**	👑
1885-86	"	"	**B**	"
1886-87	"	"	**C**	"
1887-88	"	"	**D**	"
1888-89	"	"	**E**	"
1889-1 May 1890	"	"	**F**	"
2 May 1890 5 July 1890	"	"	"	
1890-91	"	"	**G**	
1891-92	"	"	**H**	
1892-93	"	"	**I**	
1893-94	"	"	**K**	
1894-95	"	"	**L**	
1895-96	"	"	**M**	
1896-97	"	"	**N**	
1897-98	"	"	**O**	
1898-99	"	"	**P**	
1899-1900	"	"	**Q**	
1900-1	"	"	**R**	

CYCLE XI

	LION PASSANT GUARDANT	TOWN MARK	DATE LETTER
EDW.VII 1901-2	🦁	🛡	*A*
1902-3	"	"	*B*
1903-4	"	"	*C*
1904-5	"	"	*D*
1905-6	"	"	*E*
1906-7	"	"	*F*
1907-8	"	"	*G*
1908-9	"	"	*H*
1909-10	"	"	*I*
GEO.V 1910-11	"	"	*K*
1911-12	"	"	*L*
1912-13	"	"	*M*
1913-14	"	"	*N*
1914-15	"	"	*O*
1915-16	"	"	*P*
1916-17	"	"	*Q*
1917-18	"	"	*R*
1918-19	"	"	*S*
1919-20	"	"	*T*
1920-21	"	"	*U*
1921-22	"	"	*V*
1922-23	"	"	*W*
1923-24	"	"	*X*
1924-25	"	"	*Y*
1925-26	"	"	*Z*

CYCLE XII

	LION PASSANT GUARDANT	TOWN MARK	DATE LETTER
1926-27	🦁	🛡	**a**
1927-28	"	"	**k**
1928-29	"	"	**c**
1929-30	"	"	**d**
1930-31	"	"	**e**
1931-32	"	"	**ff**
1932-33	"	"	**g**
1933-34	"	"	**h**
1934-35*	"	"	**i**
1935-36*	"	"	**k**
EDW.VIII 1936-37	"	"	**l**
GEO.VI 1937-38	"	"	**m**
1938-39	"	"	**n**
1939-40	"	"	**o**
1940-41	"	"	**p**
1941-42	"	"	**q**
1942-43	"	"	**r**
1943-44	"	"	**s**
1944-45	"	"	**t**
1945-46	"	"	**u**
1946-47	"	"	**v**
1947-48	"	"	**w**
1948-49	"	"	**x**
1949-50	"	"	**y**
1950-51	"	"	**z**

CYCLE XIII

	LION PASSANT GUARDANT	TOWN MARK	DATE LETTER
1951-52	🦁	🛡	**A**
ELIZ.II 1952-53 †	"	"	**B**
1953-54 †	"	"	**C**
1954-55	"	"	**D**
1955-56	"	"	**E**
1956-57	"	"	**F**
1957-58	"	"	**G**
1958-59	"	"	**H**
1959-60	"	"	**J**
1960-61	"	"	**K**
1961-62	"	"	**L**
1 July- 24 Aug. 1962	"	"	**M**

* Jubilee mark optional.

† Coronation mark optional.

The Chester Assay Office closed on 24 August, 1962.

MARKS ON CHESTER GOLD WARES PRIOR TO 1932

Examples for 1907

22ct.	
18ct.	
15ct.	
12ct.	
9ct.	

IMPORT MARKS (Post 1904)

From 1904 to the closure of the Assay Office in 1962 an 'acorn and two leaves' replaced the 'letter F' and the 'town mark' for both gold (canted square punch) and silver (oval punch).

	IMPORTED GOLD		
22ct.		916	+ date letter and sponsor's mark
20ct.	"	833	"
18ct.	"	75	"
15ct.	"	625	"
12ct.	"	5	"
9ct.	"	375	"

	IMPORTED SILVER		
Britannia		9584	+ date letter and sponsor's mark
Sterling	"	925	"

1932-62

The alteration in gold standards in 1932 led to the following changes to the gold import marks.

	IMPORTED GOLD		
22ct.		916	+ date letter and sponsor's mark
18ct.	"	750	"
14ct.	"	585	"
9ct.	"	375	"

Chester Makers' Marks

One family, the Richardsons, produced the majority of silver in 18th C Chester. Since they nearly all were Richardsons, and variations of makers' mark RR are numerous, a selection is included below. (Reference to both *Jackson's* Chester section and Maurice Ridgway's *Chester Silver 1727-1837* is strongly recommended.) After the Richardsons the Lowes are the most prolific and are still in Chester today.

MARK	MAKER	PERIOD	COMMENTS
	George Lowe I	Late 18th/Early 19th C	Large variety of plate
	George Lowe II	Late 1st ¼/Early 2nd ¼ 19th C	Large variety of plate
	George Lowe, jun	Mid 19th C	Large variety of plate
	John Lowe	Mid 19th C	Flatware
	John Sutter (Liverpool)	2nd ¼ 19th C	Flatware
	Richard Richardson I	1st ¼ 18th C	Large variety of plate
	Robert Lowe	Mid 19th C	Flatware
	Richard Richardson I & II	Early 2nd ¼ 18th C	Large variety of plate
	Richard Richardson II	Mid 18th C	Large variety of plate
	" "	" "	
	" "	" "	
	Richard Richardson II & III	3rd ¼ 18th C	Large variety of plate
	Richard Richardson IV	4th ¼ 18th C	Large variety of plate

Note: Much work from the mid 19th C and on is found with Chester marks. The vast majority of this was only hallmarked there, not made there. Most originated from manufacturing centres of which Birmingham was the most important.

CHAPTER IV

Dublin

Cycles of Hallmarks

Where more than one version of a mark is shown in the following cycles, these are variations and will not be found together on one piece.

CYCLE I

CYCLE II

	HARP CROWNED	DATE LETTER
CHAS.I 1636		
1638-39*		𝐀
1639-40*		𝐁
1640-41	"	𝐂
1641-42	"	𝐃
1642-43		E
1643-44		F
1644-45*		G
1645-46*		H
1646-47*		I
1647-48*		K
1648-49*		L
COMWTH. 1649-50		M
1650-51		N
1651-52		O
1652-53		P
1653-54		Q
1654-55*		𝐑
1655-56*		𝐒
1656-57*	"	𝐓
1657-58		U

	HARP CROWNED	DATE LETTER
1658-59		a
1659-60*		b
CHAS.II 1660-61		c
1661-62		d
1662-63		e
1663-64*		f
1664-65	"	g
1665-66		h
1666-67		i
1667-68		k
1668-69		l
1669-70		m
1670-71		n
1671-72		o
1672-73		p
1673-74		q
1674-75		r
1675-76		s
1676-77		t
1677-78		u

* Date letter recorded.

CYCLE III

	HARP CROWNED	DATE LETTER
1678-79		
1679-80		
1680-81		
1681-82	"	
1682-83	"	
1683-84		
JAS.II 1685-87		
1688-93		
WM.III 1694-95		
1696-98	"	
1699-1700		
1700-1		
1701-2		
ANNE 1702-3		
1703-4		
1704-5		
1706-7		
1708-9		
1710-11		
1712-13		
GEO.I 1714-15	"	
1715-16		
1716-17		

CYCLE IV

	HARP CROWNED	DATE LETTER
1717-18		
		"
1718-19	"	
1719-20		

CYCLE V

	HIBERNIA	HARP CROWNED	DATE LETTER
1720-21		🛡	A
1721-22		"	B
1722-23		"	C
1723-24		"	D / D
1724-25		🛡	E
1725-26		"	F
1726-27		"	G
GEO.II 1727-28		🛡	H
1728-29		"	J
1729-30		🛡	K
1730-31		"	L
1731-32	🛡	🛡	L
1732-33	🛡	"	M
1733-34	"	"	N
1734-35	🛡	🛡	O
1735-36	"	"	P
1736-37	"	"	Q
1737-38	"	"	R
1738-39	"	"	S
1739-40	"	"	T
1740-41	"	"	U
1741-43	"	"	W / W
1743-44	"	"	Y
1745	"	"	Y
1746	"	"	Z

CYCLE VI

	HIBERNIA	HARP CROWNED	DATE LETTER
1747	🛡	🛡	A
1748	"	"	B
1749	"	🛡	C
1750	"	"	D
1751-52	"	🛡	E E
1752-53	🛡 *	"	F
1753-54	"	"	G
1754-56	🛡	"	H
1757	"	"	I
1758	"	🛡	K
1759	"	"	L
GEO.III 1760	"	"	M
1761	"	"	N
1762	"	🛡	O
1763	"	"	P
1764	"	"	Q
1765	"	"	R
1766	"	"	S
1767	"	🛡	T
1768	"	"	U
1769	🛡	🛡	W
1770	"	"	X
1771	"	🛡	Y
1772	"	"	Z

* The Hibernia stamp of this form was used between 1752 and 1754 as well as one of oval outline.

CYCLE VII

	HIBERNIA	HARP CROWNED	DATE LETTER
1773			A
1774	"	"	B
1775	"	"	C
1776*	"		D
1777	"	"	E
1778	"	"	F
1779*	"	"	G
1780	"	"	H
1781	"	"	I
1782	"	"	K
1783	"	"	L
1784	"	"	M
1785	"	"	N
1786	"	"	O
1787	"	"	P
			"
1788	"	"	Q
1789	"	"	R
1790	"	"	S
1791	"	"	T
1792	"	"	U
1793	"	"	W
1794			X
1795	"	"	Y
1796	"	"	Z

CYCLE VIII

	HIBERNIA	HARP CROWNED	DATE LETTER	DUTY MARK
1797			A	
1798	"	"	B	
1799	"	"	C	
1800	"	"	D	
1801	"	"	E	
1802	"	"	F	
1803	"	"	G	
1804	"	"	H	
1805	"	"	I	
1806			K	
1807	"	"	L	
1808	"	"	M	"
1809	"	"	NN	
	DATE LETTER	HARP CROWNED	HIBERNIA	DUTY MARK
1810	OO			"
1811	P	"	"	"
1812	Q	"	"	"
1813	R	"	"	"
1814	S	"	"	"
1815	T	"	"	"
1816	U	"	"	"
1817	W	"	"	"
1818	X	"	"	"
1819	Y	"	"	"
GEO.IV 1820	Z	"	"	"

* D and G are sometimes found without pellet.

CYCLE IX

	DATE LETTER	HARP CROWNED	HIBER-NIA	DUTY MARK
1821	A			
1822	B	"	"	
1823	C	"	"	"
1824	D	"	"	"
1825-26	E e	"	"	
1826-27	F	"	"	
1827-28	G			
1828-29	H			
1829-30	I I			
WM.IV 1830-31	K			
1831-32	L			
1832-33	M			
1833-34	N N			"
1834-35*	O O			
1835-36	P P	"	"	"
1836-37	Q Q	"	"	"
VICT. 1837-38	R R	"	"	"
1838-39	S			
1839-40	T			"
1840-41	U U	"	"	"
1841-42	V	"	"	"
1842-43	W			"
1843-44	X	"	"	"
1844-45	Y			"
1845-46	Z			"

CYCLE X

	HIBER-NIA	HARP CROWNED	DATE LETTER	DUTY MARK
1846-47			a	
1847-48	"	"	b	"
1848-49	"	"	c	"
1849-50	"	"	d	"
1850-51	"	"	e	"
1851-52	"	"	f f	"
1852-53	"	"	g g	"
1853-54	"	"	h h	"
1854-55	"	"	j	"
1855-56	"	"	k	"
1856-57	"	"	l	"
1857-58	"	"	m	"
1858-59	"	"	n	"
1859-60	"	"	o	"
1860-61	"	"	p	"
1861-62	"	"	q	"
1862-63	"	"	r	"
1863-64	"	"	s	"
1864-65		"	t	"
1865-66	"	"	u	"
1866-67	"	"	v	"
1867-68	"	"	w	"
1868-69	"	"	x	"
1869-70	"	"	y	"
1870-71	"	"	z	"

CYCLE XI

	HARP CROWNED	HIBER-NIA	DATE LETTER	DUTY MARK
1871-72	🦁	🧍	**A**	👑
1872-73	"	"	**B**	"
1873-74	"	"	**C**	"
1874-75	"	"	**D**	"
1875-76	"	"	**E**	"
1876-77	"	"	**F**	"
1877-78	"	"	**G**	"
1878-79	"	"	**H**	"
1879-80	"	"	**I**	"
1880-81	"	"	**K**	"
1881-82	"	"	**L**	"
1882-83	"	"	**M**	"
1883-84	"	"	**N**	"
1884-85	"	"	**O**	"
1885-86	"	"	**P**	"
1886-87	"	"	**Q**	"
1887-88	"	"	**R**	"
1888-89	"	"	**S**	"
1889-90	"	"	**T**	"
1890-91	"	"	**U**	
1891-92	"	"	**V**	
1892-93	"	"	**W**	
1893-94	"	"	**X**	
1894-95	"	"	**Y**	
1895-96	"	"	**Z**	

CYCLE XII

	HARP CROWNED	HIBER-NIA	DATE LETTER
1896-97	🦁	🧍	**A**
1897-98	"	"	**B**
1898-99	"	"	**C**
1899-1900	"	"	**D**
1900-1	"	"	**E**
EDW.VII 1901-2	"	"	**F**
1902-3	"	"	**G**
1903-4	🦁	🧍	**H**
1904-5	"	"	**I**
1905-6	"	"	**K**
1906-7	"	"	**L**
1907-8	"	"	**M**
1908-9	"	"	**N**
1909-10	"	"	**O**
1910-11	"	"	**P**
1911-12	"	"	**Q**
1912-13	"	"	**R**
1913-14	"	"	**S**
1914-15	"	"	**T**
1915-16	"	"	**U**

CYCLE XIII

	HARP CROWNED	HIBER-NIA	DATE LETTER
1916			
1917	"	"	b
1918	"	"	C
1919	"	"	O
1920	"	"	e
1921	"	"	f
1922	"	"	g
1923	"	"	h
1924	"	"	i
1925	"	"	k
1926	"	"	l
1927	"	"	m
1928	"	"	n
1929	"	"	o
1930-31	"	"	p
1932	"	"	q
1933	"	"	r
1934	"	"	s
1935	"	"	t
1936	"	"	u
1937	"	"	v
1938	"	"	w
1939	"	"	x
1940	"	"	y
1941	"	"	z

CYCLE XIV

	HIBER-NIA	HARP CROWNED	DATE LETTER
1942			A
1943	"	"	B
1944	"	"	C
1945			D
1946	"	"	E
1947	"	"	F
1948	"	"	G
1949			H
1950	"	"	I
1951	"	"	J
1952	"	"	K
1953	"	"	L
1954	"	"	M
1955	"	"	N
1956	"	"	O
1957	"	"	P
1958	"	"	Q
1959	"	"	R
1960	"	"	S
1961	"	"	T
1962	"	"	U
1963	"	"	V
1964	"	"	W
1965	"	"	X
1966*		"	Y
1967	"	"	Z

* Jubilee mark.

CYCLE XV

	HARP CROWNED	HIBER-NIA	DATE LETTER
1968	🔲	🔲	**a**
1969	"	"	**b**
1970	"	"	**c**
1971	🔲	🔲	**d**
1972	"	"	**e**
1973*	"	🔲	**f**
1974	"	"	**g**
1975	"	"	**h**
1976	"	"	**i**
1977	"	"	**l**
1978	"	"	**m**
1979	"	"	**n**
1980	"	"	**o**
1981	"	"	**p**
1982	"	"	**R**
1983	"	"	**s**
1984	"	"	**t**
1985	"	"	**u**

CYCLE XVI

	HARP CROWNED	HIBER-NIA	DATE LETTER
1986	🔲	🔲	*A*
1987**	"	"	*B*
1988 †	"	"	*C*
1989	"	"	*D*
1990	"	"	*E*
1991	"	"	*F*

*   Additional mark to commemorate Ireland's entry into the European Community.

**   To denote the 350th Anniversary of the founding of the Company of Goldsmiths, the Company authorised the striking of a special mark to be put on all items of Irish manufactured gold, silver and platinum, other than jewellery and watch cases, manufactured and hallmarked during the period, 1 January to 31 December 1987. The mark consists of a shield from the Coat of Arms of the Company and appears in addition to the appropriate regular hallmarks.

†   To denote the Dublin City Millennium Year the Company of Goldsmiths authorised the striking of a special mark to be put on all items of Irish manufactured gold, silver and platinum, other than jewellery and watch cases, manufactured and hallmarked during the period, 1 January to 31 December 1988. The mark represents the Dublin Coat of Arms and appears in addition to the appropriate regular hallmarks.

MARK	MAKER	PERIOD	COMMENTS
	Abel Ram	2nd ½ 17th C	Fine work
	" "	" "	
	" "	" "	
	Charles Leslie	2nd ¼ 18th C	One of the finest of all makers
	Charles Townsend	Late 18th C	Good work
	Daniel Egan	Early 19th C	Good maker
	David King	Early 18th C	Fine maker
	" "	" "	
	Isaac D'Olier	Mid 18th C	Good maker
	John Hamilton	1st ½ 18th C	Important maker
	James Keating	Late 18th C	Many boxes
	John Laughlin	Mid 18th C	Interesting maker
	James Le Bass	Early 19th C	Good maker
	Joseph Stoaker (or John Slicer)	2nd ½ 17th C	Fine work
	John Pittar	Late 18th C	Good work
	J R Neill	Mid 19th C	Important retail firm
	John Tuite	Early 18th C	Moved to London where he used the same mark
	Joseph Walker	Late 17th/Early 18th C	Important maker
	" "	" "	
LAW	William Law	Late 18th/Early 19th C	Good work
	Michael Keating	Late 18th C	Good work
	" "	" "	
	Matthew Walker	2nd ¼ 18th C	Good maker

MARK	MAKER	PERIOD	COMMENTS
MW	Matthew Walsh	Late 18th C	Good work
MW	Michael Walsh	2nd ½ 18th C	Good work
MW&S	M West & Sons	19th C	Important retail firm
NEILL	J R Neill	Mid 19th C	Important retail firm
RC	Robert Calderwood	Mid 18th C	Very important maker
R•C	" "	" "	
R•C	" "	" "	
B	Thomas Bolton	Late 17th/Early 18th C	Important maker
B	" "	" "	
TW	Thomas Walker	1st ½/Mid 18th C	Very fine maker
TW	" "	" "	
TW	" "	" "	
W&Co	Alderman West & Co	19th C	Important retail firm
W&R	Weir & Rogers	Late 19th C	Retailers
W&S	West & Son	Late 19th C	Important retail firm
W&S	" "	" "	
W&S	" "	Early 20th C	
WB	William Bond	2nd ½ 18th C	Prolific maker
WEST	Alderman West	Early 19th C	Important retail firm
WL	William Law	Late 18th/Early 19th C	Good work
W•T	William Townsend	Mid 18th C	Good work
WT	" "	" "	
WW	William Williamson	2nd ¼ 18th C	Fine maker

CHAPTER V
Edinburgh

Cycles of Hallmarks

Pre 1681

	TOWN MARK CASTLE	DEACON'S MARK
1556-67 or 1561-62		
1563-64	"	
1565-67	"	
c.1575?	"	
1576		
1577-79		
1585-86	"	
1592-93	"	
1598-1601	"	
1603-4		
1608-10	"	
1611-13		
1613-21		
1617	"	
c.1617		
1617-19	"	
1633		
1637-39		

	TOWN MARK CASTLE	DEACON'S MARK
1640-42		
1642	"	
1643		"
1644-46	"	
1648-57	"	
c.1650?	"	
1651-59	"	
1660	"	
1663-81	"	
1665	"	
1665-67	"	
1669-75	"	
1675-77	"	

CYCLE I

	TOWN MARK CASTLE	ASSAY MASTER'S MARK	DATE LETTER
1681-82	🏰	ℬ	𝖆
1682-83	"	ℬ	𝖇
1683-84	"	"	𝖈
1684-85	"	"	𝖉
1685-86	"	"	𝖊
1686-87	"	"	𝖋
1687-88*	"	"	𝖌
1688-89	"	"	𝖍
WM.& MY. 1689-90	"	"	𝖎
1690-91	"	"	𝖐
1691-92	"	"	𝖑
1692-93	"	"	𝖒
1693-94	"	"	𝖓
1694-95	"	"	𝖔
WM.III 1695-96	"	"	𝖕
1696-97	"	"	𝖖
1697-98 †	"	𝓟**	𝖗
1698-99	🏰	"	𝖘
1699-1700	"	"	𝖙
1700-1	"	"	𝖚
1701-2	"	"	𝖜
ANNE 1702-3	"	"	𝖝
1703-4	"	"	𝖞
1704-5	"	"	𝖟

* Date letter variation: 🄶 1687-88

† Date letter variation: 𝖗 1697-98

** Penman did not become Assay Master until 13 Sept., 1697.

CYCLE II

	TOWN MARK CASTLE	ASSAY MASTER'S MARK	DATE LETTER
1705-6	🏰	𝓟	𝐀
1706-7	"	"	𝐁
1707-8	"	𝐄𝐏	𝐂
1708-9	"	"	𝐃
1709-10	"	"	𝐄
1710-11	"	"	𝐅
1711-12	"	"	𝐆
			𝐆
1712-13	"	"	𝐇
1713-14	"	"	𝐈
GEO.I 1714-15	🏰	"	𝐊
1715-16	"	"	𝐋
1716-17	"	"	𝐌
1717-18	"	"	𝐍
			𝐍
	🏰	𝐄𝐏	𝐍
1718-19	"	"	𝐎
		𝐄𝐏	𝐏
1719-20	🏰	"	𝐏
		𝐄𝐏	𝐏
1720-21	"	"	𝐐
1721-22	"	"	𝐑
1722-23	"	"	𝐒
1723-24	"	"	𝐓
1724-25	"	"	𝐔
1725-26	"	"	𝐕
1726-27	"	"	𝐖
GEO.II 1727-28	"	"	𝐗
1728-29	"	"	𝐘
1729-30	"	"	𝐙
		𝐀𝐔	𝐙

CYCLE III

	TOWN MARK CASTLE	ASSAY MASTER'S MARK	DATE LETTER
1730-31	🏰	AU	𝕬
1731-32	"	"	𝕭
1732-33	"	"	𝕮
1733-34	"	"	𝕯
1734-35	"	"	𝕰
1735-36	"	"	𝕱
1736-37	"	"	𝕲
1737-38	🏰	"	𝕳
1738-39	"	"	𝕵
1739-40	"	"	𝕶
1740-41	"	" / GED	𝕷
1741-42	"	"	𝕸
1742-43	"	EL	𝕹
1743-44	"	"	𝕺
1744-45	🏰	HG	𝕻
1745-46	"	"	𝕼
1746-47	"	"	𝕽
1747-48	"	"	𝕾
1748-49	"	"	𝕿
1749-50	"	"	𝖀
1750-51	"	"	𝖁
1751-52	"	"	𝖂
1752-53	"	"	𝖃
1753-54	"	"	𝖄
1754-55	"	"	𝖅

CYCLE IV

	TOWN MARK CASTLE	ASSAY MASTER'S MARK	DATE LETTER
1755-56	🏰	HG	𝔄
1756-57	"	"	𝔅
1757-58	"	"	ℭ
1758-59	"	"	𝔇
1759-60	"	THISTLE 🏵	𝔈
GEO.III 1760-61	"	"	𝔉
1761-62	"	"	𝔊
1762-63	"	"	𝔍
1763-64	"	"	𝔍
1764-65	"	"	𝔎
1765-66	"	"	𝔏
1766-67	"	"	𝔐
1767-68	"	"	𝔑
1768-69	"	"	𝔒
1769-70	"	"	𝔓
1770-71	"	"	𝔔
1771-72	"	"	𝔕
1772-73	"	"	𝔖
1773-74	"	"	𝔗
1774-75	"	"	𝔘
1775-76	"	"	𝔙
1776-77	"	"	𝔛
1777-78	"	"	𝔜
1778-79	"	"	𝔷
1779-80	"	"	𝔥

CYCLE V

	DUTY MARK	TOWN MARK CASTLE	THISTLE	DATE LETTER
1780-81		[castle]	[thistle]	A
1781-82		"	"	B
1782-83		"	"	C
1783-84		"	"	D
1784-85	[head]	"	"	E
1785-86	"	"	"	F
1786-88	[head]	"	"	G
1788-89	"	"	"	H
1789-90	"	"	"	I
1789-90	"	"	"	J
1790-91	"	"	"	K
1791-92	"	"	"	L
1792-93	"	"	"	M
1793-94	"	"	"	N
1794-95	"	"	"	O
1795-96	"	"	"	P
1796-97	"	"	"	Q
1797-98	[head]	"	"	R
1798-99	"	"	"	S
1799-1800	"	[castle]	[thistle]	T
1800-1	"	"	"	U
1801-2	"	"	"	V
1802-3	"	[castle]	"	W
1803-4	"	"	"	X
1804-5	"	"	"	Y
1805-6	"	"	"	Z

CYCLE VI

	DUTY MARK	TOWN MARK CASTLE	THISTLE	DATE LETTER
1806-7	[head]	[castle]	[thistle]	a
1807-8	"	"	"	b
1808-9	"	"	"	c
1809-10	"	[castle]	"	d
1810-11	"	"	"	e
1811-12	"	"	"	f
1812-13	"	"	"	g
1813-14	"	"	"	h
1814-15	"	"	"	i
1815-16	"	"	"	j
1816-17	"	"	"	k
1817-18	"	"	"	l
1818-19	"	"	"	m
1819-20	"	"	"	n
GEO.IV 1820-21	"	[castle]	[thistle]	o
1821-22	"	"	"	p
1822-23	"	"	"	q
1823-24	[head]	"	"	r
1824-25	"	"	"	s
1825-26	"	"	"	t
1826-27	"	[castle]	"	u
1827-28	"	"	"	v
1828-29	"	"	"	w
1829-30	"	"	"	x
WM.IV 1830-31	"	"	"	y
1831-32	"	"	"	z

CYCLE VII

	DUTY MARK	TOWN MARK CASTLE	THISTLE	DATE LETTER
1832-33				A
1833-34	"	"	"	B
1834-35	"	"	"	C
1835-36	"	"	"	D
1836-37	"	"	"	E
VICT. 1837-38	"	"	"	F
1838-39	"	"	"	G
1839-40	"	"	"	H
1840-41	"	"	"	I
1841-42		"	"	K
1842-43	"	"	"	L
1843-44	"	"	"	M
1844-45	"	"	"	N
1845-46	"	"	"	O
1846-47	"	"	"	P
1847-48	"	"	"	Q
1848-49	"	"	"	R
1849-50	"	"	"	S
1850-51	"	"	"	T
1851-52	"	"	"	U
1852-53	"	"	"	V
1853-54	"	"	"	W
1854-55	"	"	"	X
1855-56	"	"	"	Y
1856-57	"	"	"	Z

CYCLE VIII

	DUTY MARK	TOWN MARK CASTLE	THISTLE	DATE LETTER
1857-58				A
1858-59	"	"	"	B
1859-60	"	"	"	C
1860-61	"	"	"	D
1861-62	"	"	"	E
1862-63	"	"	"	F
1863-64	"	"	"	G
1864-65	"	"	"	H
1865-66	"	"	"	I
1866-67	"	"	"	K
1867-68*	"	"	"	L
1868-69	"	"	"	M
1869-70	"	"	"	N
1870-71	"	"	"	O
1871-72	"	"	"	P
1872-73	"	"	"	Q
1873-74	"	"	"	R
1874-75	"	"	"	S
1875-76	"	"	"	T
1876-77	"	"	"	U
1877-78	"	"	"	V
1878-79	"	"	"	W
1879-80	"	"	"	X
1880-81	"	"	"	Y
1881-82	"	"	"	Z

* was struck on imported wares in addition to the marks shown from 1867-1904.

CYCLE IX

	DUTY MARK	TOWN MARK CASTLE	THISTLE	DATE LETTER
1882-83	◉	🏰	🌣	**a**
1883-84	"	"	"	**b**
1884-85	"	"	"	**c**
1885-86	"	"	"	**d**
1886-87	"	"	"	**e**
1887-88	"	"	"	**f**
1888-89	"	"	"	**g**
1889-90*	"	"	"	**h**
1890-91		🏰	🌣	**i**
1891-92		"	"	**k**
1892-93		"	"	**l**
1893-94		"	"	**m**
1894-95		"	"	**n**
1895-96		"	"	**o**
1896-97		"	"	**p**
1897-98		"	"	**q**
1898-99		"	"	**r**
1899-1900		"	"	**s**
1900-1		"	"	**t**
EDW.VII 1901-2		"	"	**u**
1902-3		"	"	**v**
1903-4 †		"	"	**w**
1904-5		"	"	**x**
1905-6		"	"	**z**

* Duty Mark is deleted as from 1890.

† **F** was struck on imported wares in addition to the marks shown from 1867-1904.

CYCLE X

	TOWN MARK CASTLE	THISTLE	DATE LETTER
1906-7	🏰	🌣	**A**
1907-8	"	"	**B**
1908-9§	"	"	**C**
1909-10	"	"	**D**
GEO.V 1910-11	"	"	**E**
1911-12	"	"	**F**
1912-13	"	"	**G**
1913-14	"	"	**H**
1914-15	"	"	**I**
1915-16	"	"	**K**
1916-17	"	"	**L**
1917-18	"	"	**M**
1918-19	"	"	**N**
1919-20	"	"	**O**
1920-21	"	"	**P**
1921-22	"	"	**Q**
1922-23**	"	"	**R**
1923-24**	"	"	**S**
1924-25**	"	"	**T**
1925-26	"	"	**U**
1926-27	"	"	**V**
1927-28	"	"	**W**
1928-29**	"	"	**X**
1929-30	"	"	**Y**
1930-31	"	"	**Z**

§ New Britannia mark: 🯄

** Date letters exist for these years but are not recorded on the surviving registration plates.

CYCLE XI

	TOWN MARK CASTLE	THISTLE	DATE LETTER
1931-32	(castle)	(thistle)	A
1932-33	"	"	B
1933-34	"	"	C
1934-35 †	"	"	D
1935-36 †	"	"	E
EDW.VIII 1936-37	"	"	F
GEO.VI 1937-38	"	"	G
1938-39	"	"	H
1939-40	"	"	I
1940-41	(castle)	(thistle)	K
1941-42	"	"	L
1942-43	"	"	M
1943-44	"	"	N
1944-45	"	"	O
1945-46	"	"	P
1946-47	"	"	Q
1947-48	"	"	R
1948-49**	"	"	S
1949-50**	"	"	T
1950-51**	"	"	U
1951-52	"	"	V
ELIZ.II 1952-53§	"	"	W
1953-54§	"	"	X
1954-55	"	"	Y
1955-56	"	"	Z

CYCLE XII

	TOWN MARK CASTLE	THISTLE	DATE LETTER
1956-57	(castle)	(thistle)	A
1957-58	"	"	B
1958-59	"	"	C
1959-60	"	"	D
1960-61	"	"	E
1961-62	"	"	F
1962-63	"	"	G
1963-64	"	"	H
1964-65	"	"	I
1965-66	"	"	k
1966-67	"	"	L
1967-68	"	"	M
1968-69	"	"	N
1969-70	"	"	O
1970-71	"	"	P
1971-72	"	"	Q
1972-73	"	"	R
1973-74	"	"	S

† Optional Jubilee Mark:

** Date letters exist for these years but are not recorded on the surviving registration plates.

§ Optional Coronation Mark:

CYCLE XIII

	TOWN MARK CASTLE	LION RAMPANT	DATE LETTER
1975 ‡	🏰	🦁	𝒜
1976	"	"	ℬ
1977 †	"	"	𝒞
1978	"	"	𝒟
1979	"	"	ℰ
1980	"	"	ℱ
1981	"	"	𝒢
1982*	"	"	ℋ
1983	"	"	𝒥
1984	"	"	𝒦
1985	"	"	ℒ
1986	"	"	ℳ
1987	"	"	𝒩
1988	"	"	𝒪
1989	"	"	𝒫
1990	"	"	𝒬
1991	"	"	ℛ

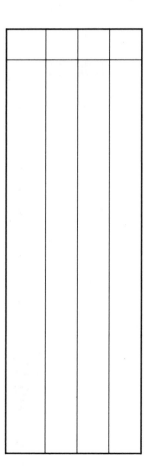

PLATINUM FROM 1982

	TOWN MARK CASTLE	PLATINUM MARK	DATE LETTER
Date as Above	🏰	⬠	ℋ

‡   Britannia mark from 1975 on:

†   Optional Jubilee Mark:

GOLD MARKS

These follow almost exactly those used in London from 1798 on with the obvious substitution of the castle mark for the leopard's head (the sun in splendour for 22ct. was not used in Edinburgh).

IMPORT MARKS 1904-32

GOLD			IMPORTED SILVER		
22ct.		·916	Britannia		·9584 + Date letter & sponsor's mark
		+ Date letter & sponsor's mark			
20ct.	"	·833 "	Sterling	"	·925 "
18ct.	"	·75 "			
15ct.	"	·625 "			
12ct.	"	·5			
9ct.	"	·375 "			

1932-74*

GOLD			SILVER
22ct.		916 + Date letter & sponsor's mark	(As 1904-32)
18ct.	"	750 "	
14ct.	"	585 "	
9ct.	"	375 "	

From 1975 on

Platinum**		950	+ Date letter & sponsor's mark
Gold 22ct.		916	"
18ct.	"	750	"
14ct.	"	585	"
9ct.	"	375	"
Silver Britannia		958	"
Sterling	"	925	"

CONVENTION MARKS 1976 on

PRECIOUS METAL	ASSAY OFFICE MARK	COMMON CONTROL MARK	FINENESS MARK
Platinum**		950	950
Gold 18ct.	"	750	750
14ct.	"	585	585
9ct.	"	375	375
Silver (Sterling)	"	925	925

Convention marking on imported wares

PRECIOUS METAL	ASSAY OFFICE MARK	COMMON CONTROL MARK	FINENESS MARK
Platinum**		950	950
Gold 18ct.		750	750
14ct.	"	585	585
9ct.	"	375	375
Silver (Sterling)		925	925

* In 1932 and from then on 14ct. replaced 15ct. and 12ct.

** Note platinum 1982 onwards

Since universally high standards were maintained by all the makers listed here, individual comments such as, 'Fine/Good maker' would be simply repetitive and are therefore not given.

MARK	MAKER	PERIOD	COMMENTS
AU	Archibald Ure	Early 18th C	
AZ	Alexander Zeigler	Late 18th/Early 19th C	
B&S	Brook & Son	Very late 19th C on	
EL	Edward Lothian	2nd ¼ 18th C	
H&I	Hamilton & Inches	Late 19th C to present day	
H&I	" "	" "	
HB	Harry Beathune	Early 18th C	
HG	Hugh Gordon	2nd ¼ 18th C	
ID	James Dempster	Last ¼ 18th C	
IK	James Ker	2nd ¼ 18th C	
IM	James Mitchellsone	Early 18th C	
IZ	John Zeigler	Very late 18th/Early 19th C	
J&WM	James & William Marshall	1st ½ & Mid 19th C	
JC&C	J Crichton & Co	Late 19th C	
JC&C	" "	Very late 19th C on	
JN	James Nasmyth	2nd ¼ 19th C	Boxes
JM	J McKay	1st ½ 19th C	
JH&C	James Nasmyth & Co	2nd ¼ 19th C	Boxes

MARK	MAKER	PERIOD	COMMENTS
K&D	Ker & Dempster	Mid 18th C	
L&R	Lothian & Robertson	Mid 18th C	
M&C	Mackay & Chisholm	Mid 19th C	
M&S	Marshall & Sons	2nd ¼ 19th C	
MK	Colin McKenzie	Late 17th/Early 18th C	
MY	Mungo Yorstoun	Early 18th C	
PC &S	P Cunningham & Son	Early 19th C	
PM	Patrick Murray	Early 18th C	
PR	Patrick Robertson	3rd ¼ 18th C	
RG	Robert Gordon	Mid 18th C	
RG &S	Robert Gray & Son (Glasgow)	Early 19th C	
T	James Taitt	Early 18th C	
T·K	Thomas Ker	Early 18th C	
W& PC	William & Patrick Cunningham	Last ¼ 18th C	
WA	William Auld	Late 18th/Early 19th C	
WA	William Aytoun	c.2nd ¼ 18th C	
W·C PC	William & Patrick Cunningham	Last ¼ 18th C	
WPC	W & P Cunningham	Late 18th C	
W Z	William Zeigler	1st ½ 19th C	

CHAPTER VI
Exeter

Cycles of Hallmarks

TABLE I

APPROXIMATE DATE	MARKS
1575	
1600	
1620	
1635	
1660	
1660	

The above is a small selection of the pre-1701 Exeter marks intended only to give an idea of the types of mark in use. See *Jackson's* pp.289/291 for full list.

CYCLE I

	CASTLE	BRIT-ANNIA	LION'S HEAD ERASED	DATE LETTER
1701-2	🏰	🦁	👤	**A**
ANNE 1702-3	🏰	"	"	**B**
1703-4	🏰	"	"	**C**
1704-5	"	"	"	**D**
1705-6	"	"	"	**E**
1706-7	"	"	"	**F**
1707-8	"	"	"	**G**
1708-9	🏰	"	"	**H**
1709-10	🏰	"	"	**I**
1710-11	"	"	"	**K**
1711-12	"	"	"	**L**
1712-13	"	"	"	**M**
1713-14	🏰	"	"	**N**
GEO.I 1714-15	"	"	"	**O**
1715-16	"	"	"	**P**
1716-17	"	"	"	**Q**
1717-18	"	"	"	**R**
1718-19	"	"	"	**S**
1719-20	"	"	"	**T**
1720-21	"	"	"	**V**

	CASTLE	LEOPARD'S HEAD CROWNED	LION PASSANT	DATE LETTER
1720-21	🏰	👑	🦁	"
1721-22	"	"	"	**W**
1722-23	"	"	"	**X**
1723-24	"	"	"	**Y**
1724-25	"	"	"	**Z**

CYCLE II

	CASTLE	LEOPARD'S HEAD CROWNED	LION PASSANT	DATE LETTER
1725-26	🏰	👑	🦁	**a**
1726-27	"	"	"	**b**
GEO.II 1727-28	"	"	"	**c**
1728-29	"	"	"	**d**
1729-30	"	"	"	**e**
1730-31	"	"	"	**f**
1731-32	"	"	"	**g**
1732-33	"	"	"	**h**
1733-34	"	"	"	**i**
1734-35	"	"	"	**k**
1735-36	"	"	"	**l** / **L**
1736-37	"	"	"	**m**
1737-38	"	"	"	**n**
1738-39	"	"	"	**o**
1739-40	"	"	"	**p**
1740-41	"	"	"	**q**
1741-42	"	"	"	**r**
1742-43	"	"	"	**s**
1743-44	"	"	"	**t**
1744-45	"	"	"	**u**
1745-46	"	"	"	**w**
1746-47	"	"	"	**x**
1747-48	"	"	"	**y**
1748-49	"	"	"	**z**

CYCLE III

	CASTLE	LEOPARD'S HEAD CROWNED	LION PASSANT	DATE LETTER
1749-50	🏰	👑	🦁	**A**
1750-51	"	"	"	**B**
1751-52	"	"	"	**C**
1752-53	"	"	"	**D**
1753-54	"	"	"	**E**
1754-55	"	"	"	**F**
1755-56	"	"	"	**G**
1756-57	"	"	"	**H**
1757-58	"	"	"	**I**
1758-59	"	"	"	**K**
1759-60	"	"	"	**L**
GEO.III 1760-61	"	"	"	**M**
1761-62	"	"	"	**N**
1762-63	"	"	"	**O**
1763-64	"	"	"	**P**
1764-65	"	"	"	**Q**
1765-66	"	"	"	**R**
1766-67	"	"	"	**S**
1767-68	"	"	"	**T**
1768-69	"	"	"	**U**
1769-70	"	"	"	**W**
1770-71	"	"	"	**X**
1771-72	"	"	"	**Y**
1772-73	"	"	"	**Z**

CYCLE IV

	CASTLE	LEOPARD'S HEAD CROWNED	LION PASSANT	DATE LETTER
1773-74	🏰	👑	🦁	**A**
1774-75	"	"	"	**B**
1775-76	"	"	"	**C**
1776-77	"	"	"	**D**
1777-78	"	"	"	**E**
1778-79	"	"	🦁	**F**
1779-80	"		"	**G**
1780-81	"		"	**H**
1781-83	"		"	**I**
1783-84	"		"	**K**
1784-85	"	🌑	"	**L**
1785-86	"	"	"	**M**
1786-87	"	🌑	"	**N**
1787-88	"	"	"	**O**
1788-89	"	"	"	**P**
1789-90	"	"	"	**q**
1790-91	"	"	"	**r**
1791-92	"	"	"	**f**
1792-93	"	"	"	**t**
1793-94	"	"	"	**u**
1794-95	"	"	"	**W**
1795-96	"	"	"	**X**
1796-97	"	"	"	**y**

CYCLE V

	CASTLE	LION PASSANT	DATE LETTER	DUTY MARK
1797-8*	🏰	🦁	**A**	👑
1798-9 †	"	"	**B**	"
1799-1800	"	"	**C**	"
1800-1	"	"	**D**	"
1801-2	"	"	**E**	"
1802-3	"	"	**F**	"
1803-4	"	"	**G**	"
1804-5	"	"	**H**	"
1805-6	🏰	🦁	**I**	"
1806-7	"	"	**K**	"
1807-8	"	"	**L**	"
1808-9	"	"	**M**	"
1809-10	"	"	**N**	"
1810-11	"	"	**O**	"
1811-12	"	"	**P**	"
1812-13	"	"	**Q**	"
1813-14	"	"	**R**	"
1814-15	"	"	**S**	"
1815-16	"	"	**T**	"
1816-17	"	"	**U**	"

CYCLE VI

	CASTLE	LION PASSANT	DATE LETTER	DUTY MARK
1817-18	🏰	🦁	**a**	👑
1818-19	"	"	**b**	"
1819-20	"	"	**c**	"
GEO.IV 1820-21	"	"	**d**	"
1821-22	"	"	**e**	"
1822-23	"	"	**f**	👑
1823-24	"	"	**g**	"
1824-25	"	"	**h**	"
1825-26	"	"	**i**	"
1826-27	"	"	**k**	"
1827-28	"	"	**l**	"
1828-29	"	"	**m**	"
1829-30	"	"	**n**	"
WM.IV 1830-31	"	"	**o**	"
1831-32	🏰	🦁	**p**	👑
1832-33	"	"	**q**	"
1833-34	🏰	🦁	**r**	"
1834-35	"	"	**s**	👑
1835-36	"	"	**t**	"
1836-37	"	"	**u**	"

* This date letter also appears with a canted square punch.

† The date letter appears with alternative punch shape. **B**

CYCLE VII

	CASTLE	LION PASSANT	DATE LETTER	DUTY MARK
VICT. 1837-38				
1838-39	"	"		
1839-40	"	"		
1840-41	"	"		"
1841-42		"		"
1842-43	"	"		"
1843-44		"		"
1844-45	"	"		"
1845-46	"	"		"
1846-47	"	"		"
1847-48	"	"		"
1848-49	"	"		"
1849-50	"	"		"
1850-51	"	"		"
1851-52	"	"		"
1852-53	"	"		"
1853-54	"	"		"
1854-55	"	"		"
1855-56	"	"		"
1856-57	"	"		"

CYCLE VIII

	CASTLE	LION PASSANT	DATE LETTER	DUTY MARK
1857-58*				
1858-59	"	"		"
1859-60	"	"		"
1860-61	"	"		"
1861-62	"	"		"
1862-63	"	"		"
1863-64	"	"		"
1864-65	"	"		"
1865-66	"	"		"
1866-67	"	"		"
1867-68	"	"		"
1868-69	"	"		"
1869-70	"	"		"
1870-71	"	"		"
1871-72	"	"		"
1872-73	"	"		"
1873-74	"	"		"
1874-75	"	"		"
1875-76	"	"		"
1876-77	"	"		"

*   Variation of date letter

CYCLE IX

	CASTLE	LION PASSANT	DATE LETTER	DUTY MARK
1877-78	🏰	🦁	**A**	👑
1878-79	"	"	**B**	"
1879-80	"	"	**C**	"
1880-81	"	"	**D**	"
1881-82	"	"	**E**	"
1882-83	"	"	**F**	"

Assay Office closed 1883.

MARK	MAKER	PERIOD	COMMENTS
	John Elston	Early 18th C	Fine work, wide range
	George Ferris	1st ½ 19th C	Mostly flatware
	George Turner	Early 19th C	Mostly flatware
	John Elston, jun	1st ½ 18th C	Fine work, wide range
	Thomas Eustace	Late 18th C	Mostly flatware
	Joseph Hicks	Late 18th/Early 19th C	Mostly flatware
	John Osment	1st ½ 19th C	Flatware
	" "	" "	
	John Stone	Mid 19th C	Mostly flatware
	" "	" "	
	James Williams	Mid 19th C	Flatware
	Josiah Williams & Co	Mid 19th C	The firm of Williams made vast quantities of flatware in Bristol
	James & Josiah Williams	" "	
	Pentecost Symonds (of Plymouth) — sterling mark	1st ½ 18th C	Fine work, wide range
	Richard Ferris	Late 18th/Early 19th C	Mostly flatware
	Robert, James & Josiah Williams	Mid 19th C	The firm of Williams made vast quantities of flatware in Bristol
	Samuel Blachford (Plymouth)	1st ½ 18th C	Good work, wide range
	W R Sobey	Mid 19th C	Flatware
	Pentecost Symonds (of Plymouth) see PS for his sterling mark	1st ½ 18th C	Fine work, wide range
	Thomas Blake	Mid 18th C	Mostly flatware
	Thomas Eustace	Late 18th C	Mostly flatware
	William Rawlings Sobey	Mid 19th C	Flatware
	William Woodman (Bristol)	1st ½ 19th C	Mostly flatware
		" "	

Glasgow

Cycles of Hallmarks

CYCLE I

	TREE FISH & BELL	DATE LETTER
1681-82	(mark)	a
1682-83		b
1683-84	(mark)	C
1684-85		d
1685-86	"	E
1686-87		f
1687-88		g
1688-89		h
1689-90	(mark)	I
1690-91	"	K
1691-92		l
1692-93		m
1693-94		n
1694-95	(mark)	O
1695-96		p
1696-97	"	Q
1697-98		r
1698-99	(mark)	S
1699-1700	(mark)	t
1700-1	(mark)	U
1701-2	"	V
1702-3		W
1703-4		x
1704-5	"	Y
1705-6	"	Z

'CYCLE' II

	TREE FISH & BELL	DATE LETTER
1706-7		A
1707-8	(mark)	B
1709-10	"	D
	(mark)	"
1709-20	(mark)	
1717-49	"	
1728-31	"	S
1725-35	"	S
1743-52	(mark)	S
1747-60		S
1756-76	"	S
	"	Z
1757-80	(mark)	
	(mark)	"
	(mark)	O
1761-65	"	S
1763-84	(mark)	
	"	E
	"	F
1776-84	(mark)	
1777-84	(mark)	S
1781-84	(mark)	S
1782-84	(mark)	
1783-84	(mark)	"
1784-85	(mark)	S
	"	O

CYCLE III

	TREE FISH & BELL	LION RAMPANT	DATE LETTER	DUTY MARK
1819-20	🛡	🛡	**A**	🛡
GEO.IV 1820-21	🛡	"	**B**	"
1821-22	"	"	**C**	"
1822-23	"	"	**D**	"
1823-24	"	"	**E**	"
1824-25	"	"	**F**	"
1825-26	"	"	**G**	"
1826-27	"	"	**H**	"
1827-28	"	"	**I**	"
1828-29	"	"	**J**	"
1829-30	"	"	**K**	"
WM.IV 1830-31	"	"	**L**	"
1831-32	"	"	**M**	"
1832-33	"	"	**N**	🛡
1833-34	"	"	**O**	"
1834-35	"	"	**P**	"
1835-36	"	"	**Q**	"
1836-37	"	"	**R**	"
VICT. 1837-38	"	"	**S**	"
1838-39	"	"	**T**	"
1839-40	"	"	**U**	"
1840-41	"	"	**V**	"
1841-42	"	"	**W**	🛡
1842-43	"	"	**X**	"
1843-44	"	"	**Y**	"
1844-45	"	"	**Z**	"

CYCLE IV

	TREE FISH & BELL	LION RAMPANT	DATE LETTER	DUTY MARK
1845-46	🛡	🛡	**A**	🛡
1846-47	"	"	**B**	"
1847-48	"	"	**C**	"
1848-49	"	"	**D**	"
1849-50	"	"	**E**	"
1850-51	"	"	**f**	"
1851-52	"	"	**G**	"
1852-53	"	"	**H**	"
1853-54	"	"	**I**	"
1854-55	"	"	**J**	"
1855-56	"	"	**K**	"
1856-57	"	"	**L**	"
1857-58	"	"	**M**	"
1858-59	"	"	**N**	"
1859-60	"	"	**O**	"
1860-61	"	"	**P**	"
1861-62	"	"	**Q**	"
1862-63	"	"	**R**	"
1863-64	"	"	**S**	"
1864-65	"	"	**T**	"
1865-66	"	"	**U**	"
1866-67	"	"	**V**	"
1867-68*	"	"	**W**	"
1868-69	"	"	**X**	"
1869-70	"	"	**Y**	"
1870-71	"	"	**Z**	"

* 🅕 struck in addition to the above on imported wares from 1867-1904.

CYCLE V

	TREE FISH & BELL	LION RAMPANT	DATE LETTER	DUTY MARK
1871-72	🛡	🦁	A	●
1872-73	"	"	B	"
1873-74	"	"	C	"
1874-75	"	"	D	"
1875-76	"	"	E	"
1876-77	"	"	F	"
1877-78	"	"	G	"
1878-79	"	"	H	"
1879-80	"	"	I	"
1880-81	"	"	J	"
1881-82	"	"	K	"
1882-83	"	"	L	"
1883-84	"	"	M	"
1884-85	"	"	N	"
1885-86	"	"	O	"
1886-87	"	"	P	"
1887-88	"	"	Q	"
1888-89	"	"	R	"
1889-90	"	"	S	"
1890-91	"	"	T	
1891-92	"	"	U	
1892-93	"	"	V	
1893-94	"	"	W	
1894-95	"	"	X	
1895-86	"	"	Y	
1896-97	"	"	Z	

CYCLE VI

	TREE FISH & BELL	LION RAMPANT	THISTLE	DATE LETTER
1897-98	🛡	🦁		A
1898-99	"	"		B
1899-1900	"	"		C
1900-1	"	"		D
EDW.VII 1901-2	"	"		E
1902-3	"	"		F
1903-4*	"	"		G
1904-5	"	"		H
1905-6	"	"		I
1906-7	"	"		J
1907-8	"	"		K
1908-9	"	"		L
1909-10	"	"		M
1910-11	"	"		N
1911-12	"	"		O
1912-13	"	"		P
1913-14	"	"		Q
1914-15	"	"	🌸	R
1915-16	"	"	"	S
1916-17	"	"	"	T
1917-18	"	"	"	U
1918-19	"	"	"	V
1919-20	"	"	"	W
1920-21	"	"	"	X
1921-22	"	"	"	Y
1922-23	"	"	"	Z

* **F** struck in addition to the above on imported wares from 1867-1904.

CYCLE VII

	TREE FISH & BELL	LION RAMPANT	THISTLE	DATE LETTER
1923-24	🛡	🛡	⬡	**a**
1924-25	"	"	"	**b**
1925-26	"	"	"	**c**
1926-27	"	"	"	**d**
1927-28	"	"	"	**e**
1928-29	"	"	"	**f**
1929-30	"	"	"	**g**
1930-31	"	"	"	**h**
1931-32	"	"	"	**i**
1932-33	"	"	"	**j**
1933-34	"	"	"	**k**
1934-35	"	"	"	**l**
1935-36	"	"	"	**m**
1936-37	"	"	"	**n**
1937-38	"	"	"	**O**
1938-39	"	"	"	**P**
1939-40	"	"	"	**q**
1940-41	"	"	"	**r**
1941-42	"	"	"	**s**
1942-43	"	"	"	**t**
1943-44	"	"	"	**u**
1944-45	"	"	"	**v**
1945-46	"	"	"	**w**
1946-47	"	"	"	**x**
1947-48	"	"	"	**y**
1948-49	"	"	"	**Z**

CYCLE VIII

	TREE FISH & BELL	LION RAMPANT	THISTLE	DATE LETTER
1949-50	🛡	🛡	⬡	**A**
1950-51	"	"	"	**B**
1951-52	"	"	"	**C**
1952-53	"	"	"	**D**
1953-54	"	"	"	**e**
1954-55	"	"	"	**F**
1955-56	"	"	"	**G**
1956-57	"	"	"	**h**
1957-58	"	"	"	**I**
1958-59	"	"	"	**L**
1959-60	"	"	"	**M**
1960-61	"	"	"	**N**
1961-62	"	"	"	**O**
1962-63	"	"	"	**P**
1963-64	"	"	"	**R**

The Glasgow Assay Office closed in 1964.

GOLD MARKS

From 1819 onwards Glasgow follows the same pattern as Edinburgh with the obvious substitution of town marks.

IMPORTED WARES ASSAYED AT GLASGOW

1904-06

GOLD			SILVER		
22ct.	🏛	22·916	+ Date letter & sponsor's mark	Britannia	🏛	·9584	+ Date letter & sponsor's mark
20ct.	"	20·833	"	Sterling	"	·925	"
18ct.	"	18·75	"				
15ct.	"	15·625	"				
12ct.	"	12·5	"				
9ct.	"	9·375	"				

GOLD 1906-32			SILVER 1906-64		
22ct.	🔲	22·916	+ Date letter & sponsor's mark	Britannia	🔲	·9584	+ Date letter & sponsor's mark
20ct.	"	20·833	"	Sterling	"	·925	"
18ct.	"	18·75	"				
15ct.	"	15·625	"				
12ct.	"	12·5	"				
9ct.	"	9·375	"				

GOLD 1932-64*

22ct.	🔲	22 916	+ Date letter & sponsor's mark
18ct.	"	18 750	"
14ct.	"	14 585	"
9ct.	"	9 375	"

* In 1932 and from then on 14ct. replaced 15ct. and 12ct.

MARK	MAKER	PERIOD	COMMENTS
AG	Adam Graham	2nd ½ 18th C	
AM	Alxr. Mitchell	2nd ¼ 19th C	
AT&S	A. Taylor & Son	2nd ½ 19th C	
DMᶜC	D. McCallum	2nd ½ 19th C	
GLN	James Glen	Mid 18th C	
H&L	Hamilton & Laidlaw	2nd ½ 19th C	
H&M	Hyslop & Marshall	2nd ½ 19th C	
HM	Henry Muirhead	Mid 19th C	
IG	James Glen	Mid 18th C	
IL	John Luke II	Early 18th C	
I·L	" "	" "	
IL	" "	" "	
J&Cᵒ	Johnston & Co.	2nd ½ 19th C	
J.C	Jas. Crichton	2nd ½ 19th C	
JM	John Mitchell	2nd ¼ 19th C	
JM&S	J. Muirhead & Sons	2nd ½ 19th C	
J.MᶜA	J. McArthur	2nd ½ 19th C	
J.MᶜD	J. McDonald	2nd ½ 19th C	
JMᶜG	J. McGregor	2nd ½ 19th C	
J.MᶜI	J. McInnes	2nd ½ 19th C	
J&WM	J. & W. Mitchell	Mid 19th C	
M&A	Muirhead & Arthur	2nd ½ 19th C	
M&C	Milne & Campbell	Mid 18th C	
M&R	Mitchell & Russell	1st ¼ 19th C	
M&S	Mitchell & Son	2nd ¼ 19th C	
M&T	Miller & Thompson	2nd ½ 19th C	

MARK	MAKER	PERIOD	COMMENTS
M.BROS	Mitchell Bros.	2nd ½ 19th C	
R&G	Reed & Garrick	2nd ½ 19th C	
RG	Robert Gray	Last ¼ 18th C	
RG	" "	" "	
RG &S	Robt. Gray & Son	1st ½/Mid 19th C	
RG&S	" "	" "	
S&R	Smith & Rait	2nd ½ 19th C	
SB GG	Barclay & Goodwin	2nd ½ 19th C	
WA&S	W. Alexander & Son	2nd ½ 19th C	
W.M	W. Mitchell	2nd ½ 19th C	
W.M&C°	W. Miller & Co.	2nd ½ 19th C	

CHAPTER VIII

Newcastle

Cycles of Hallmarks

DATE APPROX.	MARKS
1650	
1655	
1664	
1675	
1686-87	
1690	
1695	

The above is a selection of Pre-Assay Office marks intended to give a general idea of the type of marking most usually found. See *Jackson's* pp.492-3 for a comprehensive list.

CYCLE I

	THREE CASTLES	BRIT-ANNIA	LION'S HEAD ERASED	DATE LETTER
ANNE 1702-3	![castles]	![britannia]	![lion head]	𝕬
1703-4	"	"	"	𝕭
1704-5	"	"	"	𝕮
1705-6	"	"	"	𝕯
1706-7	"	"	"	𝕰
1707-8	![castles]	"	"	𝕱
1708-9				†
1709-10				†
1710-11				†
1711-12				𝕭
1712-13*	![castles]	![britannia]	![lion head]	𝕸
1713-14				
GEO.I 1714-15				
1715-16				
1716-17				𝕺
1717-18*	![castles]	"	"	𝕻
1718-19*	"	"	"	𝕼
1719-20*	"	"	"	𝕯
1720-21*	"	"	"	𝕰

CYCLE II

	THREE CASTLES	LION PASSANT	LEOPARD'S HEAD CROWNED	DATE LETTER
1721-22*	![castles]	![lion]	![leopard]	𝖆
1722-23*	![castles]	![lion]	"	𝕭
1723-24*	"	![lion]	"	𝕮
1724-25*	"	"	"	𝕯
1725-26*	![castles]	![lion]	![leopard]	𝕰
1726-27*	"	"	"	𝕱
GEO.II 1727-28*	![castles]	"	![leopard]	𝕲
1728-29*	"	![lion]	"	𝕳
1729-30*	"	"	"	𝕴
1730-31*	"	"	"	𝕶
1731-32*	"	"	"	𝕷
1732-33*	"	"	"	𝕸
1733-34*	"	"	"	𝕹
1734-35*	"	"	"	𝕺
1735-36*	"	"	"	𝕻
1736-37*	"	"	"	𝕼
1737-38*	"	"	"	𝕽
1738-39*	"	"	"	𝕾
1739-40*	"	"	"	𝕿

* Asterisks indicate date-letters recorded in the Newcastle Goldsmiths' Company minute books.

† F was probably used during these years (i.e. F from 1707-1711).

CYCLE III

	THREE CASTLES	LION PASSANT	LEOPARD'S HEAD CROWNED	DATE LETTER
1740-41*				A
1741-42*	"	"	"	B
1742-43*	"	"	"	C
1743-44*	"	"	"	D
1744-45*	"	"	"	E
1745-46*	"	"	"	F
1746-47*				G
1747-48*	"	"	"	H
1748-49	"	"	"	I
1749-50*	"	"	"	K
1750-51*	"			L
1751-52*	"	"	"	M
1752-53*	"	"	"	N
1753-54*	"	"	"	O
1754-55*	"	"	"	P
1755-56*	"	"	"	Q
1756-57*	"	"	"	R
1757-58*		"		S
1758-59				‡

* Asterisks indicate date letters recorded in the Newcastle Goldsmiths' Company minute books.

‡ S was probably used for 1758/59 (i.e. S from 1757-59)

CYCLE IV

	THREE CASTLES	LION PASSANT	LEOPARD'S HEAD CROWNED	DATE LETTER	DUTY MARK
1759-60*				A	
GEO.III 1760-61 to 1768	"	"	"	B	
1769-70*	"	"	"	C	
1770-71*		"		D	
1771-72*	"	"	"	E	
1772-73*		"	"	F	
1773-74*	"	"	"	G	
1774-75*	"	"	"	H	
1775-76*	"	"	"	I	
1776-77*	"	"	"	K	
1777-78*	"	"	"	L	
1778-79*	"	"	"	M	
1779-80*	"			N	
1780-81*	"	"	"	O	
1781-82	"	"	"	P	
1782-83	"	"	"	Q	
1783-84	"	"	"	R	
1784-85	"	"	"	S	
1785-86*	"	"	"	T	"
1786-87*	"	"	"	U	
1787-88*	"			W	"
1788-89*	"	"	"	X	"
1789-90*	"	"	"	Y	"
1790-91*	"	"	"	Z	"

CYCLE V

	LION PASSANT	THREE CASTLES	LEOPARD'S HEAD CROWNED	DUTY LETTER	DATE LETTER
1791-92*	🦁	🏰	👑	😊	**A**
1792-93*	"	"	"	"	**B**
1793-94*	"	"	"	"	**C**
1794-95*	"	"	"	"	**D**
1795-96*	"	"	"	"	**E**
1796-97*	"	"	"	"	**F**
1797-98*	"	"	"	"	**G**
1798-99	"	"	"	😊	**H**
1799-1800*	"	"	"	"	**I**
1800-1*	🦁	🏰	👑	😊	**K**
1801-2*	"	"	"	"	**L**
1802-3*	"	"	"	"	**M**
1803-4*	"	"	"	"	**N**
1804-5*	🦁	"	"	😊	**O**
1805-6*	"	"	"	"	**P**
1806-7*	"	"	"	"	**Q**
1807-8*	"	"	"	"	**R**
1808-9*	"	"	"	"	**S**
1809-10*	🦁	🏰	👑	😊	**T**
1810-11*	"	"	"	"	**U**
1811-12*	"	"	"	"	**W**
1812-13*	"	"	"	"	**X**
1813-14*	"	"	"	"	**Y**
1814-15*	"	"	"	"	**Z**

CYCLE VI

	DATE LETTER	DUTY MARK	LION PASSANT	THREE CASTLES	LEOPARD'S HEAD CROWNED
1815-16*	**A**	😊	🦁	🏰	👑
1816-17*	**B**	"	"	"	"
1817-18*	**C**	"	"	"	"
1818-19*	**D**	"	"	"	"
1819-20*	E	"	"	"	"
GEO.IV 1820-21*	**F**	"	"	"	"
1821-22*	**G**	😊	"	"	"
1822-23*	**H**	"	"	"	"
1823-24*	**I**	"	"	"	"
1824-25*	**K**	"	"	"	"
1825-26*	L	"	"	"	"
1826-27*	M	"	"		"
1827-28*	N	"	"	"	"
1828-29*	O	"	"	"	"
1829-30*	**P**	😊	🦁	🏰	"
WM.IV 1830-31*	Q	"	"	"	"
1831-32*	R	"	"	"	"
1832-33*	**S**	😊	"	"	"
1833-34*	T	"	"	"	"
1834-35*	**U**	"	"	"	"
1835-36*	W	"	"	"	"
1836-37*	X	"	"	"	"
VICT. 1837-38*	**Y**	"	"	"	"
1838-39*	**Z**	"	"	"	"

* Asterisks indicate date letters recorded in the Newcastle Goldsmiths' Company minute books.

CYCLE VII

	DUTY MARK	LION PASSANT	THREE CASTLES	LEOPARD'S HEAD CROWNED	DATE LETTER
1839* †	Ⓞ	🦁	🏰	🐆	**A**
1840-41*	"	"	"	"	**B**
1841-42*	Ⓠ	"	"	"	**C**
1842-43*	"	"	"	"	**D**
1843-44*	"	"	"	"	**E**
1844-45*	"	"	"	"	**F**
1845-46*	"	"	"	"	**G**
1846-47* ‡	"	🦁	🏰	🐆	**H**
1847-48*	"	"	"	"	**I**
1848-49*	"	"	"	"	**J**
1849-50*	"	"	"	"	**K**
1850-51*	"	"	"	"	**L**
1851-52*	Ⓖ	"	"	🐆	**M**
1852-53*	"	"	"	"	**N**
1853-54*	"	"	"	"	**O**
1854-55*	"	"	"	"	**P**
1855-56*	"	"	"	"	**Q**
1856-57*	"	"	"	"	**R**
1857-58*	"	"	"	"	**S**
1858-59*	"	"	"	"	**T**
1859-60*	"	"	"	"	**U**
1860-61*	"	"	"	"	**W**
1861-62*	"	"	"	"	**X**
1862-63*	"	"	"	"	**Y**
1863-64*	"	"	"	"	**Z**

CYCLE VIII

	DUTY MARK	LION PASSANT	THREE CASTLES	LEOPARD'S HEAD CROWNED	DATE LETTER
1864-65*	Ⓞ	🦁	🏰	🐆	**a**
1865-66*	"	"	"	"	**b**
1866-67*	"	"	"	"	**c**
1867-68*	"	"	"	"	**d**
1868-69*	"	"	"	"	**e**
1869-70*	"	"	"	"	**f**
1870-71*	"	"	"	"	**g**
1871-72*	"	"	"	"	**h**
1872-73*	"	"	"	"	**i**
1873-74*	"	"	"	"	**k**
1874-75*	"	"	"	"	**l**
1875-76*	"	"	"	"	**m**
1876-77*	"	"	"	"	**n**
1877-78*	"	"	"	"	**o**
1878-79*	"	"	"	"	**p**
1879-80*	"	"	"	"	**q**
1880-81*	"	"	"	"	**r**
1881-82*	"	"	"	"	**s**
1882-83*	"	"	"	"	**t**
1883-84*	"	"	"	"	**u**

The office was closed in 1884.

* Asterisks indicate date letters recorded in the Newcastle Goldsmith's Company minute books.

† Head of William IV has been noted as late as 1842-43.

‡ From 1846 both crowned and uncrowned leopard's heads have been found.

MARK	MAKER	PERIOD	COMMENTS
AC	Alexander Cameron (of Dundee)	2nd ¼ 19th C	Much flatware
A·R	Ann Robertson	Early 19th C	Wide range
Ba	Francis Batty I	Late 17th/Very Early 18th C	Fine maker, wide range of pieces
Ba	Francis Batty II	Early 18th C	Wide variety
CAM ERON	Alexander Cameron (of Dundee)	2nd ¼ 19th C	Much flatware
CJR	Reid & Sons	Mid 19th C	Mostly retailing by this date
CJR	" "	" "	
CR	Christian Ker Reid I	Very late 18th/Early 19th C	
CR DR	Reid & Son	Early 19th C	The last large silversmiths in Newcastle
CR DR	" "	2nd ¼ 19th C	
CR DR CR	Reid & Sons	" "	
DC	David Crawford	3rd ¼ 18th C	Wide range; much flatware
D·D	David Darling	Very late 18th/Early 19th C	Mostly small pieces
D·L	Dorothy Langlands	Early 19th C	Prolific maker
DR	Reid & Sons	Mid 19th C	Mostly retailing by this date
DR	" "	" "	
FB	Francis Batty II	Early 18th C	Wide variety
I·C	Isaac Cookson	2nd ¼ 18th C	Prolific maker
IC	" "	" "	
IC	" "	Mid 18th C	
IC	James Crawford	2nd ½ 18th C	Wide range

MARK	MAKER	PERIOD	COMMENTS
I·K	James Kirkup	1st ½ 18th C	Wide variety, good maker
I·L	John Langlands II	Very late 18th C	Prolific maker
I·L I·R	John Langlands I & John Robertson I	Last ¼ 18th C	Prolific makers, many tankards and mugs
I·L I·R	" "	" "	
I·L	John Langlands I	2nd ½ 18th C	
I·R	James Kirkup	1st ½ 18th C	Wide variety, good maker
I·R	John Robertson I	Very late 18th C	Wide range
IR	John Robertson II	Early 19th C	Wide range
J·L	John Langlands I	2nd ½ 18th C	Prolific maker, many tankards and mugs
JR	John Robertson I	Very late 18th C	Wide range
Ki	James Kirkup	1st ½ 18th C	Wide variety, good maker
Ma Ba	Robert Makepeace I & Francis Batty II	Early 18th C	
R·M	Robert Makepeace I	2nd ¼ 18th C	Fine maker
R·M	" "	Mid 18th C	
T·W	Thomas Watson	Late 18th C	Prolific maker, wide range
TW	" "	Early 19th C mark	
W·B	William Beilby	Mid 18th C	Father of the famous Ralph Beilby

Norwich

Cycles of Hallmarks

	CASTLE OVER LION	DATE LETTER
1565-66		**A**
1566-67	"	**B**
1567-68		**C**
1568-69		**D**
1569-70		**E**
1570-71		**F**

DATE (ABOUT)	CASTLE OVER LION
c.1572	
c.1580	
1590	
1600-10	

	CASTLE OVER LION	ROSE CROWNED	DATE LETTER
1624-25			**A**
1625-26	"	"	**B**
1626-27		"	**C**
1627-28	"	"	**D**
1628-29		"	**E**
1629-30			**F**
1630-31	"		**G**
1631-32	"	"	**H**
1632-33	"	"	**I**
1633-34	"	"	**K**
1634-35	"	"	**L**
1635-36			**M**
1636-37			**N**
1637-38			**O**
1638-39	"	"	**P**
1639-40			**Q**
1640-41	"	"	**R**
1641-42	"	"	**S**
1642-43	"	"	**T**

DATE (ABOUT)	MARKS
1645	
1650	

DATE (ABOUT)	MARKS
1661	
1665	
1670	
1675	
1676	" "
1679	" "
1680	
1685	"
c.1685	

DATE (ABOUT)	ROSE CROWNED	CASTLE OVER LION	DATE LETTER
1688			a
1689			b
1690			c
1691			d
1692			E
1693			F
1694			G
1695			H
1696	"	"	I "
1697*	"	"	K

* Up to 27 March, 1697.

DATE (ABOUT)	MARKS
c.1697/1701	
	"
	'EH' "

DATE (ABOUT)	MARKS
1702/3	

The makers given below produced a variety of pieces, however, spoons will mostly be found.

MARK	MAKER	PERIOD	COMMENTS
	Arthur Haselwood	Mid 17th C	
	" "	" "	
	Arthur Haselwood II	3rd ¼ 17th C	
	Elizabeth Haselwood	Late 17th C	
	" "	" "	
	James Daniel	Late 17th C	
	" "	" "	
	Thomas Havers	Last ¼ 17th C	
	Timothy Skottowe	2nd ¼ 17th C	
	" "	" "	

CHAPTER X

Sheffield

Cycles of Hallmarks

CYCLE I

STANDARD MARKS

	LION PASSANT	CROWN	DATE LETTER	DUTY MARK
1773-74	🦁	👑	𝕬	
1774-75	"	"	𝕱	
1775-76	"	"	𝕻	
1776-77	"	"	𝕽	
1777-78	"	"	𝕳	
1778-79	"	"	𝕾	
1779-80	"	"	𝕬	
1780-81	"	"	𝕮	
1781-82	"	"	𝕯	
1782-83	"	"	𝕲	
1783-84	"	"	𝕭	
Up to 30 Nov 1784	"	"	𝕴	
From 1 Dec 1784-85	"	"	"	👤
1785-86	"	"	𝕻	"
1786-87	"	👑	𝕶	"
	"	"	"	👤
1787-88	"	"	𝕮	"
1788-89	"	"	𝕸	"
1789-90	"	"	𝕹	"
1790-91	"	"	𝕷	"
1791-92	"	"	𝕻	"
1792-93	🦁	👑	𝖀	"
1793-94	"	"	𝐎	"
1794-95	"	"	𝐦	"
1795-96	"	"	𝐪	"
1796-97*	"	"	𝐙	"
1797	"	"	𝐗	"
15 July 1797 to end of Aug 1798	"	"	"	👤👤
1798-99	"	"	𝐕	👤

MARKS ON SMALL ARTICLES

	LION PASSANT	CROWN & DATE LETTER	DUTY MARK
1780-81	🦁	𝑒	
1781-82	"	𝑑	
1782-83	"	𝑐	
1783-84	"	𝐵	
Up to 30 Nov 1784	"	𝑓	
From 1 Dec 1784-85	"	"	👤
1785-86	"	𝑝	"
	"	"	👤
1786-87	"	𝑘	"
1787-88	"	𝑡	"
1788-89	"	𝑤	"
1789-90	"	𝑠	"
1790-91	"	𝐿	"
1791-92	"	𝑃	"
1792-93		𝑢	"
1793-94	"	𝑜	"
1794-95	"	𝑚	"
1795-96	"	𝑞	"
1796-97	"	𝑧	"
1797	"	𝑥	"
15 July 1797 to end of Aug 1798	"	"	👤👤
1798-99	"	𝑣	👤

* A teapot of 1796-97 is stamped with a variation of the Z 𝐙

CYCLE II

STANDARD MARKS

	LION PASSANT	CROWN	DATE LETTER	DUTY MARK
1799-1800	🦁	👑	**E**	👤
1800-1	"	"	**N**	"
1801-2	"	"	**H**	"
1802-3	"	"	**M**	"
1803-4	"	"	**F**	"
1804-5	"	"	**G**	"
1805-6	"	"	**B**	👤
1806-7	"	"	**A**	👤
1807-8	"	"	**S**	"
1808-9	"	"	**P**	"
1809-10	"	"	**K**	"
1810-11	"	"	**L**	"
1811-12*	"	"	**C**	👤
1812-13	"	"	**D**	"
1813-14	"	"	**R**	"
1814-15	"	"	**W**	👤
1815-16	"	"	**O**	"
1816-17	"	"	**T**	"
1817-18	"	"	**X**	"
1818-19	"	"	**I**	"
1819-20	"	"	**V**	"
GEO.IV 1820-21	"	"	**Q**	"
1821-22	"	"	**Y**	"
1822-23	"	"	**Z**	"
1823-24	"	"	**U**	"

MARKS ON SMALL ARTICLES

	LION PASSANT	CROWN & DATE LETTER	DUTY MARK
1799-1800	🦁	Ⓔ	👤
1800-1	"	Ⓝ	"
1801-2	"	Ⓗ	"
1802-3	"	Ⓜ	"
1803-4	"	Ⓕ	"
1804-5	"	Ⓖ	"
1805-6	"	Ⓑ	👤
1806-7	"	Ⓐ	👤
1807-8	"	Ⓢ	"
1808-9	"	Ⓟ	"
1809-10	"	Ⓚ	"
1810-11	"	Ⓛ	"
1811-12*	"	Ⓒ	👤
1812-13	"	Ⓓ	"
1813-14	"	Ⓡ	"
1814-15	"	Ⓦ	👤
1815-16	"	Ⓞ	"
1816-17	"	Ⓣ	"
1817-18	"	Ⓧ	"
1818-19	"	Ⓘ	"
1819-20	"	Ⓥ	"
GEO.IV 1820-21	"	Ⓠ	"
1821-22	"	Ⓨ	"
1822-23	"	Ⓩ	"
1823-24	"	Ⓤ	"

* Alternative duty mark for this year 👤

CYCLE III

STANDARD MARKS

	LION PASSANT	CROWN	DATE LETTER	DUTY MARK
1824-25	🦁	👑	**a**	👤
1825-26	"	"	**b**	"
1826-27	"	"	**c**	"
1827-28	"	"	**d**	"
1828-29	"	"	**e**	"
1829-30	"	"	**f**	"
WM.IV 1830-31	"	"	**g**	"
1831-32	"	"	**h**	👤
1832-33	"	"	**K**	"
1833-34	"	"	**l**	"
1834-35	"	"	**m**	"
1835-36	"	"	**p**	👤
1836-37	"	"	**q**	"
VICT. 1837-38	"	"	**r**	"
1838-39	"	"	**S**	"
1839-40	"	"	**t**	"
1840-41	"	"	**u**	👤
1841-42	"	"	**V**	"
1842-43	"	"	**X**	"
1843-44	"	"	**Z**	"

MARKS ON SMALL ARTICLES

	LION PASSANT	CROWN & DATE LETTER	DUTY MARK
1824-25	🦁	**a**	👤
1825-26	"	**b**	"
1826-27	"	**c**	"
1827-28	"	**d**	"
1828-29	"	**e**	"
1829-30	"	**f**	"
WM.IV 1830-31	"	**g**	"
1831-32	"	**h**	👤
1832-33	"	**k**	"
1833-34	"	**l**	"
1834-35	"	**m**	"
1835-36*	"	**p**	👤
1836-37	"	**q**	"
VICT. 1837-38	"	**r**	"
1838-39	"	**S**	"
1839-40	"	**t**	"
1840-41	"	**u**	👤
1841-42	"	**V**	"
1842-43	"	**X**	"
1843-44	"	**Z**	"

* Variation: 🔵P

CYCLE IV

STANDARD MARKS

	CROWN	DATE LETTER	LION PASSANT	DUTY MARK
1844-45	👑	A	🦁	👤
1845-46	"	B	"	"
1846-47	"	C	"	"
1847-48	"	D	"	"
1848-49	"	E	"	"
1849-50	"	F	"	"
1850-51	"	G	"	"
1851-52	"	H	"	"
1852-53	"	I	"	"
1853-54	"	K	"	"
1854-55	"	L	"	"
1855-56	"	M	"	"
1856-57	"	N	"	"
1857-58	"	O	"	"
1858-59	"	P	"	"
1859-60	"	R	"	"
1860-61	"	S	"	"
1861-62	"	T	"	"
1862-63	"	U	"	"
1863-64	"	V	"	"
1864-65	"	W	"	"
1865-66	"	X	"	"
1866-67	"	Y	"	"
1867-68	"	Z	"	"

MARKS ON SMALL ARTICLES

	CROWN & DATE LETTER	LION PASSANT	DUTY MARK
1844-45	A👑	🦁	👤
1845-46	B👑	"	"
1846-47	C👑	"	"
1847-48	D👑	"	"
1848-49	E👑	"	"
1849-50	F👑	"	"
1850-51	G👑	"	"
1851-52	H👑	"	"
1852-53	I👑	"	"
1853-54	K👑	"	"

CYCLE V

	CROWN	LION PASSANT	DATE LETTER	DUTY MARK
1868-69	👑	🦁	**A**	👤
1869-70	"	"	**B**	"
1870-71	"	"	**C**	"
1871-72	"	"	**D**	"
1872-73	"	"	**E**	"
1873-74	"	"	**F**	"
1874-75	"	"	**G**	"
1875-76	"	"	**H**	"
1876-77	"	"	**J**	"
1877-78	"	"	**K**	"
1878-79	"	"	**L**	"
1879-80	"	"	**M**	"
1880-81	"	"	**N**	"
1881-82	"	"	**O**	"
1882-83	"	"	**P**	"
1883-84	"	"	**Q**	"
1884-85	"	"	**R**	"
1885-86	"	"	**S**	"
1886-87	"	"	**T**	"
1887-88	"	"	**U**	"
1888-89	"	"	**V**	"
1889-90	"	"	**W**	"
June 1890	"	"	"	
1890-91	"	"	**X**	
1891-92	"	"	**Y**	
1892-93	"	"	**Z**	

CYCLE VI

	CROWN	LION PASSANT	DATE LETTER
1893-94	👑	🦁	**a**
1894-95	"	"	**b**
1895-96	"	"	**c**
1896-97	"	"	**d**
1897-98	"	"	**e**
1898-99	"	"	**f**
1899-1900	"	"	**g**
1900-1	"	"	**h**
EDW.VII 1901-2	"	"	**i**
1902-3	"	"	**k**
1903-4	"	"	**l**
1904-5	"	"	**m**
1905-6	"	"	**n**
1906-7	"	"	**o**
1907-8	"	"	**p**
1908-9	"	"	**q**
1909-10	"	"	**r**
GEO.V 1910-11	"	"	**s**
1911-12	"	"	**t**
1912-13	"	"	**u**
1913-14	"	"	**v**
1914-15	"	"	**w**
1915-16	"	"	**x**
1916-17	"	"	**y**
1917-18	"	"	**z**

CYCLE VII

	CROWN	LION PASSANT	DATE LETTER
1918-19	♔	🦁	**a**
1919-20	"	"	**b**
1920-21	"	"	**c**
1921-22	"	"	**d**
1922-23	"	"	**e**
1923-24	"	"	**f**
1924-25	"	"	**g**
1925-26	"	"	**h**
1926-27	"	"	**i**
1927-28	"	"	**k**
1928-29	"	"	**l**
1929-30	"	"	**m**
1930-31	"	"	**n**
1931-32	"	"	**o**
1932-33	"	"	**p**
1933-34*	"	"	**q**
1934-35*	"	"	**r**
1935-36	"	"	**s**
EDW.VIII 1936-37	"	"	**t**
GEO.VI 1837-38	"	"	**u**
1938-39	"	"	**v**
1939-40	"	"	**w**
1940-41	"	"	**x**
1941-42	"	"	**y**
1942-43	"	"	**z**

CYCLE VIII

	CROWN	LION PASSANT	DATE LETTER
1943-44	♔	🦁	**A**
1944-45	"	"	**B**
1945-46	"	"	**C**
1946-47	"	"	**D**
1947-48	"	"	**E**
1948-49	"	"	**F**
1949-50	"	"	**G**
1950-51	"	"	**H**
1951-52	"	"	**I**
ELIZ.II 1952-53*	"	"	**K**
1953-54	"	"	**L**
1954-55	"	"	**M**
1955-56	"	"	**N**
1956-57	"	"	**O**
1957-58	"	"	**P**
1958-59	"	"	**Q**
1959-60	"	"	**R**
1960-61	"	"	**S**
1961-62	"	"	**T**
1962-63	"	"	**U**
1963-64	"	"	**V**
1964-65	"	"	**W**
1965-66	"	"	**X**
1966-67	"	"	**Y**
1967-68	"	"	**Z**

* Optional Silver Jubilee mark:

* Optional coronation mark:

CYCLE IX

	CROWN	LION PASSANT	DATE LETTER
1968-69			𝒜
1969-70	"	"	ℬ
1970-71	"	"	𝒞
1971-72	"	"	𝒟
1972-73	"	"	ℰ
1973-74*	"	"	ℱ
1974 up to 31 Dec	"	"	𝒢

* To commemorate the bicentenary of the Sheffield Assay Office, a copy of the date letter for 1773 was used (in a different field to avoid confusion).

CYCLE X

	ROSE	LION PASSANT	DATE LETTER
1975			𝒜
1976	"	"	ℬ
1977 †	"	"	𝒞
1978	"	"	𝒟
1979	"	"	ℰ
1980	"	"	ℱ
1981	"	"	𝒢
1982	"	"	ℋ
1983	"	"	𝒥
1984	"	"	𝒦
1985	"	"	ℒ
1986	"	"	ℳ
1987	"	"	𝒩
1988	"	"	𝒪
1989	"	"	𝒫
1990	"	"	𝒬
1991	"	"	ℛ

† Optional Silver Jubilee mark:

Marks reproduced courtesy The Worshipful Company of Goldsmiths.

PLATINUM FROM 1975 ON

	ROSE	PLATINUM MARK	DATE LETTER
Date as Left			𝒜

GOLD MARKS

22ct.	⚜	♛	22	C
18ct.	"	"	18	"
15ct.			15 ·625	"
12ct.			12 ·5	"
9ct.			9 ·375	"

Sheffield has put hallmarks on gold since 1904. The examples given are for 1920-1. In 1932 15 and 12 carats were abolished and replaced by 14 carats (marked 14·585). From 1932 to the end of 1974 the four carat values of 22, 18, 14, and 9 will be found marked 22, 18, 14·585 and 9·375 respectively.

From 1 January, 1975 to the present day 22 carat is represented by 916, 18 carat by 750, 14 by 585 and 9 carat by 375. As with the earlier gold marks these punches will be struck with a crown, the rose for Sheffield and the date letter.

IMPORTED WARES ASSAYED AT SHEFFIELD

The letter F was added, as for example:

	CROWN	LION PASSANT	DATE LETTER	IMPORT MARK
1893-94	♛	🦁	a	F

IMPORT MARKS 1904-06

	GOLD				SILVER			
22ct.	✳	22·916	+ Date letter & sponsor's mark	Britannia	✳	·9584	+ Date letter & sponsor's mark
20ct.	"	20·833	"	Sterling	"	·925	"
18ct.	"	18·75	"				
15ct.	"	15·625	"				
12ct.	"	12·5	"				
9ct.	"	9·375	"				

	GOLD 1906-32				SILVER 1906 to end of 1974			
22ct.	Ω	22·916	+ Date letter & sponsor's mark	Britannia	Ω	·9584	+ Date letter & sponsor's mark
20ct.	"	20·833	"	Sterling	"	·925	"
18ct.	"	18·75	"				
15ct.	"	15·625	"				
12ct.	"	12·5	"				
9ct.	"	9·375	"				

IMPORT MARKS (continued)

GOLD 1932 to end of 1974

22ct.	Ω	916
18ct.	"	750
14ct.	"	585
9ct.	"	375

1975 and on

Platinum	Ω 950
Gold 22ct.	Ω 916
18ct.	" 750
14ct.	" 585
9ct.	" 375

Silver Britannia	Ω 958
Sterling	" 925

CONVENTION HALLMARKS

Precious Metal		Town Mark	Fineness Mark	Common Control Mark
Platinum		🛡	950	950
Gold	18ct.	"	750	750
	14ct.	"	585	585
	9ct.	"	375	375
Silver	Sterling	"	925	925

ON IMPORTED WARES

Precious Metal		Town Mark	Fineness Mark	Common Control Mark
Platinum		Ω	950	950
Gold	18ct.	Ω	750	750
	14ct.	"	585	585
	9ct.	"	375	375
Silver	Sterling	Ω	925	925

MARK	MAKER	PERIOD	COMMENTS
AG&Cº	Alex Goodman & Co	(First entered 1797; this mark 1801)	Large range
DH&Cº	Daniel Holy & Co	(Entered 1783)	Large range
EM&Cº	Elkington Mason & Co	(Entered 1859)	Large variety
GA &Cº	George Ashworth	(Entered 1773)	Large range
GE &Cº	George Eadon & Co	(Entered 1795)	Large range
H&H	Howard & Hawksworth	(Entered 1835)	Large variety
HE &Cº	Hawkesworth, Eyre & Co	(Entered 1833)	Large variety
HT&Cº	Hy Tudor & Co	(Entered 1797)	Large range
HL TL	Tudor & Leader	(Entered 1773)	Large range
HW &Cº **HW &Cº**	Hy Wilkinson & Co	(Entered 1831)	Large variety
I&IW &Cº	Waterhouse, Hodson & Co	(Entered 1822)	Candlesticks
IG&Cº	John Green & Co	(Entered 1793)	Prolific maker of candlesticks
IH&Cº **IH &Cº**	J Hoyland & Co	(Entered 1773) " "	Large range
I·K·I·W&Cº	Kirkby, Waterhouse & Co	(Entered c.1813)	Prolific maker, wide range
I·P&Cº	John Parsons & Co	(Entered 1783)	Prolific maker of candlesticks
I·R&Cº	John Roberts & Co	(Entered 1805)	Prolific maker, large range
ITY &Cº	J T Younge & Co	(Entered 1797)	Large range
ITY&Cº	John Younge & Sons	(Entered 1788)	Large range
IW&Cº	John Winter & Co	(Entered 1773)	Large range
JD &S	James Deakin & Sons	(Entered 1894)	Large variety
J·D&S	James Dixon & Son	(Entered 1867)	Large variety

MARK	MAKER	PERIOD	COMMENTS
J D W D	James Deakin & Sons	(Entered 1878)	Large variety
J R	John Round & Son Ltd	(Entered 1874)	Large variety
M&W	Mappin & Webb	(Entered 1892)	Large variety
M B	Mappin Bros	(Entered 1859)	Large variety
MF &Cº	M Fenton & Co	(Entered c.1790)	Large range
MF RC	Fenton Creswick & Co	(Entered 1773)	Large range
M H &Co	Martin Hall & Co	(Entered 1854)	Large variety
M&R&Cº	Mappin & Webb	(Entered 1864)	Large variety
N·S&Cº	Nathaniel Smith & Co	(Entered 1780)	Large range
R&B	Roberts & Belk	(Entered 1892)	Large variety
R·M	Richard Morton & Co	(Entered 1773 & 1781)	Large range
R·M &Cº	" "	(Entered 1773)	
R M E H	Martin Hall & Co	(Entered 1863)	Large variety
R M E H	Martin Hall & Co Ltd	(Entered 1880)	
SR&Cº	S Roberts & Co	(Entered 1773)	Large range
ST N&H	Smith, Tate & Co (Nicholson & Hoult)	(Entered 1812)	Prolific maker, wide range
TB &S	Thomas Bradbury & Sons	(Entered 1892)	Large variety
TJ NC	T J & N Creswick	(Entered c.1827)	Candlesticks
TJ&NC	" "	(Entered 1819)	Prolific maker, wide range
T·LAW	Thomas Law	(Entered 1773)	Large range
TW&Cº	Thomas Watson & Co	(Entered c.1801)	Prolific maker, wide range
W&H	Walker & Hall	(Entered 1862)	Large variety
W&H	" "	(Entered 1896)	
WS GS	W & G Sissons	(Entered 1858)	Large variety

CHAPTER XI

York

Cycles of Hallmarks

Example of pre-1559 Town Mark

DATE	MARK
c.1475-1500	

CYCLE I

	TOWN MARK	DATE LETTER
ELIZ.I 1559-60		**A**
1560-61		**B**
1561-62	″	**C**
1562-63		**D**
1563-64		**E**
1564-65		**F**
1565-66		**G**
1566-67		**H**
1567-68		**I**
1568-69		**K**
1569-70		**L**
1570-71		**M**
1571-72		**N**
1572-73		**O**
1573-74		**P**
1574-75	″	**Q**
1575-76		**R**
1576-77		**S**
1577-78	″	**T**
1578-79		**V**
1579-80		**W**
1580-81		**X**
1581-82		**Y**
1582-83	″	**Z**

CYCLE II

	TOWN MARK	DATE LETTER
1583-84		**a**
1584-85		**b**
1585-86		**c**
1586-87		**d**
1587-88	″	**e**
1588-89		**f**
1589-90		**g**
1590-91	″	**h**
1591-92		**i**
1592-93		**k**
1593-94	″	**l**
1594-95	″	**m**
1595-96		**n**
1596-97		**o**
1597-98	″	**p**
1598-99		**q**
1599-1600	″	**r**
1600-1		**s**
1601-2	″	**t**
1602-3		**u**
JAS.I 1603-4		**w**
1604-5	″	**x**
1605-6		**y**
1606-7		**z**

CYCLE III

	TOWN MARK	DATE LETTER
1607-8		**A**
1608-9		**B**
1609-10	″	**C**
1610-11	″	**D**
1611-12	″	**E**
1612-13	″	**F**
1613-14		**G**
1614-15	″	**H**
1615-16		**I**
1616-17	″	**K**
1617-18		**L**
1618-19	″	**M**
1619-20	″	**N**
1620-21	″	**O**
1621-22	″	**P**
1622-23		**Q**
1623-24		**R**
1624-25		**S**
CHAS.I 1625-26		**T**
1626-27	″	**U**
1627-28	″	**W**
1628-29		**x**
1629-30	″	**Y**
1630-31	″	**Z**

CYCLE IV

	TOWN MARK	DATE LETTER
1631-32	⬤	*a*
1632-33	⬤	*b*
1633-34	"	*c*
1634-35	"	*d*
1635-36	"	*e*
1636-37	⬤	*f*
1637-38	⬤	*g*
1638-39	"	*h*
1639-40	"	*i*
1640-41	"	*k*
1641-42	"	*l*
1642-43	"	*m*
1643-44		*n*
1644-45	"	*o*
1645-46		*p*
1646-47		*q*
1647-48		*r*
1648-49	⬤	*s*
COMWTH. 1649-50	⬤	*t*
1650-51	"	*u*
1651-52		*w*
1652-53	"	*x*
1653-54	"	*y*
1654-55	"	*z*

CYCLE V

	TOWN MARK	DATE LETTER
1655-56	⬤	A
1656-57	⬤	B
1757-58	⬤	C
1658-59	"	D
1659-60	"	E
CHAS.II 1660-61	⬤	F
1661-62	⬤	G
1662-63	"	H
1663-64	"	J
1664-65	⬤	K
1665-66	"	L
1666-67	"	M
1667-68	"	N
1668-69	⬤	O
1669-70	"	P
1670-71	⬤	Q
1671-72	"	R
1672-73	"	S
1673-74	"	T
1674-75	"	V
1675-76	"	W
1676-77	⬤	X
1677-78	"	Y
1678-79	"	Z

CYCLE VI

	TOWN MARK	DATE LETTER
1679-80	⬤	A
1680-81	"	B
1681-82	⬤	C
1682-83		D
1683-84	"	E
1684-85	"	F
JAS.II 1685-86	"	G
1686-87	"	H
1687-88		J
1688-89	⬤	K
WM.& MY. 1689-90	"	L
1690-91	"	M
1691-92		N
1692-93	⬤	O
1693-94	"	P
1694-95	"	Q
1695-96	"	R
WM.III 1696-97		S

CYCLE VII

	TOWN MARK	BRIT-ANNIA	LION'S HEAD ERASED	DATE LETTER
1701-2				
ANNE 1702-3				Ⓑ
1703-4	"	"	"	Ⓒ
1704-5	"	"	"	Ⓓ
1705-6				
1706-7	"	"	"	Ⓕ
1707-8	"	"	"	Ⓖ
1708-9				
1709-10	"	"	"	
1710-11				
1711-12				
1712-13	"	"	"	𝔪
1713-14				
GEO.I 1714-15	"	"	"	
1715-16				

CYCLE VIII

	TOWN MARK	LION PASSANT	LEOPARD'S HEAD CROWNED	DATE LETTER	DUTY MARK
1776-77				A	
1777-78				B	
1778-79				C	
1779-80				Ⓓ	
1780-81	"	"	"	Ⓔ	
1781-82	"	"	"	Ⓕ	
1782-83	"	"	"	Ⓖ	
1783-84		"	"	Ⓗ	
1784-85	"	"	"	Ⓙ	
1785-86		"			"
1786-87		"		"	

*CYCLE IX

	TOWN MARK	LION PASSANT	LEOPARD'S HEAD CROWNED	DUTY MARK	DATE LETTER
1787-88		🦁	👑		Ⓐ
1788-89					Ⓑ
1789-90	🛡	"	👑	"	Ⓒ
1790-91	🛡	"	"	"	ⓓ
1791-92		"	"	"	ⓔ
1792-93					"
1793-94		"	"	"	ⓖ
1794-95		"	"	"	ⓗ
1795-96	"	"	"	"	ⓘ
1796-97		"	"	"	ⓚ
1797-98	"	"	"	👑	ⓛ
1798-99	✠	"	"	"	Ⓜ
1799-1800		"	"	"	Ⓝ
1800-1	🛡	"	"	"	Ⓞ
1801-2		"	"	"	Ⓟ
1802-3	"	"	"	"	Ⓠ
1803-4	"	"	"	"	Ⓡ
1804-5		"	"	"	Ⓢ
1805-6		"	"	"	Ⓣ
1806-7		"	"	"	Ⓤ
1807-8	"	"	"	"	Ⓥ
1808-9		"	"	"	Ⓦ
1809-10		"	"	"	Ⓧ
1810-11		"	"	"	Ⓨ
1811-12		"	"	"	Ⓩ

* From 1793-1808 the lion passant is sometimes found facing right.

Other variations stamped on small brass plate from the assay office:

1805-6   1807-8 **Ⓥ**   1809-10 **Ⓧ**

 Sometimes used from 1790 onwards.

CYCLE X

	TOWN MARK	LION PASSANT	LEOPARD'S HEAD CROWNED	DUTY MARK	DATE LETTER
1812-13*		▦	♛	●	**a**
1813-14*					"
1814-15					"
1815-16*		"	"	"	**d**
1816-17					"
1817-18	⊕	"	"	"	**f**
1818-19	"	"	"	"	**g**
1819-20*		"	"	"	**h**
GEO.IV 1820-21*		"	"	"	**i**
1821-22*		"	"	"	**k**
1822-23		"	"		"
1823-24*					"
1824-25	"	"	"	"	**n**
1825-26	"	"	"	"	**o**
1826-27		"	"	"	**p**
1827-28§		"	"	"	**q**
1828-29		"	"	"	**r**
1829-30	"	"	"	"	**s**
WM.IV 1830-31		"	"	●	**t**
1831-32		"	"	"	**u**
1832-33*		"	"	●	**u**
1833-34*		"	"	"	**w**
1834-35		"	"	"	**x**
1835-36		"	"	"	**z**

* In examples of marks from 1812 onwards, the leopard's head is sometimes found with whiskers and sometimes without. Other variations stamped on small brass plate from the assay office:

1812-15 **a**   1813-14 **b**   1815-17 **d**

1819-20 **h**   1820-21 **i**   1821-24 **k**

1832-33 **u**   1833-34 **w**

§ Alternative date letter for 1827-8: (See 'Any Old Ladle', *Antique Collecting*, Dec. 1987.) **q**

CYCLE XI

	TOWN MARK	LION PASSANT	LEOPARD'S HEAD CROWNED	DUTY MARK	DATE LETTER
1836-37					**A**
1837-38		"	"		**B**
1838-39		"	"	"	**C**
1839-40		"	"		**D**
1840-41		"	"	"	**E**
1841-42	"	"	"	"	**F**
1842-43		"	"	"	**G**
1843-44		"	"	"	**H**
1844-45		"	"	"	**I**
1845-46					**K**
1846-47		"	"	"	**L**
1847-48		"		"	**M**
1848-49	"	"		"	**N**
1849-50		"	"	"	**O**
1850-51		"	"	"	**P**
1851-52		"	"	"	**Q**
1852-53		"		"	**R**
1853-54		"	"	"	**S**
1854-55		"	"	"	**T**
1855-56		"	"	"	**U**
1856-57	"	"	"	"	**V**
1857-58		"	"	"	**W**
1858-59		"		"	**X**

It is thought that the York Assay Office ended its active life by the end of 1858.

MARK	MAKER	PERIOD	COMMENTS
H&P	John Hampston & John Prince	Last ¼ 18th C	Variety of plate
HP &C	Hampston, Prince & Cattles	Very early 19th C	Variety of plate, mostly flatware
I·H I·P, **I·H P**, **I·H P**	John Hampston & John Prince	Last ¼ 18th C	Variety of plate
	" "	" "	
	" "	" "	
JB	James Barber	Mid 19th C	Mostly flatware
JB GC WN	James Barber, George Cattle & William North	2nd ¼ 19th C	Mostly flatware
JB WN	James Barber & William North	2nd ¼ 19th C	Mostly flatware
JB WW	James Barber & William Whitwell	Early 19th C	Variety of plate, mostly flatware
LA	John Langwith	Queen Anne period	Variety of plate
RC JB	Robert Cattle & James Barber	Early 19th C	Variety of plate, mostly flatware

NOTE: There are several variations of the above. Reference to either *Jackson's* York section or Martin Gubbins' *York Silversmiths* is recommended.

English Provincial Marks

The marks given below are intended as a selective guide to the sort of marks to be found in these centres. For a comprehensive list with names of makers and other marks, reference should be made to the appropriate section in the main volume.

Barnstaple

DATE	MARKS
c.1585	
1630-40	
1670-80	

Bridgwater

DATE	MARKS
c.1680	

Bristol

DATE	MARKS
c.1620	
c.1735	

Coventry

DATE	MARKS
Early 17th C	

Dorchester

DATE	MARKS
c.1575	

Falmouth

DATE	MARKS
c.1685-1700	

Gloucester

DATE	MARKS
c.1660-90	

Gt. Yarmouth

DATE	MARKS
c.1680	

Hull

DATE	MARKS
1629	
1651	
1697	

King's Lynn

DATE	MARKS
c.1600-20	

Launceston

DATE	MARKS
c.1695	

Leeds

DATE	MARKS
1650	
1690	

Leicester

DATE	MARKS
1570	

Lewes

DATE	MARKS
c.1640	

Lincoln

DATE	MARKS
c.1570	

Liverpool

DATE	MARKS
Early 18th C	
c.1710	

Plymouth

DATE	MARKS
1600-50	
c.1695	
1697-1700	

Salisbury

DATE	MARKS
Late 16th e.17th C	
1620-40	
1640-50	
1670	

Sherborne

DATE	MARKS
Early 17th C	

Southampton

DATE	MARKS
c.1680	

Taunton

DATE	MARKS
c.1660-80	
c.1690	

Truro

DATE	MARKS
c.1610-20	

Waveney Valley

DATE	MARKS
c.1650	

CHAPTER XIII

168

Scottish Provincial Marks

The marks given below are intended as a selective guide to the sort of marks to be found in these centres. For a comprehensive list with names of makers and other marks, reference should be made to the appropriate section in the main volume.

Aberdeen

DATE (ABOUT)	MARKS
1650	
1691-97	
1718-27	
1778-1801	
1824-91	
1871	

Arbroath

DATE (ABOUT)	MARKS
1835-50	

Banff

DATE (ABOUT)	MARKS
1698	
1750	
1820-40	
1825	

Canongate

DATE (ABOUT)	MARKS
1625	
1696	
1740	
1770-75	
1775	

Cupar

DATE (ABOUT)	MARKS
Mid 19th C	

Dumfries

DATE (ABOUT)	MARKS
1794-1817	
1820	
1834-44	

Dundee

DATE (ABOUT)	MARKS
1628-36	AL ⚜ AL
1667	TL ⚜ TL
1734-35	GD ⚜ GD E
1790-1800	EL ⚜ EL m
1820-40	CAM ERON ⚜ C ⚜ DUN DEE
1865	RN ⚜ ⚜ ⚜

Inverness

DATE (ABOUT)	MARKS
1708	M INS M
1760	RA 🐾 C INS
1830	RN INS J RN
1840	TS INS 🐪
1890	F&M 🐫 INVS

Elgin

DATE (ABOUT)	MARKS
1708	VS ELGIN D
1755	IH ELN 🦌 A
1813	TS ELN ▦
1835	JS ELN

Montrose

DATE (ABOUT)	MARKS
1671	◉ 🌹 ◉
1752	TI B ✿
1790	✳ EL ✳
1835	🌹 ◉ PL ◉ 🌹
1860	🌹 🌹 🌹

Forres

DATE (ABOUT)	MARKS
1817-36	⬛ IPR ⬛
1850-67	RH ⬛ RH

Paisley

DATE (ABOUT)	MARKS
1790-1820	IA 🦁 IA ⬌ T I&GH WH 🐟 ⬌

Greenock

DATE (ABOUT)	MARKS
1775-80	IT ⚓ IT S
1800-30	IH ⚓ 🌳 C

Perth

DATE (ABOUT)	MARKS
1687	RG 🦅 RG
1772-85	IC ✿ IC ✿
1839-56	RK ✿ RK ✿

Peterhead

DATE (ABOUT)	MARKS
1825	WF PHD WF

St. Andrews

DATE (ABOUT)	MARKS
1670	PG ⊗ PG

Tain

DATE (ABOUT)	MARKS
1740	H·R TAIN S·D ℒ
1835	RW TAIN

Wick

DATE (ABOUT)	MARKS
1825	JS WICK

Irish Provincial Marks

The marks given below are intended as a selective guide to the sort of marks to be found in these centres. For a comprehensive list with names of makers and other marks, reference should be made to the appropriate section in the main volume.

Cork

DATE	MARKS
1663	
1679	
1686	
1692	
1698	
1710	
1715-25	STERLING
1745-70	STARLING G✾H
1795	WT STERLING
1808-20	•CORBETT• STERLING

Galway

DATE	MARKS
1695	
1730	MF

Kinsale

DATE	MARKS
1712	W W

Youghal

DATE	MARKS
1644	IG
1683	BF
1712	EG

Limerick

DATE	MARKS
1685	RS
1710	
1730-62	STERLING
1784	P•C STER P•C
1784	TB STERLING
1798	WW STER WW
1810-20	S★P STERLING

Bibliography

Other than *Jackson's Silver & Gold Marks of England, Scotland & Ireland,* the following works will be found to be particularly useful.

General

Report of Departmental Committee on Hallmarking Board of Trade, 1959.

Touching Gold and Silver, Exhibition Catalogue, Goldsmiths Hall, 1978.

Castro, J.P. de, The Law and Practice of Marking Gold and Silver Wares, 1926.

D.T.W., Hallmarks on Gold and Silver Plate, J.M. Dent and Sons Ltd., 1925.

Dove, A.B.L., "Some New Light on Plate Duty and its Marks", Antique Collecting, Sept. 1984.

Dove, A.B.L., "Some Observations on Gold and its Hallmarks", Antique Collecting, Sept. 1986.

How, G.E.P. and J.P., English and Scottish Silver Spoons and Pre-Elizabethan Hallmarks on English Plate, 3 vols., privately printed, 1952.

How, G.E.P., The Ellis Collection of Provincial Spoons, Sotheby and Co. Catalogue, 1935.

London

Culme, J., The Directory of Gold and Silversmiths, Jewellers and Allied Traders 1838-1914, Antique Collectors' Club, 1987.

Goldsmiths' Hall — see General section.

Grimwade, A.G., London Goldsmiths 1697-1837, Their Marks and Lives, Faber and Faber, 3rd edition 1990.

How, G.E.P. and J.P. — see General section.

Kent, T.A., London Silver Spoonmakers 1500-1697, The Silver Society, 1981.

Birmingham

Jones, K.C., (ed.), The Silversmiths of Birmingham and their Marks 1750-1980, N.A.G. Press, 1981.

Chester

Ridgway, M.H., Chester Goldsmiths from early times to 1726, Sherratt, 1968.

Ridgway, M.H., Chester Silver 1727-1837, Phillimore, 1985.

Cornwall

Douch, H.L., "Cornish Goldsmiths", Journal of the Royal Institution of Cornwall, 1970.

Exeter

Exeter Museum, Exeter and West Country Silver, 1978.

Kent, T.A., Early West Country Spoons, Exeter Museum, 1977.

Ireland

Bennett, D., Irish Georgian Silver, Cassell and Co. Ltd., 1972.

Ticher, K., and Delamer, I., Hallmarks on Dublin Silver 1730-1772, National Museum of Ireland, 1968.

King's Lynn

Lynn Silver, Exhibition Catalogue, King's Lynn Preservation Trust.

Liverpool

Grosvenor Museum, The, Chester Silver, Loan Exhibition Catalogue, Sotheby's, 1984.

Newcastle

Gill, M.A.V., A Directory of Newcastle Goldsmiths, Goldsmiths Hall, 1980.

Gill, M.A.V., A Handbook of Newcastle Silver, 1978.

Norwich

Barrett, G.N., Norwich Silver and its Marks, 1565-1702.

Barrett, G.N., The Goldsmiths of Norwich 1141-1750, The Wensum Press, 1981.

Norfolk Museums Service, Norwich Silver in the Collection of Norwich Castle Museum, 1981.

Sheffield

Bradbury, F., History of Old Sheffield Plate, Northend Publications, 1968.

Sheffield Assay Office, The Sheffield Assay Office Register, 1911.

York

Gubbins, M., York Assay Office and Silversmiths 1776-1858, William Sessions Ltd., 1983.

Lee, W., York Silver 1475-1858, Catalogue of the William Lee Collection in the York Undercroft, 1972.

Other books available on silver and gold ware from the
Antique Collectors' Club

JACKSON'S SILVER AND GOLD MARKS OF ENGLAND, SCOTLAND AND IRELAND
edited by Ian Pickford
766 pp., ISBN 0 907462 63 4
For over 80 years this has been the book on antique silver essential to dealers, scholars and collectors. Now half a century of research is incorporated in this **new edition** which contains some 10,000 corrections to the original material as well as much vital extra information. A key reference book.

19TH CENTURY AUSTRALIAN SILVER
by J.B. Hawkins
2 volumes. Vol I, 344 pp. Vol. II, 376 pp. Over 80 colour plates. Over 700 b. & w. illustrations. ISBN 1 85149 002 7
The first comprehensive book on the fascinating but hitherto neglected wares of 19th century Australian silversmiths. It contains detailed biographies of all known Australian craftsmen with a photographic index of their marks, lavishly illustrated throughout. While a strong European design influence predominates, Australian flora and fauna play an important part in the manufacture of the more exotic pieces. An essential reference as without it, a good deal of Australian silver, usually many times more valuable than its European equivalent, will go unrecognised or wrongly ascribed. This will be the standard work for many years.

STARTING TO COLLECT SILVER

by John Luddington

228 pp., 345 b. & w. illus. ISBN 0 907462 48 0

John Luddington, an experienced dealer of long standing, describes the importance of the many varied aspects of quality both in terms of aesthetics and hard cash, and analyses the value of pieces.

This fascinating book describes in an easy to read manner the many problems and pitfalls which face the novice and includes copious illustrations of interesting items. It guides the reader through the pitfalls of the silver trade and discusses the pieces to avoid.

THE PRICE GUIDE TO ANTIQUE SILVER

2nd edition with 1992 prices
by Peter Waldron

368 pp., 1,172 b. & w. illus. ISBN 1 85149 165 1

One of our most popular titles. The head of Sotheby's silver department has used the huge number of photographs at his disposal to advise collectors on what to buy and what to avoid. Detailed examination of fakes is an important feature of this classic work.

For details of these and other books on jewellery, antique furniture, horology, architecture and gardening contact:

Antique Collectors' Club

5 Church Street
Woodbridge, Suffolk IP12 1DS, UK
Tel: 0394 385501 Fax: 0394 384434

Market Street Industrial Park
Wappingers' Falls, NY 12590, USA
Tel: 914 297 0003 Fax: 914 297 0068